# THE COVENANT PATH

## IN THE BIBLE & THE BOOK OF MORMON

# THE COVENANT PATH

## IN THE BIBLE & THE BOOK OF MORMON

TAYLOR HALVERSON, PhD

Text © 2020 by Taylor Halverson
All rights reserved.

No part of this book may be reproduced in any form whatsoever, whether by graphic, visual, electronic, film, microfilm, tape recording, or any other means, without prior written permission of the authors, except in the case of brief passages embodied in critical reviews and articles.

This is not an official publication of The Church of Jesus Christ of Latter-day Saints. The opinions and views expressed herein belong solely to the authors. Permission for the use of sources, graphics, and photos is also solely the responsibility of the author.

ISBN 978-1-951341-03-9

Published by Line of Sight Publishing.

Cover image © 2020 by Anthony Fitzgerald
Cover design © 2020 by Shawnda Craig and Taylor Halverson
Copyedited by Deborah Spencer

# DEDICATION

This book is dedicated to God, who has always been faithful and loyal to His covenants.

# OTHER BOOKS BY TAYLOR HALVERSON

*Beautiful Truths from the First Vision* (with Lisa Halverson)

*Learning at the Feet of the Savior: Additional Insights from New Testament Background, Culture, and Setting* (with David Ridges)

*Scriptural Insights and Commentary: The New Testament*

*Scriptural Insights and Commentary: The Book of Mormon*

*Scriptural Insights and Commentary: The Doctrine & Covenants* (forthcoming)

*Scriptural Insights and Commentary: The Old Testament (forthcoming)*

*Knowing Why: 137 Evidences that the Book of Mormon is True* (with Jack Welch, Neal Rappleye, Stephen Smoot, and David Larsen)

*Knowing Why: 127 MORE Evidences that the Book of Mormon is True* (with Jack Welch, Neal Rappleye, Jamin G. Rappleye, and Jonathan Riley)

*History of Creativity in the Arts, Science, and Technology: Pre-History to 1500, 3rd edition* (with Brent Strong and Mark Davis)

*History of Creativity in the Arts, Science, and Technology: 1500 to Present, 3rd edition* (with Brent Strong and Mark Davis)

*"Finding Myself Alone": Positive Thoughts, Insights, & Discoveries of LDS Singles* (with Mike Agrelius)

*Millions Shall Know Brother Joseph Again: Daily Inspiration from the Prophet Joseph Smith* (with Tyler Griffin)

*Letters from a Christmas Elf: Unexpected Humor for Any Season* (with Kirsten Johnston and Kurt Johnston)

*Memoirs of the Ward Rumor Control Coordinator* (with Richard Halverson)

*Distance Education Innovations and New Learning Environments: Combining Traditional Teaching Methods and Emerging Technologies*

*Preparing Tomorrow's Missionaries Today: Teaching Skills for Disciples of Christ* (with Rob Cornilles)

*Learning for Eternity: Best BYU Speeches and Articles on Learners and Learning* (with Brad Wilcox and Lisa Halverson, forthcoming)

# CONTENTS

Preface . . . . . . . . . . . . . . . . . . . . . . . . . . . . . . . . . . . . . . . . . . . . . 1

*Part 1: Mount Moriah and the Unconditional Covenant God Made to Abraham*

Chapter 1: The Covenant Path in the Bible Starts with Father Abraham . . . . . . . . . . . . . . . . . . . . . . . . . . . . . . . . . . . . . . . . 13

Chapter 2: Genesis 15 as the Origin Story of God's Unconditional Covenant . . . . . . . . . . . . . . . . . . . . . . . . . . . . . . . . . . . . . . 18

Chapter 3: God's Faithfulness to Abraham as Fulfillment of the Covenant. The Purpose of the Abraham Story in Genesis 12–25 . . . . . . . . . . 29

*Part 2: Mount Sinai and the Covenant God Offered the House of Israel*

Chapter 4: God Fulfills His Covenant with Abraham by Saving Israel from Egypt . . . . . . . . . . . . . . . . . . . . . . . . . . . . . . . . . . . . 56

Chapter 5: The Second Covenant of the Covenant Path Revealed at Mount Sinai . . . . . . . . . . . . . . . . . . . . . . . . . . . . . . . . . . . 71

*Part 3: The Covenant Path between Mount Moriah and Mount Sinai in Select Old Testament and New Testament Passages*

Chapter 6: The Old Testament Is Structured on and Preserves the Interactions of the Two Mountain Covenants . . . . . . . . . . . . 106

Chapter 7: The Covenant Path in the New Testament . . . . . . . . . 126

Chapter 8: Expressions of the Two Mountain Covenants Elsewhere in the New Testament. . . . . . . . . . . . . . . . . . . . . . . . . . . . . . . . . 134

*Part 4: The Covenant Path in the Book of Mormon*

Chapter 9: Book of Mormon Title Page: The Book of Mormon Restored the Covenant Path . . . . . . . . . . . . . . . . . . . . . . . . . . . 142

Chapter 10: 1 Nephi as a Record of the Covenant Path . . . . . . . . . 149

Chapter 11: Isaiah in the Book of Mormon: The Interweaving of the Abrahamic and Mosaic Covenants . . . . . . . . . . . . . . . . . . . . . 188

Chapter 12: The Small Plates of Nephi as Torah or Instructional Manual for the Covenant Path . . . . . . . . . . . . . . . . . . . . . . . . 202

Chapter 13: The Book of Mosiah: The Book of Three Kings and the Story of Their Covenant Paths . . . . . . . . . . . . . . . . . . . . . . 212

Chapter 14: Alma 1–4: The Promised Land Is Challenged by a False King . . . . . . . . . . . . . . . . . . . . . . . . . . . . . . . . . . . . . . . . . . . . . 230

Chapter 15: Alma 5–16: God's Covenantal Representatives Teach the People How and Why to Be Covenantally Faithful to God . . . 236

Chapter 16: Alma 17–27: Those Who Have Discovered the Covenant Path Labor to Invite Others to the Path . . . . . . . . . . . . . . . . . 245

Chapter 17: Alma 28–35: The Mission to Reclaim Those Who Have Fallen Off the Covenant Path . . . . . . . . . . . . . . . . . . . . . . . . . 251

Chapter 18: Alma 36–42: Alma Models and Teaches the Covenant Path . . . . . . . . . . . . . . . . . . . . . . . . . . . . . . . . . . . . . . . . . . . . . . 256

Chapter 19: Alma 43–63: Threats to the Promised Land. . . . . . . . 263

Chapter 20: The Book of Helaman: Covenant Keepers and Covenant Counterfeiters. . . . . . . . . . . . . . . . . . . . . . . . . . . . . . . . . . . . . . 272

Chapter 21: 3 Nephi: The Covenant Is Fulfilled in Jesus Christ. . . . 290

Chapter 22: 4 Nephi: The Rise and Fall of God's Covenant People. . . . . . . . . . . . . . . . . . . . . . . . . . . . . . . . . . . . . . . . . . . . . 308

Chapter 23: Mormon: Our Covenantal Instructor and Guide. . . . 311

Chapter 24: Ether: Second Witness of the Covenant Path . . . . . . . 321

Chapter 25: Moroni: Exhortation to Experience the Preserved
    Covenant Path . . . . . . . . . . . . . . . . . . . . . . . . . . . . . . . . . . 332

Concluding Thoughts and Resources for the Covenant Path in the
    Bible and the Book of Mormon . . . . . . . . . . . . . . . . . . . . . . 339

Appendix 1: Some Thoughts on the Restoration of the Covenant
    Path. . . . . . . . . . . . . . . . . . . . . . . . . . . . . . . . . . . . . . . . . . 345

Appendix 2: Why Does My Book Not Include More References to the
    Book of Abraham and the Pearl of Great Price? . . . . . . . . . . . 351

Appendix 3: Glossary of Covenantal Terms in Scripture . . . . . . . . 353

Appendix 4: Foundational Readings on Covenants in Scripture . . . 360

Appendix 5: List of References to the Name Abraham in the Book of
    Mormon . . . . . . . . . . . . . . . . . . . . . . . . . . . . . . . . . . . . . . 362

Appendix 6: List of References to the Name Moses in the Book of
    Mormon . . . . . . . . . . . . . . . . . . . . . . . . . . . . . . . . . . . . . . 363

Appendix 7: List of References to the Word Covenant in the Book of
    Mormon . . . . . . . . . . . . . . . . . . . . . . . . . . . . . . . . . . . . . . 365

About the Author. . . . . . . . . . . . . . . . . . . . . . . . . . . . . . . . . . . . 368

NOTA BENE:

For an overview of covenantal words throughout scripture start with *Appendix 3: Glossary of Covenantal Terms in Scripture*.

The book cover image symbolizes the two mountain covenants with the covenant path running in between on the spine. The image is of Mount Sinai at sunrise.

# PREFACE

Who am I and why am I writing this book?

I've been thinking about, researching, and planning for this book for about fifteen years. On November 22, 2019, I woke up early feeling the urging that now was the time to complete this book.

I never aspired to be a writer or to publish books. As a teenager, I didn't think I had much to say either in writing or in teaching. I still haven't kicked that feeling all these years later. Still, I feel this pressing need to share my voice of understanding the gospel and the scriptures. Though I find it way easier and pleasing to be in conversation with my wife, go on a walk, or play games, I have felt constrained to write this and many other things. My hope is that what I share here will illuminate the gospel and scriptures in new and profound ways, that the reader will find renewed joy and understanding of the gospel, that the covenant path will be seen clearly and purposefully, and that the binding cord of the covenant path that is woven throughout the Bible and the Book of Mormon and the Restoration will be clearly seen.

When I was young, I never aspired to master Biblical languages, literature, culture, or context. As a teenager I was far too focused on sports, girls, and food (and not always in that order). I was blithely unaware of the larger world around me, of the beauties of culture and history, of the meaning of the scriptures, of the power of covenants. Sure, I was a dedicated church goer, faithfully and usually energetically attending early morning seminary in Minnesota (can you say torture and cruel and unusual punishment when winter temperatures would be as low as 20 below zero?). My apologies to my 10th Grade Old Testament seminary teacher, Scott Burton, who, because I sometimes treated class time as social hour with my friends where the teacher's talking was the background music at a restaurant, walked out on us several times. I've tried to repent and be more serious about studying the Old Testament and the scriptures. What I share here is a portion of nearly three decades of intense study and learning.

But my dreams changed. The summer I returned home from my mission, I found a copy of *Isaiah and the Prophets* in my mom's library. My mind and spirit were stirred by the capable expounding of scripture by those who had studied seriously and deeply for some years. I felt a strong stirring in my soul to want to learn Hebrew. How to do so? Having returned from a mission in Chile where I learned Spanish, I reasoned that I needed to go to Israel to learn Hebrew. About a year later, after much planning and exerted effort and sacrifice, I found myself in the Fall 1994 BYU Jerusalem program. That experience changed my life forever. I didn't learn much Hebrew. But I did drink deeply of and learn tremendously about the culture, history, and context of the Bible and the Middle East. When I returned to the BYU Provo campus, I walked away from my chemical engineering degree and embarked on an adventure to professionally study the ancient and modern Middle East. Little did I foresee the price to be paid to gain mastery. Over more years than I can count on my two hands, I studied some dozen languages, plumbed the depths of human civilization from the dawn of writing to the modern day, explored the world's greatest literature, minutely picked apart Biblical passages under the guidance of seasoned experts, sat in the libraries containing much of the world's accumulated wisdom, and stretched my mind, spirit, and soul to comprehend all that I was experiencing.

One of the powerful discoveries I experienced was to learn about the foundational meaning, purpose, and narrative thread of the covenant path found in the Old Testament, New Testament, and the Book of Mormon. Since President Nelson came to his role as President of the Church, and has emphasized the covenant path, I've felt a stirring that I should lend my voice in support of his mission to encourage all of us along that covenant path. The scriptures were written, in part, to record God's covenants to and with His people. Many of the stories and narratives in the scriptures are case studies of how God, or His people, responded to covenantal opportunities and challenges along the covenant path. Because I had been immersively studying the covenantal thread throughout scriptures, I knew that I needed to add my voice in support of our journey on the covenant path.

I still remember the day I was reading a biblical scholar's book on two major covenant types in the Bible, Jon Levenson's *Sinai and Zion: An Entry into the Jewish Bible* (1987). It was like a revelation. Suddenly, the structure and purpose of all the scriptures fell into place around these covenants. All at once, the forward movement of the history of God's people made storyline sense because of the covenants.

What I learned, and I'll simplify this for the sake of brevity and clarity, is that there are two major covenant types, represented by two symbolic mountains, which permeate and animate the biblical text marking the covenant path. I later realized that the Book of Mormon was also thoroughly saturated with and in conversation with these covenants. The two basic covenants are these:

## First Covenant: God's Unconditional Covenant to Give Abraham Property, Posterity, and Priesthood

Mount Moriah / Mount Zion in Jerusalem represents this unconditional covenant.

God is covenantally obligated to make these promises available to all of Abraham's children. God will never break this covenant. This covenant can best be summarized by the scripturally repeated refrain, "The God of Abraham, the God of Isaac, and the God of Jacob." This is the God who will never waver in His commitment or loyalty to make the promises to Abraham available to all his posterity, by blood or adoption.

## Second Covenant: The Mosaic Covenant Promises Are Conditional According to Our Loyalty or Faithfulness to God

Mount Sinai in the wilderness represents this conditional covenant.

Our ongoing and continued access to God's promises to Abraham depend on our loyalty to God. When we are loyal, we have His presence and promises. When we are not loyal and faithful, we no longer have access. This conditional covenant can best be summarized by a statement repeated throughout the Book of Mormon: "If ye keep my commandments, ye shall prosper in the land." The Book of Mormon is a record of how well children of Abraham did or did not keep God's commandments and the consequences of those choices.

The covenant path has two main components: what to believe (orthodoxy) and what to do or what to practice (orthopraxis).

*Covenantally what to believe (orthodoxy)*—God's unconditional promises and covenant to Abraham show us what to believe: God is a God of covenants. God is faithful. God is believable. God is trustworthy. God will be our God.

*Covenantally what to do (orthopraxis)*—The Sinai covenant instructs us on what we should do to demonstrate our loving belief in and loyalty to God. Those instructions for that covenant have been updated from time to time by new prophets and revelation, most notably the Sermon of the Mount delivered by Jesus Christ and revelations provided in the Book of Mormon and the Doctrine and Covenants. In our dispensation the key ways to practice showing our love to God are faith, repentance, baptism, reception of the Holy Ghost, and endurance to the end.

That is the covenant path.

Know what it is, what to believe, and then do it. I hope that this book can support readers along their journey on the covenant path.

## Basic Overview of the Covenant Path between the Covenantal Mountains

In order to understand the Book of Mormon and the Bible, we have to understand the covenant path marked by the two covenantal mountains in the Old Testament.

| Abrahamic Covenant<br>Mount Moriah | Mosaic Covenant<br>Mount Sinai |
|---|---|
| God is the covenant maker and keeper | God's people are (or should be) the covenant makers and keepers |
| God shows us loyalty | We show loyalty to God |
| This covenant protects our rights | This covenant protects God's rights |
| Summary statement of the covenant: The God of Abraham, Isaac, and Jacob | Summary statement of the covenant: If ye keep my commandments, ye shall prosper in the land |
| God's promises to Abraham<br>• Property<br>• Posterity<br>• Priesthood<br>• Prosperity | Promises we make to God<br>• Show love<br>• Show faithfulness<br>• Show devotion<br>• Show trust<br>• Stay within the covenant |

| | |
|---|---|
| God is trustworthy<br>God shares stories and instructions to demonstrate that He is a covenant-making and a covenant-keeping God<br>• Abraham stories (Genesis)<br>• Isaac stories (Genesis)<br>• Jacob stories (Genesis)<br>• Joseph stories (Genesis) | Torah (5 books of Moses, especially Exodus, Leviticus, Numbers, Deuteronomy) are the instruction manual for covenants. They teach us how to show covenantal loyalty<br>• Ten Commandments and the Law of Moses are God's expectations for us to show loyalty to Him<br>• God updates this covenant and the instructions through new revelation, sent via Jesus and His prophets<br>• At the Sermon on the Mount, Jesus is the new Moses who, from a mountain, delivers the higher law, or updated covenantal instructions |

This book focuses on the covenant path in the Book of Mormon and the Bible.

Because much of the Old Testament text pre-dates the Book of Mormon and because the source of the two mountain boundaries—Abraham at Mount Moriah (later known as Mount Zion) and Moses at Mount Sinai—that mark the covenant path are found in the Bible (initially in the Torah or the Five Books of Moses)—my book will begin by exploring in depth the Abraham story, where God's unconditional covenant originated, and the story of Moses and the children of Israel at Sinai, where the conditional covenant originated. After laying the groundwork for these two covenant traditions, I'll show examples of how these two covenants are enacted throughout Israelite history during the Old Testament, New Testament, and then in the Book of Mormon. The last portion of the book will demonstrate that the Book of Mormon is a true, ancient, authentic witness of Jesus Christ, best read through the lens of its expression of the covenant path originally revealed in the Bible. When we read the Book of Mormon as a covenantal text, we help to fulfill Mormon and Moroni's vision and purpose for the book, as stated on the title page.

> [The Book of Mormon was written and preserved] to show unto the remnant of the house of Israel what great things the Lord hath done for their fathers; and **that they may know the covenants of the Lord,** that they are not cast off forever— And also to the convincing of the Jew and Gentile that Jesus is the Christ, the Eternal God, manifesting himself unto all nations. (Book of Mormon Title Page; emphasis added)

When we read the Book of Mormon as a covenantal text, we help to remove the curse from the earth that requires the antidote of the Book of Mormon: "And they shall remain under this condemnation until they repent and remember the new covenant, even the Book of Mormon and the former commandments which I have given them, not only to say, but to do according to that which I have written" (D&C 84:57).

This book is a small representative portion of some of the treasures I've discovered over the years. I hope this book helps you to treasure the covenants of God more fully. I cannot contain between the covers of this book all I've discovered. So if you wish for more updates from me, find regular updates at taylorhalverson.com and join my email list at taylor.halverson@gmail.com. To be honest, if you have a choice in how to use your time, I hope that you'd spend more time reading and pondering, and living the truths of the scriptures and the words of living-day prophets. ☺

Additional note: In this book I use the name Abraham even though he was originally called Abram until God covenantally changed his name to Abraham in Genesis 17. Similarly, Sarah's name was changed from Sarai in Genesis 17. I'll use their more familiar, though later covenantally revealed, names of Abraham and Sarah throughout this book.

## The Book of Mormon Is a Miraculous Book: My Testimony after Writing This Book

I wrote the words of this book at about the same speed that Joseph Smith translated the Book of Mormon. Trust me when I say that writing this book over the course of about twenty writing days was very difficult. I made mistakes and changed things along the way. I had editors reviewing my work looking for errors and inconsistencies. Whenever I took a break, I had to reread where I left off so that I could pick up the thread of the argument. Also whenever I took a break I would think of ways to better explain something or reword it so that when I went back to writing I would revise and edit. In some cases I would use the algorithms available in Word to search for a particular repeated word, phrase, or grammatical feature so that I could fix or update it. While writing, I had access to the entire World Wide Web and a world class research library at Brigham Young University. These things represented my very own Urim and Thummim. I've had two decades more of life experience when I wrote this book than Joseph Smith did. More importantly, I have spent more than twenty-five years intensively studying and researching the topic I'm presenting in this book. This is my area of expertise. I've read everything on the topic and researched, presented, and written on the topic for years, gaining feedback from my audience along the way to improve the final product. I've been practicing and preparing for this moment for more years than Joseph Smith was alive when he brought forth the Book of Mormon. The biggest distractions I had to my writing were Thanksgiving and Christmas holidays in 2019. I had the glorious invention of Minecraft to keep my kids occupied for hours at a time when I needed to focus on writing (Please don't tell my wife!). I wasn't harassed by enemies. I didn't move. I didn't need to find a co-writer. I didn't need to fear for my life. I didn't have fifty pounds of sacred scripture written on gold plates to preserve and protect. I didn't have to fight over copyright. Finding a willing publisher was rather simple. I didn't have to mortgage my home, or anyone's farm, to acquire the money to publish this book. No one stole the equivalent of a quarter of my manuscript so that I had to start over from scratch and *not* repeat anything to be found in the stolen manuscript. I have had all the worldly advantages that Joseph Smith never had. And still I found the process of writing and producing my book to consume my very best energies and be a very challenging task. I didn't even produce anywhere the number of words Joseph Smith did with the Book of Mormon. My manuscript is more than 115,000 words while the Book of Mormon has more than 273,000 words.

I cannot fathom a viable explanation for the Book of Mormon other than what Joseph Smith always testified of. From my personal experience, the only way that the Book of Mormon came forth is as Joseph Smith claimed it did, by the gift and power of God, a marvelous work and a wonder. And as we'll see in this book, the word "wonder" is a covenantal term referring to the great deeds of God delivering truth and salvation to His people. The Book of Mormon is that—a latter-day message to share the truth and salvation of the covenant path with all of God's children.

> *"Wherefore, the fruit of thy loins shall write; and the fruit of the loins of Judah shall write; and that which shall be written by the fruit of thy loins, and also that which shall be written by the fruit of the loins of Judah, shall grow together, unto the confounding of false doctrines and laying down of contentions, and establishing peace among the fruit of thy loins, and bringing them to the knowledge of their fathers in the latter days, and also to the knowledge of my covenants, saith the Lord." (2 Nephi 3:12)*

# PART 1

## MOUNT MORIAH AND THE UNCONDITIONAL COVENANT GOD MADE TO ABRAHAM

# CHAPTER 1

## THE COVENANT PATH IN THE BIBLE STARTS WITH FATHER ABRAHAM

The story of Abraham is so unexpected.

Open to Genesis 12 and start reading. What do we find? God makes these seven stunning promises to Abraham.

1. And I will make of thee a great nation,
2. and I will bless thee,
3. and make thy name great;
4. and thou shalt be a blessing:
5. And I will bless them that bless thee,
6. and curse him that curseth thee:
7. and in thee shall all families of the earth be blessed. (Genesis 12:2–3)

Why did God make these promises to Abraham? Why weren't these promises given to Adam & Eve, or to Enoch, or to Noah, some of God's greatest and most stalwart faithful followers? If we search in the Bible for an answer to that question, the context is missing. Restoration revelation via the Book of Abraham offers strong rationale for why God chose to make these covenantal promises to Abraham. Abraham was deliberately, purposely, and devotedly loyal to God despite significant suffering, trial, and persecution (see also Abraham 1:1–19).

From a narrative construction standpoint, the Abraham story in the Bible seems to come out of nowhere. With nearly zero introduction to who Abraham is and why God would choose Abraham, God declares to this rather unknown character the most desirable blessings one could aspire to experience in this life or the next. Before this revelatory disclosure in Genesis 12:2–3, what do we know of Abraham in the Bible? Hardly anything. The first we hear of Abraham is in Genesis 11. This is the sum total of everything we know about Abraham from the Bible before God delivers the Abrahamic promises:

> And Terah lived seventy years, and begat Abram, Nahor, and Haran. Now these are the generations of Terah: Terah begat Abram, Nahor, and Haran; and Haran begat Lot. And Haran died before his father Terah in the land of his nativity, in Ur of the Chaldees. And Abram and Nahor took them wives: the name of Abram's wife was Sarai; and the name of Nahor's wife, Milcah, the daughter of Haran, the father of Milcah, and the father of Iscah. But Sarai was barren; she had no child. And Terah took Abram his son, and Lot the son of Haran his son's son, and Sarai his daughter in law, his son Abram's wife; and they went forth with them from Ur of the Chaldees, to go into the land of Canaan; and they came unto Haran, and dwelt there. And the days of Terah were two hundred and five years: and Terah died in Haran. Now the LORD had said unto Abram, Get thee out of thy country, and from thy kindred, and from thy father's house, unto a land that I will shew thee. (Genesis 11:26–12:1)

These verses are rather spare about Abraham. From these verses, what do we really know about Abraham? Do we know that he is faithful to God? Devoted? Loving? Kind? We don't know anything of these things. Here's all that we know about Abraham from these verses:

- His father is Terah.
- His brothers are Nahor and Haran.
- His nephew is Lot.

- His wife is Sarai.
- Abraham and Sarai have no children.
- He moved from Ur of the Chaldees to go to Canaan and stopped in Haran along the way.
- God commanded Abraham to leave his country, family, and home.

Do we really know Abraham at this point? No, not really. This spare narrative introduction of Abraham in the Bible makes God's promises to Abraham in Genesis 12:2–3 all the more stunning. God essentially chose one man out of everyone on earth and declared that His most valuable promises would live through this man and his posterity. As mentioned earlier, the beautiful revelation of the Book of Abraham teaches us that Abraham was one of the most stalwart and committed of God's children, details not disclosed in the Bible before God delivered His promises to Abraham.

If God was making a modern-day drama movie and wanted to grab everyone's attention, this is perfect story telling. We are immediately drawn into the story of Abraham. Who is this hero? Why is he a hero? Why are we focused on him? How will his story unfold?

It seems clear that the inspired writers of the Bible crafted this narrative purposely, structuring this story right next to another famous and compelling story in the Bible that is the opposite of the Abraham story: The Tower of Babel.

Turn one chapter back from Genesis 12 to Genesis 11. Look at the stark and instructive differences between Genesis 11:1–9 and Genesis 12:1–6. It is no accident that these two narratives are placed back to back in the Bible. We are supposed to read them in comparison and contrast. Such contrasting stories create vivid and memorable insights through highlighted differences. Consider how clearly we learn from the paired contrast found in the Cain and Abel story. Or how worthy of emulation Nephi's example becomes when compared to his murderous and rebellious brothers Laman and Lemuel. Opposites, when purposely brought together, are vividly instructive. The Abraham story follows closely on the heels of the Tower of Babel story. And that is no accident.

> And the whole earth was of one language, and of one speech. And it came to pass, as they journeyed from the east, that they found a plain in the land of Shinar; and they dwelt there. And they said one to another, Go to, let us make brick, and burn them thoroughly. And they had brick for stone, and slime had they for morter. And they said, Go to, let us build us a city and a tower, whose top may reach unto heaven; and let us make us a name, lest we be scattered abroad upon the face of the whole earth. And the LORD came down to see the city and the tower, which the children of men builded. And the LORD said, Behold, the people is one, and they have all one language; and this they begin to do: and now nothing will be restrained from them, which they have imagined to do. Go to, let us go down, and there confound their language, that they may not understand one another's speech. So the LORD scattered them abroad from thence upon the face of all the earth: and they left off to build the city. Therefore is the name of it called Babel; because the LORD did there confound the language of all the earth: and from thence did the LORD scatter them abroad upon the face of all the earth. (Genesis 11:1–9)

## Comparing and Contrasting the People of the Tower of Babel to Abraham

Let's list some of the instructive contrasts between the story of the people of the Tower of Babel and the introduction of Abraham in Genesis.

| Tower of Babel (Genesis 11:1–9) | Abraham's Introduction (Genesis 12:1–6) |
|---|---|
| Large group of people | Solitary individual |
| Unnamed | Named |

| | |
|---|---|
| Try to get to heaven on their own | God offers the blessings of heaven |
| People wanted to make their own name great | God promises to make the name of one man great |
| Initially gathering to a city | Initially leaving the city (and moving out into the wilderness) |
| Focus on the things of the earth | Focus on the things of God |
| Worshiping the work of their own hands | Worshiping God |
| Avoiding the voice of God | Obeying the voice of God |
| Building a tower | Building a people |
| Confusion | Clarity |
| Scattering | Gathering |
| Curses | Covenants |

God chose Abraham. He called Abraham out from among the nations and gave to Abraham His special promises and covenant. What exactly is the covenant that was made? If we jump ahead a few chapters to Genesis 15 we find what seems to be a puzzling incident. Most of us read over this interaction between Abraham and God, not fully understanding its significance or why it was included in the Biblical narrative. Yet Genesis 15 is absolutely crucial for understanding the covenant path. Understanding the covenantal conversations and actions in Genesis 15 is essential for comprehending the foundation of the covenants in the Biblical story which then weave throughout the Book of Mormon and the Restoration and, ultimately, throughout our place in this grand adventure of the plan of salvation animated by covenants.

# CHAPTER 2

## GENESIS 15 AS THE ORIGIN STORY OF GOD'S UNCONDITIONAL COVENANT

Because Genesis 15 is the first lynchpin for understanding God's covenant to His people, I'll spend more time on an in-depth review of this chapter than most other chapters in scripture. Genesis 15 is not well-known and even less well understood. But because we love God and His covenants, this chapter deserves careful attention and consideration. The chapter offers amazing insights about the nature of God and his role in the unconditional covenant.

The format of discussion here is to quote a verse (or set of verses) from Genesis 15 and then provide an extended explanation of what that verse means and its relationship to the covenant path.

**Genesis 15:1.** *After these things the word of the Lord came unto Abram in a vision, saying, Fear not, Abram: I am thy shield, and thy exceeding great reward.*

In ancient covenant making, the person initiating the covenant would identify themselves to the individual who was receiving the covenant. We see here in Genesis 15:1 that God introduces himself to Abraham with these descriptions, "I am thy shield, and thy exceeding great reward." God will protect Abraham, as He originally promised in Genesis 12:3. God is also Abraham's great reward. Remember that God promised to make Abraham's name great (see Genesis 12:2). In some sense, that divine promise has been fulfilled, for Abraham is known as the father of the faithful by some four billion people worldwide, among Jews, Christians, and Muslims (the three great Abrahamic and monotheistic faith traditions). But there is more about God being the great reward through making Abraham's name great. And we have the same promise. Ultimately, we will become great by taking on the greatest name of all, the name of God. At some time in the future, all titles will fade away and all that will remain is our identity as children of God and followers of Jesus Christ. So too for Abraham. His name will be great, because he will be one with God and will be as God is. That is the promise to Abraham, and all of us, if we are faithful.

**Genesis 15:2–3.** *And Abram said, LORD God, what wilt thou give me, seeing I go childless, and the steward of my house is this Eliezer of Damascus? And Abram said, Behold, to me thou hast given no seed: and, lo, one born in my house is mine heir.*

Abraham remembered the promises God delivered to him (see Genesis 12:1–3). So he spoke to God in humility and trust. God had promised Abraham posterity, but Abraham still had no children. Thinking he would need to act for himself to ratify this covenant, Abraham decided to adopt as his son one of the servants in his home, Eliezer. We can hear Abraham wondering aloud to the Lord "Didn't you promise that I would have children? And yet I have no children of my own, unless I count this servant."

**Genesis 15:4.** *And, behold, the word of the LORD came unto him, saying, This shall not be thine heir; but he that shall come forth out of thine own bowels shall be thine heir.*

God corrected Abraham. Abraham still did not fully understand God's covenantal role and obligations in the covenant. God reminded Abraham again that he would truly at some future day have his own flesh and blood son who would be his heir.

**Genesis 15:5.** *And he brought him forth abroad, and said, Look now toward heaven, and tell the stars, if thou be able to number them: and he said unto him, So shall thy seed be.*

To convince Abraham of the endless possibilities awaiting him, and in an effort to help Abraham believe His promises, God tutored Abraham. He had Abraham observe the night skies, something that in our modern world we may know little about with so much light pollution. There on a grand scale to overwhelm Abraham were the innumerable stars representing what God wanted to give to Abraham in posterity. What a beautiful metaphor God chose to depict the power and vastness of His covenants. Every evening as light faded from the earth, the enormity of God's promise to Abraham would twinkle down at him from billions upon billions of uncountable stars.

**Genesis 15:6.** *And he believed in the LORD; and he counted it to him for righteousness.*

Abraham was a good learner. He believed God. He knew that God would not lie. What we usually miss in this verse is the covenantally significant word "believe." It comes from the Hebrew word *aman*, as does the word "amen" that we use at the end of blessings, prayers, or whenever we assent our agreement to something. *Aman* means to be covenantally faithful, which demonstrates belief. So our word "amen" literally means "faithful," that is, I concur that what I just heard was faithfully and truthfully stated, therefore I agree. So Abraham was not simply believing

God. Abraham was demonstrating faithfulness and truthful commitment to God—righteousness. Furthermore, the word "righteous," or "righteousness," is a covenantal term. It does not simply mean "not committing sin" or "keeping the commandments." In the Bible, the word "righteous" is best understood as faithful commitment to a covenant or trusting dedication or loyal allegiance. Abraham trusted God. Abraham demonstrated loyal allegiance. Abraham was faithfully committed to God. These descriptors are the essence of righteousness. And this is the righteousness of Abraham so succinctly expressed in Genesis 15:6.

**Genesis 15:7.** *And he said unto him, I am the LORD that brought thee out of Ur of the Chaldees, to give thee this land to inherit it.*

Posterity is meaningless if you have no place, or no land, to be with that posterity. Without land, your posterity cannot survive. Posterity and property are intimately tied up in God's covenantal promises to Abraham. Because God had promised Abraham more than posterity, God continued instructing Abraham in His covenant. What we see in this verse is similar to verse 1 above. God identified Himself again to Abraham and reminded Abraham of the incredible deeds He had already done for him. Further, God made the point about what He was doing unmistakable for Abraham: "[I] brought thee out of Ur of the Chaldees, to give thee this land to inherit it." God had not forgotten His promise made to Abraham in Genesis 12. Perhaps Abraham felt like a wander lost in a foreign land. But God had a plan and a purpose. The land where Abraham resided would be his land, the land where his posterity would be enveloped in the protecting shield of God's covenant.

**Genesis 15:8.** *And he said, LORD God, whereby shall I know that I shall inherit it?*

Abraham was still looking for assurances that God would fulfill His promises. What trusting faith does it take to ask God, "How will I know you will be faithful and true to your word?" Abraham was not looking for a vain, or empty, sign. Abraham was looking for the tokens of a covenantal commitment upon which he could be sure.

**Genesis 15:9.** *And he said unto him, Take me an heifer of three years old, and a she goat of three years old, and a ram of three years old, and a turtledove, and a young pigeon.*

God had just spent the early portion of this chapter reviewing His promises to Abraham. We discussed that Abraham was faithfully committed to God. What Abraham now wanted was covenantal assurances. He wanted to know how he was to inherit these incredible blessings. How was God going to do these marvelous works and wonders? This is where the story in Abraham gets a little interesting and confusing, mostly because we no longer practice animal sacrifice and so the covenantal significance, symbolism, and purposefulness may be less apparent to us than it was to Abraham in his day. Abraham had asked God for evidence of His commitment to His promises. God commanded Abraham to gather a heifer (a young female cow that had never born a calf), a female goat, and male goat, a turtledove and a pigeon.

**Genesis 15:10.** *And he took unto him all these, and divided them in the midst, and laid each piece one against another: but the birds divided he not.*

Abraham faithfully complied gathering each of these animals. Notice carefully that Abraham now does something that God did not command him to do. Abraham cut the animals in half (except for the birds) and then arranged them in a line with one half on the right side and one half on the left with a pathway in the middle. Why did Abraham cut up these animals when God never commanded it? Because in Abraham's culture and day covenants were made, ratified, and empowered by the sacrificial cutting in half and death of animals. This is known as "cutting a covenant." Abraham knew that God was making a covenant to Abraham to fulfill the promises. And Abraham knew what needed to be done with the animals. God did not need to explain to Abraham what was already culturally understood in covenant making.

**Genesis 15:11.** *And when the fowls came down upon the carcases, Abram drove them away.*

After preparing the animals, Abraham protected the carcasses as sacred objects necessary for the enlivening of the covenant.

**Genesis 15:12.** *And when the sun was going down, a deep sleep fell upon Abram; and, lo, an horror of great darkness fell upon him.*

But after some time, the day progressed, the sun went down and Abraham fell asleep. Then God appeared. The Bible writers describe Abraham's encounter with God as a horror of darkness. I know this sounds strange to our ears, but in the ancient world, they saw God as awesome and terrifying power; how else would you describe the most powerful being in the universe? Perhaps what really happened is that the adversary attacked Abraham, just as he did Joseph Smith before the grand revelatory First Vision. Whatever the case may be, God appeared. Before the covenant was enacted God delivered a series of prophecies to Abraham.

**Genesis 15:13.** *And he said unto Abram, Know of a surety that thy seed shall be a stranger in a land that is not theirs, and shall serve them; and they shall afflict them four hundred years;*

God spoke to Abraham and prophesied that his posterity would be taken into captivity. God knew this. He foresaw it.

There was a plan. The God of heaven and earth had a plan for fulfilling his covenants.

**Genesis 15:14.** *And also that nation, whom they shall serve, will I judge: and afterward shall they come out with great substance.*

God's plan included allowing the Israelites to suffer as foreigners in a strange land so that God could show his marvelous powers of salvation and covenant-keeping to bring them into the land of promise laden with the spoils of other nations.

**Genesis 15:15.** *And thou shalt go to thy fathers in peace; thou shalt be buried in a good old age.*

God further promised Abraham that he would die in peace.

**Genesis 15:16.** *But in the fourth generation they shall come hither again: for the iniquity of the Amorites is not yet full.*

And then when the time was ripe, God would lead the children of Abraham to the promised land, to inherit lands that were at that point occupied by other people.

**Genesis 15:17.** *And it came to pass, that, when the sun went down, and it was dark, behold a smoking furnace, and a burning lamp that passed between those pieces.*

Before I jump into this lengthy discussion of this verse, I want to highlight that this verse is *one of the most significant covenantal verses in all of scripture. If you truly want to understand the covenant path, you must start here.*

The Genesis narrative now returns to recounting the act of God's covenant-making with Abraham. We should pause to remind ourselves of key features of covenants in Bible times.

First, something had to die for the covenant to live.

Second, whoever passed between the divided animals, physically enacting their entering into the covenant, was duty-bound and covenantally obligated to fulfill the expectations of that covenant.

Third, if the person who put themselves under covenant, symbolized by passing through the chopped-in-half animals, did not keep the commandments, then they, too, were supposed to be cut in half as a penalty. This sounds harsh to our ears today, but it was more symbolic than anything. Consider these modern-day scenarios that remind us of the serious nature of covenant-making and -keeping. The first may seem frivolous: Have you ever heard someone say (and it's usually children saying this phrase) "Cross my heart and hope to die" when they are attempting to convince someone to believe them? Did you know that the phrase "Cross my heart and hope to die" was originally covenantal language? In translation, what this phrase really means is, "I'm telling the truth, honest! I'm even willing to have my heart cut out if it is discovered that I'm not telling the truth!" Of course, no one truly intends the explicit meaning of the phrase, especially when kids say this out on the playground. Even so this began as a phrase that underscored the serious nature of what is being said.

Or try this scenario. Do you have or do you know anyone who has a mortgage? Did you know that the word *mort*gage comes from the same word found in *mort*uary and *mort*ician? Yes, *death* is the source word for mortgage. A mortgage is literally a death pledge. When someone accepts the burden of a mortgage, they are saying to the bank, "I pledge my life to pay back all this money. If I do not pay back this money, I forfeit my life." Remember the US housing price crash around 2006–2009? Do you know of anyone who could no longer pay their mortgage? Did the bank go out and kill those people? No. Instead, the bank foreclosed on the home and the people had to move. That is the essence of the mortgage commitment: pay your money to the bank or lose your home. No one ever loses their life over this at the hands of the bank. Now, do you know of anyone who takes the literal meaning of "mortgage" seriously? I certainly hope not, since the literal meaning is not meant to be taken seriously or to be acted upon. It is language meant to convey the serious nature of the commitment. Would we call the banks mean or hateful for foreclosing on someone who has failed to keep their commitment and pay the mortgage? Nope. Nevertheless, extremely serious language is invoked to remind the oath and covenant makers of the significance of their undertaking. That is how commitments or covenants work.

Having established this covenantal context of cutting as a visual and metaphorical reminder of the solemn nature of covenant-making, we have a weighty question to consider. Who passed through the chopped up animals?

Remember, the person who passes through the animal is the one making the covenant, is the one who is responsible for the fulfillment of the covenant, is obligated to see that the covenant stays in force, and is the one who is under threat of being cut in half (metaphorically speaking) if they fail to keep the covenant.

God Himself is the Abrahamic covenant maker and keeper.

That is the stunning and revelatory knowledge disclosed in Genesis 15. Abraham was *not* under obligation in the Abrahamic covenant. Yes, he needed to show ongoing faithfulness to God, but Abraham was not the one passing through the sacrificial animals. God was.

Only God is responsible to fulfill the Abrahamic covenant. That is the thrust and purpose of the entire Abrahamic story of Genesis 12–25 and indeed the patriarchal stories of Genesis and then bleeding into the rest of the Bible and into the Book of Mormon. God made a covenant to our Father Abraham and unless God ceases to be God, He is forever obligated to fulfill the expectations of the covenant. Because God cannot lie, because God will not cease to be God, all of us as children of Abraham can believe God's faithfulness to this covenant and have it counted unto us for righteousness. God *is* and *has been* faithful to this covenant throughout human history. The stories in the Old and New Testament and in the Book of Mormon provide ample evidence of God acting faithfully to the expectations of the

Abrahamic covenant to provide posterity, property, and priesthood to the children of Abraham.

The Abrahamic covenant is an unconditional covenant. As long as God is God, this covenant is in force. It is live, it is available to all of Abraham's children or those who are grafted in through adoption.

What is the covenant path? It begins with God showing the way by passing through the sacrificial victims in a solemn ceremony that witnesses His loving obligation to fulfill the promises to Abraham and his descendants, now and always.

You may be thinking right now, "Wait a second. Do I get a free pass into the kingdom of God? Aren't there any covenantal obligations for Abraham and his children to demonstrate to God?"

To be clear, there is no free pass into the kingdom of God without faith and faithfulness. And yes, there are other covenants that we are invited to enter in, to show our faithfulness to God. From a Biblical and Book of Mormon perspective, the most important of those covenants occurred at Mt. Sinai when God had Moses deliver the enslaved Israelites to God's wilderness presence. We'll talk more in a future chapter about how the Mosaic covenant, or the Sinai covenant, is a conditional covenant whereby according to our faithfulness we have access to the Abrahamic covenant. God will always provide a way to make the Abrahamic promises available to the children of Abraham. That is His covenant, as expressed in Genesis. However, God's offering the promises to us does not automatically guarantee that any of us will receive those promises. Those promises are contingent upon our faithfulness as described in the Mt. Sinai covenant. Therefore the unconditional covenant of God to Abraham is in league with the conditional covenant first initiated at Sinai between the Israelites and God.

The covenant path is marked by the unconditional covenant God made to Abraham and the conditional covenant we make to God, first delivered through Moses to the children of Israel at Sinai.

**Genesis 15:18–21.** *In the same day the LORD made a covenant with Abram, saying, Unto thy seed have I given this land, from the river of Egypt unto the great river, the river Euphrates: The Kenites, and the Kenizzites, and the Kadmonites, And the Hittites, and the Perizzites, and the Rephaims, And the Amorites, and the Canaanites, and the Girgashites, and the Jebusites.*

These verses succinctly summarize the significant and eternal acts undertaken by God in the verse above. As God concluded the covenantal ceremony, He declared and promised to Abraham the purpose of the covenant: that Abraham would have a promised land for his posterity to live in, though as we saw earlier in Genesis 15 several generations would need to pass away before God removed the current tribes from the land and replaced them with the children of Abraham.

## Conclusion

We've seen from our close review of Genesis 15 that God willingly put Himself into an unconditional covenantal relationship with Abraham and his posterity to fulfill the promises God made in Genesis 12:1–3. To understand the covenant path, we must lay this foundational piece of God's unconditional covenant to Abraham. In a future chapter, we'll discuss another foundational piece of the covenant path: the conditional covenant God made with the Israelites at Sinai. Before we look at our covenantal obligations to God, let us explore how God was true and faithful to Abraham and His promises made. We'll see the truth and power behind the phrase "The God of Abraham, Isaac, and Jacob" that truly is about God's unswerving loyalty and covenantal commitment to bless Abraham.

# CHAPTER 3

## GOD'S FAITHFULNESS TO ABRAHAM AS FULFILLMENT OF THE COVENANT. THE PURPOSE OF THE ABRAHAM STORY IN GENESIS 12–25

What happens when we re-read the Abraham story of Genesis 12–25 through the lens of God's covenantal obligations to Abraham? What happens when we test the idea that it is God, and not Abraham, who had a duty to keep the covenant that the promises to Abraham might be fulfilled? Let's walk this path and discover fresh perspectives on the God we can trust, yes, even the God of Abraham, Isaac, and Jacob. In this chapter, we'll review Genesis 12–25, often called the Abraham cycle, through the lens of God's covenant to Abraham.

**God's Promises to Abraham**

We remember that the core summary of the promises to Abraham include property and posterity. When we include additional revelation found in the Book of Abraham from the Pearl of Great Price, we can add priesthood to that list. We learned in Genesis 15 that God is under covenant to deliver on those promises. Let's take a look at the Abraham story.

## Abraham Goes to Egypt: Genesis 12

Soon after receiving the promise of land and property, Abraham and his retinue arrived in the promised land. What did Abraham discover? A raging famine (see Genesis 12:10). That was a direct threat to God's promise to Abraham to give him property. A careful reader might wonder, "What kind of God would promise land and then lead someone to the wreckage of destitution?" That is a fair question. As we read further, we see the power and mercy of God to save and to deliver on His promises. God has a plan. God also provides opportunities for His children to learn to trust Him as the fulfillment of His promises unfold. These same opportunities allow God to show to His children that He is trustworthy and faithful, that He will do all that He covenanted to do. That is the thrust of the Abraham story. God and Abraham were in circumstances that allowed them to mutually demonstrate trust.

Because of the famine in the promised land, Abraham had to lead his family to Egypt to find food. When Abraham arrived in Egypt another threat to God's promises emerged. Abraham lost Sarah to the Egyptians. First the promise of property seemed lost since Abraham was no longer in the promised land; now it appeared he would never have posterity because His wife was taken from him. Abraham himself was close to certain death, as the Pharaoh at that time had power to take another man's wife and then kill her husband (see Genesis 12:12–13). God intervened, prompting Abraham to tell the Egyptians that Sarah was his sister. Abraham was momentarily protected from death, but the prospect of posterity looked dim with his wife abducted in a foreign land.

Yet these actions by the Pharaoh allowed God to show His mighty hand, to demonstrate to Abraham that God was his exceeding great reward (see Genesis 15:1). God brought a plague upon Pharaoh and his house. In the ancient world, the Pharaoh would have interpreted the plague as being a consequence of some erroneous and immoral thing that he had done. Recognizing that the plague occurred as soon as he had taken Sarah, the Pharaoh realized that Sarah must be married to Abraham, and that Abraham was protected by a powerful God. Pharaoh endeavored immediately and quickly to rectify the situation. The subtext of this story, which we learn through the context of the ancient world, is that Pharaoh came to realize that God was with Abraham and that Pharaoh should not stand in the way, or block, or attempt to disrupt God from fulfilling His promises to Abraham. As a sign of penitence and in recognition of God's mighty power to protect Abraham and his promises, Pharaoh returned Sarah to Abraham and gifted him enormous wealth as is depicted at the beginning of Genesis 13.

"And Abram went up out of Egypt, he, and his wife, and all that he had, and Lot with him, into the south. And Abram was very rich in cattle, in silver, and in gold" (Genesis 13:1–2).

This was all part of God's plan to help bring to pass His oath to Abraham in Genesis 12 to bless him with property and posterity. To express thanks to God for His righteousness and faithfulness, Abraham built an altar (see Genesis 13:4).

## Abraham Has Conflict in the Promised Land Over Land Ownership: Genesis 13

Once he had returned to the land of promise, Abraham discovered conflict over the land. We would think that all would be well. God had preserved Abraham and Sarah's marriage. The famine had abated and God had returned them to the promised land. But like any engaging narrative, the tension continues. There will be a few more cycles of tension and resolutions before we see the promises finally come to pass.

Abraham's nephew Lot was with Abraham. Each man had servants tending their separate flocks of animals. As is human nature, these two groups fell into quarreling about water rights and land rights. Grieved at the family strife, Abraham proposed a division of the land, letting his nephew choose first. Abraham trusted God to be faithful to His promises. So Abraham felt no worry to allow Lot to choose his portion of the land first. Abraham knew that God would bring to pass His assurance to provide land to Abraham.

Sure enough, what do we see happening in verse 14 of Genesis 13 as soon as Lot had chosen his land? God spoke to Abraham and showed Him the land that would be his. "Lift up now thine eyes, and look from the place where thou art northward, and southward, and eastward, and westward: For all the land which thou seest, to thee will I give it, and to thy seed for ever" (Genesis 13:14–15). For good measure, God also reiterated His vow to make Abraham rich in posterity: "And I will make thy seed as the dust of the earth: so that if a man can number the dust of the earth, then shall thy seed also be numbered" (Genesis 13:16).

God concluded this revelatory exchange with Abraham with the command to see the land for himself, "Arise, walk through the land in the length of it and in the breadth of it; for I will give it unto thee" (Genesis 13:17).

We should highlight the chiastic structure in these verses, with the center spot being the promise of posterity. God does care about land, but He cares more about His people. Without land, the people cannot survive. We see that concern expressed as the center of this chiastic promises.

> A God promises land to Abraham (Genesis 13:14–15)
>   B God promises posterity to Abraham (Genesis 13:16)
> A' God promises land to Abraham (Genesis 13:17)

Once again, to show his gratitude to a faithful and worthy-of-trust God, Abraham built an altar to the Lord (see Genesis 13:18).

## Abraham Enriched by the King of Heaven and Earth: Genesis 14

We are gaining insight into the covenant path. Abraham is the exemplary pilgrim on that covenant path. God came to

*The Covenant Path in the Bible and the Book of Mormon* 33

him, and by extension to all of us as his posterity, assuring him with property and posterity. The stories in the Abraham cycle (Genesis 12–25) reveal God's character, how God was faithful to Abraham, thus earning Him the epithet "The God of Abraham, Isaac, and Jacob," which means "the faithful God you can trust to keep the covenant and fulfill His promises." These stories in Genesis 12–25 also demonstrate Abraham's growing assurance of the trustworthiness of God. These stories are placed at the beginning of the Bible as orienting signals about the covenant path. That path is paved with the faithful acts of God to His people, starting with Abraham.

Given this perspective, what are we to make of the story preserved in Genesis 14? In this chapter, a war breaks out that engulfs Sodom and Gomorrah, where Lot resided. Lot and his family are captured, as were all the people and wealth of that region. Abraham raised a strike force to retrieve what was taken by the invading army. He succeeded in liberating the captives and restoring the wealth to the rightful owners. The king of Sodom wanted to reward Abraham with great wealth because of his heroic and daring deeds. But Abraham demurred, saying, "I have lift up mine hand unto the Lord, the most high God, the possessor of heaven and earth, that I will not take from a thread even to a shoelatchet, and that I will not take any thing that is thine, lest thou shouldest say, I have made Abram rich" (Genesis 14:22–23).

Abraham did not want the king of Sodom to claim that he had enriched Abraham. Rather, Abraham wanted to leave that to God, who Abraham appropriately describes as "the possessor of heaven and earth" (Genesis 14:22). Because Abraham knows that God is a faithful God of covenants, Abraham does not need an earthly king to enrich him. Abraham will be enriched by the King of Heaven and Earth. Instead of gaining wealth through his own actions, Abraham knew that it was God who would reward Abraham with wealth, lands, and posterity. As a sign of his gratitude for all that God had delivered into his hands, Abraham returned a portion back to God. His consecrated gift of ten percent was put into the hands of Melchizedek, the king of Salem and the high priest of God during the time of Abraham.

We see in Genesis 14 that the covenant path includes life experiences, trials, and challenges that God puts in front of each us. We can boldly walk that covenant path because we know that God is faithful. He will do His part to make the assurances to Abraham of property and posterity become a reality.

Because we discussed the covenantal significance of Genesis 15 earlier, we'll pursue our understanding of Abraham's covenantal journey in Genesis 16.

## God's Promises Extend to All of Abraham's Family: Genesis 16

We've talked at length about Abraham. Sarah, as his wife, was an equal inheritor of the promises God made to Abraham. Like Abraham, she too had to learn to trust that God would be loyal to His covenant, that He would come through with His promises. Sarah thought to move things along, to fulfill God's promises by her own determination and actions (similar to what Abraham had done when he adopted Eliezer as his son in an attempt to fulfill God's promise of posterity) by giving her handmaid Hagar to Abraham to bear a child. What Abraham learned, and what Sarah also learned, was that God had a plan, process, and timeline for when and how He would deliver on His promises. Just as Abraham learned from God that Eliezer was not the fulfillment of the promise, Sarah would learn that her actions to provide posterity to Abraham through her handmaid Hagar also were not the fulfillment of the promise.

Even still, God is faithful to our efforts to help Him do His work. Though it is God's responsibility to bring to pass His promises to Abraham, God will not reject our efforts, if in our limited awareness we try to bring about His will. For example, God did not disown Eliezer, Abraham's adopted servant, even though Eliezer was not the promised child. Similarly we see in

Genesis 16 that God did not disown Hagar and Ishmael or throw them out of the covenant. What we see in Genesis 16 is that God honored Sarah's efforts, even if Sarah herself had second thoughts and cast the pregnant Hagar out. The following vignette is too often overlooked in our reading of the Bible, but it cannot be ignored when we are reading through the lens of covenants.

The angel of the Lord found Hagar and communed with her. In the Bible, the phrase "angel of the Lord" is a title of God Himself (see examples in Genesis 22:11, Exodus 3:2, and 2 Kings 1:15). Remarkably, this means that Hagar had direct experience with God. In His interaction with her, God commanded Hagar to return to her place and status in the family of Abraham. Pay close attention to what God did next. He delivered a nearly identical promise to Hagar as Abraham received: "I will multiply thy seed exceedingly, that it shall not be numbered for multitude" (Genesis 16:10). Because her son, to be called Ishmael, was a child of Abraham, he and his descendants would inherit the same promises as his Father Abraham. By extension, as the mother of the child of Abraham, Hagar received God's promise of multitudes of posterity. But this was special because God delivered the news of that promise directly and personally to Hagar. Beautiful!

## God Reaffirms His Promises to Abraham by way of Covenant: Genesis 17

Genesis 17 is a thoroughly covenantal text. God once again affirmed his covenantal duties to Abraham, reassuring Abraham that even though Abraham was now nearly one hun-dred years old—and Sarah ninety—they would yet have a child of their own. As the chapter opens, God said some curious things to Abraham that are often overlooked or not understood, "The Lord appeared to Abraham, and said unto him, I am the Almighty God; walk before me, and be thou perfect" (Genesis 17:1).

There are significant insights packed into the closing statements of this verse. First, God declared one of His qualities and characteristics, "I am the Almighty God." Do we thoughtfully reflect on the reality of what He is saying? Do we recognize the magnitude and meaning of that claim? If God is who He says He is, and He is, then we have nothing to fear. God will be faithful to us, as He was faithful to Abraham. Just as Abraham needed reassurance and reminders of God's almighty trustworthiness, these Biblical stories have been preserved to reassure us as children of Abraham that we too can fully rely on God, who has all power and might.

God also commanded Abraham to walk before God and be perfect. We can reasonably retranslate "before" as "with." So God invited Abraham, and all of us by extension because we are children of Abraham, to walk *with* God. In essence, God told Abraham, "Be with me, join me at my side."

As for the word "perfect" in this verse, unfortunately, our modern-day conception of perfection leads us into fear, worry, doubt, angst, and deeply disempowering misunderstanding. Peeling back the true meaning of the word "perfect" in its ancient context is transformatively revealing and empowering. The word "perfect" here did not mean "without blemish" or "without error" or "without sin" or "without mistake." Rather, in the covenantal context "perfect" is a synonym to faithfulness, loyalty, and trustworthiness. It's covenantal perfection, that is, being loyal and faithful to covenants.

So let's rewind this verse. God came to Abraham and said, "Walk with me, by my side, and be thou a loyal, faithful, and trustworthy companion as I have been to you." Wow! Think of it. God wants to be with us as expressed in the meaning of His name Emmanuel, "God with us." He wants us to walk by His side. He wants us to be a faithful companion. He wants us to be loyally devoted to Him. So instead of reading perfect as some impossible standard that is unachievable in this life, which it is without Jesus, we now understand that God is asking us to join Him in a loyally committed relationship. Who among us can't do that? Who among us does not desire to be loyal to God? Who among us does not want to trust God? Who among us does not want to be faithful to God? See the difference? God expects us to show loyalty, not perfection, as in the meaning of fully developed and without mistake, misstep, or deficiency. God wants us as we are. Join Him by His side. If you stumble, let Him pick you up to join Him again by His side. If you fall behind, remember that if you are facing in His direction and desire to be with Him, that is what He too desires. If you find yourself wandering in forgetfulness, you can turn to God and pledge your loving loyalty again to Him and He will receive you again. God does not expect perfection in the modern rendering of that word. God will not wait until you are perfect (as in whole, complete, without blemish) before He wants you to walk with Him in companionship. He wants you now. The only thing He wants in return is your loyalty, your loving faithfulness. Even in our fallen and broken natures where we struggle to always do what we know we should, God is faithful and consistently reminds us, "Walk with me, and be thou loyal to me." One of the simplest and most powerful ways we can show that loyalty is to weekly renew the covenant, in His name, to take upon ourselves the name of His Son who died as the Perfect Lamb that the covenant path would be enlivened. We call that sacred communing meal sacrament.

A careful review of scripture shows that the word "perfect" does indeed convey this covenantal context of devotion and loyalty. Noah was introduced in the Old Testament as being covenantally loyal and devoted to God in this manner, "Noah was a just man and perfect in his generations, and Noah walked with God." (Genesis 6:9.) We see that Noah walked with God, just as Abraham did, who was commanded by God to "walk before me," meaning to "walk with God."

Other instances of the word "perfect" in the Old Testament better understood as covenantal loyalty, devotion, or trustworthiness include these:

- "Thou shalt be **perfect** [covenantally devoted] with the LORD thy God" (Deuteronomy 18:13; emphasis added).
- "As for God, his way is **perfect** [trustworthy]; the word of the LORD is tried: he is a buckler to all them that trust in him" (2 Samuel 22:31; emphasis added).
- "Let your heart therefore be **perfect** with the LORD our God, to walk in his statutes, and to keep his commandments, as at this day" (1 Kings 8:61; emphasis added). Remember that to "walk with God" means to be loyally devoted to God in covenantal relationship.
- Or the prayer of righteous Hezekiah, who pleaded with God to heal him from a malady "I beseech thee, O Lord, remember now how I have walked before thee in truth and with a **perfect** [totally devoted] heart, and have done that which is good in thy sight" (2 Kings 20:3; emphasis added).

Returning to Genesis 17, we see God giving new names. When people make covenants with God, God will give them a new name. In this chapter, God changed Abram's name to Abraham. Abram means "exalted father" and Abraham means "Father of Multitudes," a perfect name to represent the promise God made to Abraham. God also changed Sarai's name to Sarah. Sarai means "my princess" and Sarah means "princess." God also made a requirement of Abraham. He asked Abraham to covenant to circumcise all the males in his household as a witness that they had accepted God to be the God of the land for an everlasting possession, for God said, "I will be their God" (Genesis 17:8).

As God had done repeatedly throughout the Abraham stories, He once again reminded Abraham of what He would do for Abraham: "And I will give unto thee, and to thy seed after thee, the land wherein thou art a stranger, all the land of Canaan, for an everlasting possession; and I will be their God" (Genesis 17:8) and "I will bless [Sarah], and give thee a son also of her: yea, I will bless her, and she shall be a mother of nations; kings of people shall be of her" (Genesis 17:16).

In surprise, wonderment, and joy, Abraham laughed out loud while thinking to himself, "Shall a child be born unto him that is an hundred years old? and shall Sarah, that is ninety years old, bear?" (Genesis 17:17). But God, who knows the hearts of humans, responded that Abraham would call his first-born son with Sarah, Isaac. Why? Because Isaac means "laughter" in Hebrew. Isaac's name became a permanent reminder that we can laugh in joy at the miraculous way that God delivers on His promises. And we should not laugh in doubt about God's almighty powers to fulfill His promises.

Genesis 17 concludes with Abraham showing loyalty to God by circumcising all males in his household, as God asked.

## Abraham Is the Friend of God: Genesis 18

We won't detain ourselves with many of the details of this chapter. The key idea is that once again God visited Abraham (God appeared to Abraham via three angelic visitors which came to the tent of Abraham) and again confirmed the promise that Abraham and Sarah would have flesh and blood posterity. Abraham had laughed in Genesis 17 to think that in his old age he would have son. Now it was Sarah's turn to laugh when she heard the news that she and Abraham would bear a son.

How many of us laugh at promises from the Lord, outlandish as they may seem? One of the key insights from this chapter is the statement "Is any thing too hard for the Lord?" (Genesis 18:14). The underlying Hebrew word for "is anything too hard" can be translated as "wonder" and it is the same word God used in Exodus 3:20 when He promised to save the Israelites from Egyptian bondage, saying, "And I will stretch out my hand, and smite Egypt with all my **wonders** which I will do in the midst thereof: and after that he will let you go" (emphasis added). Just as God would save the children of Abraham (i.e., the Israelites) from Egyptian bondage, because of His promise to the fathers (i.e., the patriarchs Abraham, Isaac, and Jacob), God can make

Abraham and Sarah fruitful to have a son. Which is harder? Saving the teeming masses of slaves from the hard labor in the most powerful human empire the world had ever known? Or bringing a promised baby into the world? Each is miraculous and unexpected in its own right. But God Himself has the power to do these things. More importantly, He promised that he would do these things and is therefore covenantally bound to fulfill His word.

After confirming again the promise of the awaited son, God decided to counsel with Abraham. Notice that the Lord concludes His rationale for bringing Abraham into His decision-making as a way to help the Lord fulfill His promises to Abraham.

"Shall I hide from Abraham that thing which I do; Seeing that Abraham shall surely become a great and mighty nation, and all the nations of the earth shall be blessed in him? For I know him, that he will command his children and his household after him, and they shall keep the way of the Lord, to do justice and judgment; that the LORD may bring upon Abraham [the promises] that which he hath spoken of him" (Genesis 18:17–19).

So trusting was God of Abraham's faithfulness that He revealed His plans to Abraham and allowed Abraham to reason with Him. We know that Abraham was called the "Friend of God" (James 2:23; see also Isaiah 41:8 and Qur'an Surah 4:125). Genesis 18 demonstrates that God treated Abraham as a friend. And what do friends do? Even though friends are different in terms of powers and abilities, friends treat each other as equals in the relationship. That is how we see God treat Abraham in Genesis 18 (as a consequence of the covenant God had made to Abraham) when He involved Abraham in the decision to destroy (or save) Sodom and Gomorrah. Another way of seeing this relationship of Abraham as the Friend of God is to consider that Abraham had his calling and election made sure.

The Abraham cycle of Genesis 12–25 shares stories where Abraham was tested by God so that Abraham could show trust and faith that God is who He says He is (i.e., the God who keeps

His promises). And these same stories show how God is tested, or rather, how God gives Abraham testimony building experiences to trust God. Notice that the word "test" and "testimony" come from the same root word. You cannot have a testimony without a test. God needed to test Abraham to see if Abraham would trust that God would keep His covenantal commitment.

How often in our lives does God test us, to see if we will wait upon Him, trust Him, believe Him? God gives us these experiences so that we can have testimonies because of the tests we have endured. Without such tests, without such testimonies, we cannot become a "Friend of God," which is the desire we share with God. This is the essence of the Abraham cycle of Genesis 12–25. God created experiences, or tests, for Abraham's testimony to grow of God's faithfulness. Those stories have been recorded for our benefit so that we, too, can trust that God will be faithful to His covenants and promises.

Indeed, this is the core meaning of Moroni's exhortation at the end of the Book of Mormon. The Bible and the Book of Mormon were both written as witnesses of God's tender mercies to His people, that God has ever been and will always be faithful to the promises to the fathers, that is, the patriarchs, beginning with Abraham. Moroni urged us to remember these things. Without the written record, remembering would be more difficult. In addition to the written scripture record of God's tender mercies, we are invited to remember the tender mercies God has poured out upon us.

"Behold, I would exhort you that when ye shall read these things, if it be wisdom in God that ye should read them, that ye would remember how merciful the Lord hath been unto the children of men, from the creation of Adam even down until the time that ye shall receive these things, and ponder it in your hearts" (Moroni 10:3).

As we remember God's tender, covenantal mercies, we will be overwhelmed by the Spirit testifying of God's presence in our lives and His faithfulness to us.

## The Overthrow of Sodom and Gomorrah: Genesis 19

Remember that we are reading the Abraham cycle (the stories of Genesis 12–25) through the lens of the covenantal promises God made to Abraham. What we are looking for is evidence that God is committed to His promises to Abraham and is covenantally bound to act on Abraham's behalf unto the fulfillment of God's promises. In that light, the key verse in this chapter is, "God remembered Abraham [and the promises that He had made to Abraham], and sent Lot out of the midst of the overthrow, when he overthrew the cities in the which Lot dwelt" (Genesis 19:29).

So why is the story of the overthrow of Sodom and Gomorrah, and Lot's physical salvation from that destruction, included in the Biblical narrative? As evidence, as material for remembering what great things God has done (because of His covenant) for the fathers, that is for Father Abraham. We may find ourselves distracted with any number of details or questions about Genesis 19. But when we focus on the *why* of this chapter in light of God's covenantal duties, the meaning and purpose of Genesis 19 fall into place. The Abraham stories record evidence of God's faith and faithfulness to what He swore, or promised, to do.

## God Preserves the Life of Abraham and Sarah: Genesis 20

In this chapter Sarah is again taken from Abraham, this time by king Abimelech. Again we ask, "Why is this story included in the Abraham cycle? How does this story provide evidence that God can be trusted to fulfill His vows?" Like the story of Sarah being taken captive by Pharaoh of Egypt in Genesis 12, her abduction here follows a similar pattern. There are a few key differences. In the Egypt story of Genesis 12, and because of His promises to Abraham, God urged Abraham to protect Sarah (and hence God's promises of posterity to Abraham) by suggesting that Abraham call Sarah his sister. In ancient Egypt, the word "sister" also meant "wife", so this ambiguity preserved both Sarah and Abraham. Having learned the lesson, Abraham did not wait for God to make the preserving suggestion in Genesis 20 to call Sarah his sister. Abraham knew that God would protect him and Sarah. Abraham knew that God had promised a flesh and blood son. Abraham also knew he had an opportunity to show God's faithfulness and trustworthiness to those who did not yet know Him. Fortunately, God told Abimelech in a dream to not touch Sarah, and thereafter he returned her to Abraham. In some sense, Abraham took this as a missionary opportunity of sorts (though I doubt that such a strategy today would be met with much success or enthusiasm), stating "Because I thought, Surely the fear [i.e., respect and knowledge] of God is not in this place" (Genesis 20:11). What was Abimelech and his people to learn from this episode? They were to gain knowledge that God is a God of promises and protection. That God will covenant with His faithful servants, thereby preserving them.

What was the outcome of this story? Abraham received Sarah back into his life (necessary for them to have a promised son) and he was rewarded with additional land and material blessings. Remember that God promised land to Abraham. This story in Genesis demonstrates how God helped Abraham to bring the fulfillment of that blessing. Furthermore, because bareness had befallen Abimelech and his household, God healed Abimelech's family. They now had a testimony that God could open and close the doors of posterity.

## The Birth of Isaac, Banishment of Hagar, and Abraham's Covenant at Beersheba: Genesis 21

There are three major stories to consider in Genesis 21: the birth of Isaac, the banishment of Hagar and Ishmael, and Abraham's covenant with Abimelech at Beersheba.

## *The Birth of Isaac*

At long last, the key element of God's assurances to Abraham came to pass. Isaac was born. Yes, God had blessed Abraham with land, wealth, and a great name. But none of these mattered, none of these things were relevant without a posterity to share with. Only by having a promised posterity did land, wealth, and a great name matter. The story of the birth of Isaac was recorded in the Bible to show at long last, after Abraham and Sarah's much expectation and trusting of God, that God was true and faithful. Abraham called his son "Isaac," which we have said means laughter. Abraham and Sarah both laughed in disbelief that God would fulfill His promises to them. Now when the promise was realized, they both laughed in joy and gratitude. That son bore the name of what any of us will feel when we experience the culmination of God's promises in our lives. Isaac serves as a testimony to his parents and to us that God will bring us sure laughter at the delight of seeing that He is trustworthy, loyal, and faithful to His covenants.

As a faithful servant, Abraham soon thereafter fulfilled God's command to circumcise Isaac, as a sign of devoted loyalty to and covenant with God.

## *The Banishment of Hagar and Ishmael*

However, now that the promised son had arrived, Sarah once again turned to throw out Hagar and Abraham's other son, Ishmael. Once again the Lord had mercy upon Hagar, for the sake of the covenant He had made with her. As a wife of Abraham, Hagar had the same rights and privileges in the covenant. Similarly, God was under covenantal obligation to fulfill the promises of Abraham to Ishmael, who was also the seed of Abraham. Therefore, God reiterated to Hagar "What aileth thee, Hagar? fear not; for God hath heard the voice of the lad where he is [note that the name Ishmael literally means "heard of God"]. Arise, lift up the lad, and hold him in thine hand; for **I will make**

*The Covenant Path in the Bible and the Book of Mormon* 45

**him a great nation**" (Genesis 21:17–18; emphasis added). As a child of Abraham, Ishmael also received the promise of becoming a great nation.

As evidence to Hagar that God is a God to be trusted, He immediately brought her and Ishmael temporal salvation in the form of water: "And God opened her eyes, and she saw a well of water; and she went, and filled the bottle with water, and gave the lad drink" (Genesis 21:19).

The purpose of this story in the Abraham narrative is to convince the reader that God will complete His plan, even if humans get in the way. Sarah, like all of us who are prone to human nature, seemed to get in the way of God's plan and His promises to make Ishmael a great nation. Nevertheless, God can and will do His work. He does not compromise our agency, even if it appears to thwart His work, or appears to put a stumbling block in His plans to covenantally fulfill His promises to us. God will find a way to make good on His word. That is one of the major purposes for why this story is included in the Abraham cycle.

## *The Covenant at Beersheba*

God's promise of posterity had been fulfilled. Now the land needed to be secured. Abimelech had learned through experience what Abraham had also learned about God, "God is with thee in all that thou doest" (Genesis 21:22). Because there had been conflict between the people of Abimelech and the people of Abraham, and that conflict specifically flared up over water rights (still a source of controversy in the Middle East today), Abraham and Abimelech made a covenant with each other about who would occupy the land. Abraham gave seven ewe lambs to Abimelech, stating solemnly, and I translate loosely, "Take these animals as a witness that I dug this well with my own hands" (Genesis 21:30). Abimelech received the gift with a covenant and departed the land, returning to the land of the Philistines (vs. 32) and ceding the land to Abraham for him and his posterity. Beersheba literally means the "well of seven" or "the well of covenant" making. And still to this day, Beersheba is considered by the children of Abraham as one of the most significant pieces of land God granted to Abraham.

This chapter documents these stories so that the reader knows God will ultimately accomplish His promises of land and posterity and that the work of God (i.e., the Abrahamic covenant) cannot be frustrated.

## The Binding (Akedah) of Isaac: Genesis 22

This chapter opens in a very curious way, "And it came to pass after these things" (vs. 1). What are "these things" that the Biblical author invites the reader to consider? If we remember the purpose of the stories in the Abraham cycle, we realize that all of the stories we've read from Genesis 12 through Genesis 21 have prepared Abraham, *and us*, for this fateful moment when God gives one final test to Abraham. In fact, the text signals to us that God wants Abraham to be absolutely certain (to have a firm testimony) that God is to be trusted above all things, when it states, "God did [test] Abraham" (vs. 1, note that the word "tempt" in the King James translation is better translated as "test").

Notice that we often miss this significant but small detail just one chapter prior, "And Abraham planted a grove in Beersheba, and called there on the name of the Lord, the everlasting God" (Genesis 21:33). By what name, title, or description did Abraham call upon God? The everlasting God. Abraham knew that God was not a God for the day, or the week, or for the period of Abraham's life. God was from all time to all time. From one end of eternity to the other, (if we can even claim there are boundaries to eternity). The God that Abraham worshipped was everlasting. Everlasting in His power, His grace, His providence, His blessings, and, most significantly and appropriate for Abraham, everlasting in His commitment to the oath He made to Abraham to bless him with land, children, and a great name. God was a God to trust.

God had already given Abraham multiple opportunities to learn about the character of God, that God would be true and faithful to the unconditional covenant He made with Abraham in Genesis 15. God is trustworthy. Abraham could trust God. Abraham could know that God would fulfill His promises, not necessarily in the way that Abraham expected, but He would always come through.

What evidence do we have in Genesis 22 that after chapters and years of testimony building, Abraham had full, complete, and implicit trust in God's plan, promises, and covenantal duties? By this simple phrase, "And Abraham rose up early in the morning" (vs. 3).

## God Asks Abraham to Do the Unthinkable

"Take now thy son."

We can almost hear Abraham protesting, "I have two sons, Lord!"

"Thine only son Isaac," was the gentle and clarifying reply.

And as if to make the unimaginable demand more heart-rending, God added, "whom thou lovest."

Isaac was the focus of God's next command. That was unmistakable, however much Abraham, or we as readers, would crave for this dreadful episode to end. "Get thee into the land of Moriah; and offer him there for a burnt offering upon one of the mountains which I will tell thee of" (Genesis 22:2).

Of all the stories in scripture, this one causes some of the greatest pause! How could God let the beloved son die? How could God let the father watch the son die? How could God demand that father be the cause of the son's death? What kind of cruel God would do such a thing?

Over the ages, millions of people have read this story and most people have wondered these very questions. What are we to make of this story? Is this truly the God that we worship, one that seems to delight in the blood and gore of human sacrificial victims?

We should stop and ask ourselves again, "Why would this story be included?" We know that the Abraham cycle was recorded to show and witness to Abraham and to us as readers that God will fulfill His promises to Abraham to give him posterity, a land for that posterity, and make his name great. God is trustworthy. God is faithful. How does this story fit that pattern? How does this story function as a test for Abraham, and for us, to demonstrate God's faithfulness? To show us that God has a plan? To give evidence that the tender mercies of the Lord are over all who have faith in Him?

God raised the stakes so high that no one could miss the significance of God's trustworthiness. God wanted no mistake, no equivocation, no misunderstanding about His true nature. He knew that He needed a real test, something significant and dramatic that demanded the total faith of all involved, Abraham's and ours.

## *And Abraham Rose Up Early in the Morning*

And what do we discover Abraham doing after this colossally unexpected command to sacrifice his son? Do we find him dallying about with chores? Finding excuses to delay? Fleeing like Jonah into a far country to avoid the face of God?

Stunningly, we see this! "**And Abraham rose up early in the morning**, and saddled his ass, and took two of his young men with him, and Isaac his son, and clave the wood for the burnt offering, and rose up, and went unto the place of which God had told him" (vs. 3; emphasis added).

What parent, knowing they had to sacrifice their child, would get up early in the morning to get going on the task? Only a parent that knows a Divine Parent has vowed to provide an endless posterity. Therefore, that Divine Parent must have a divine plan to bring that about even if that plan currently seems inscrutable. Because Abraham had learned time and again, test after test, that God was everlastingly faithful, that God would find a way to make the promises real; Abraham was willing to get up early and without delay to embark on the task God had established.

We can only wonder at the surging emotions that must have coursed through Abraham's heart as he trudged to the appointed location of sacrifice. His human fallen-nature likely screamed out, "God cannot demand this. There must be another way. How will this bitter cup be removed?" while his test-strengthened spirit cried out, "I know you are the God of covenants who has made a never-ending, unchanging, immutable promise to grant me posterity. I put my life and the life of my beloved son into your hands. Your divine will be done. I have full faith and confidence that You will raise me up a posterity as You covenanted to do!"

Isaac asked the most natural question as he saw the ongoing preparations for sacrifice, "My father. . . . Behold the fire and the wood: but where is the lamb for a burnt offering?" (vs. 7).

Only a man of mighty faith and trust could have replied as Abraham did, his testimony forged and strengthened in the fires of ongoing Divine testing, "My son, God will provide himself a lamb for a burnt offering" (vs. 8). Appropriately and significantly, we learn later that the name of this sacrificial location was *Jehovahjireh*, which literally means "God will provide" (vs. 14, footnote *a*). Why? God was covenantally obligated to provide a solution to this situation. Since God had promised Abraham posterity, and since God had put Himself under covenantal obligation to make those promises real, God was therefore required to provide a plan, to find a path. Abraham's role was to trust, to believe, to have faith that God would be the God He had promised to Abraham to be. Because God demonstrated yet again His covenantal loyalty, the location of the near-sacrifice of Isaac was called for many long generations, "In the mount of the LORD it shall be seen" or in my alternate translation "In the mount of the Lord He shall provide a divine plan to fulfill His promises" (vs. 14).

## God Reiterates Promises to Abraham

At the climax of this divine event, God spoke to Abraham again, confirming the promises made way back at the beginning of the Abraham cycle in Genesis 12:1–3, "And the angel of the

LORD called unto Abraham out of heaven the second time, And said, By myself have I sworn, saith the Lord, for because thou hast done this thing, and hast not withheld thy son, thine only son: That in blessing I will bless thee, and in multiplying I will multiply thy seed as the stars of the heaven, and as the sand which is upon the sea shore; and thy seed shall possess the gate of his enemies; And in thy seed shall all the nations of the earth be blessed; because thou hast obeyed my voice" (Genesis 22:15–18).

Notice that God said "By myself have I sworn." This is a curious phrase. What does God mean? He made the unconditional covenant to Abraham willingly, without coercion, on His own; no one else made the covenant, no one else is committed or obligated. God alone will be the God of Abraham. God alone will be the God of the fathers. God alone will be the God of the covenant. God alone will fulfill what the covenant demands.

## Sarah Dies and Abraham Secures the Land: Genesis 23

Sarah dies in the chapter and the story captures the interactions Abraham had with the people of the land for him to secure a burying place for Sarah, and later for himself. From a covenant path perspective, the purpose of this chapter is to show how the land promised to Abraham by God was given into the hand of Abraham. Yes, Abraham had to act. But God Himself was the surety that the land would eventually be Abraham's.

## Isaac Marries Rebekah: Genesis 24

Genesis 24 records the story of how Abraham found a wife for Isaac, by sending a trusted servant on this special mission. Why is this story included in the Abraham cycle? Because it was not enough for Abraham to have a promised son. That son needed to be married within a covenantal relationship in order to continue and expand the blessings of posterity. Knowing that He had the covenantal strength and blessings of God to support him, Abraham trusted that he would succeed in finding a wife for his son Isaac, "The LORD God of heaven, which took me from my father's house, and from the land of my kindred, and which spake unto me, and that sware unto me, saying, Unto thy seed will I give this land; he shall send his angel before thee, and thou shalt take a wife unto my son from thence" (vs. 7). He therefore sent his trusted servant on an errand back to the land of Haran in Mesopotamia, where Abraham had once lived, to seek a wife from among the daughters of Laban, Abraham's grand-nephew. Rebekah's consent to the marriage was received when "they called Rebekah, and said unto her, Wilt thou go with this man? And she said, I will go" (vs. 58). In response her family blessed her with these words that align with God's promises to Abraham, "Thou art our sister, be thou the mother of thousands of millions, and let thy seed possess the gate of those which hate them" (vs. 60).

This story is included in the Abraham cycle to demonstrate how God will prosper (that means to fulfill His promises) the way of His faithful followers, as fulfillment of the covenant.

## Abraham Dies: Genesis 25

The Abraham cycle concludes in Genesis 25. This chapter lists many of the descendants of Abraham, evidence that God had indeed fulfilled His promise to give an overflowing posterity to Abraham and make his name great. We also see in this chapter the transition from Abraham as the focal point of the patriarchal promises to Isaac. When Abraham died, Isaac assumed his role as the heir of the Abrahamic promises. Without the long delay Abraham experienced in seeing God's promise of posterity fulfilled, Isaac soon had twins, Esau and Jacob. And Jacob would continue the covenantal line of promise, later being renamed to Israel.

## The God of the Fathers: The God of Abraham, Isaac, and Jacob

We've learned in the Abraham cycle that God put Himself under covenantal obligation to fulfill His promises to Abraham.

And we saw, by means of an in-depth review, that the stories found in Genesis 12–25 are each profitably read as covenantal texts. When we read through the lens of God's covenantal faithfulness to Abraham and Abraham's trust of God, these stories create a unified message that God is true and faithful.

But what happened after Abraham? How did God's covenant persist? God renewed the covenant with Abraham's son Isaac and with Jacob, the son of Isaac. I'll only share a few brief scriptural passages of how God renewed His original covenant to Abraham with Isaac and Joseph.

God first renewed His promises to Abraham with Isaac: "And the LORD appeared unto [Isaac], and said, Go not down into Egypt; dwell in the land which I shall tell thee of: Sojourn in this land, and I will be with thee, and will bless thee; for unto thee, and unto thy seed, I will give all these countries, and I will perform the oath which I sware unto Abraham thy father; And I will make thy seed to multiply as the stars of heaven, and will give unto thy seed all these countries; and in thy seed shall all the nations of the earth be blessed; Because that Abraham obeyed my voice, and kept my charge, my commandments, my statutes, and my laws" (Genesis 26:2–5). The chapter after Abraham's death, Isaac became the stand-in for Abraham in the covenant.

In the very next chapter, God extended the promise to Isaac's son Jacob, "And God Almighty bless thee, and make thee fruitful, and multiply thee, that thou mayest be a multitude of people; And give thee the blessing of Abraham, to thee, and to thy seed with thee; that thou mayest inherit the land wherein thou art a stranger, which God gave unto Abraham" (Genesis 28:3–4). Jacob's name was covenantally changed to Israel (see Genesis 32:28). He had twelve sons, who became known as the twelve tribes of Israel. These went to Egypt to avoid famine. But many years later their descendants were put into bondage and slavery by the Egyptians. Only God could save them as He was covenantally obligated to do. After He saved them from Egypt, He brought them to Sinai to offer them a new covenant to be His people and for Him to be their God. That, in essence, is the purpose of the stories found in Exodus, Leviticus, Numbers, and Deuteronomy, which we'll discuss later in the book.

The stories of Isaac and Jacob demonstrate God's efforts to fulfill His obligations to make the covenant available to Abraham's seed. Abraham, Isaac, and Jacob are the three honored patriarchs in the Genesis story. These three patriarchs (the word "patriarch" means father-leader) are the covenantal fathers.

## Summary of the Abraham Cycle (Genesis 12–25)

We come to the conclusion of the Abraham cycle, the set of stories that express God's covenantal commitment and obligations to Abraham and his posterity. The covenant to Abraham is unconditional, available to each of Abraham's children. This is one of the major covenants on God's covenant path. The mountain of Moriah (Zion) is God's mountain of unconditional commitment to Abraham's posterity. We'll see in the next section how at Mount Sinai, God put the Israelites under covenant to be loyal to Him. Their personal reception and fulfillment of the blessings of the Abrahamic covenant were conditioned on their loyalty to God as explained in the covenant at Mount Sinai.

We have reviewed the Abraham stories at length because they are core and foundational for understanding the covenant path. We have seen that God made promises to Abraham and obligated Himself to achieve those promises by entering into a solemn covenant with Abraham. We learned that sacrificial animals metaphorically represent what will happen to those who do not keep their covenants. We also learned that those who pass through the covenant path of the separated animal parts are covenantally obligated to fulfill the duties of the covenant. We came to see that only God is responsible for bringing to pass the promises to Abraham. Though we call it the Abrahamic covenant or the Abrahamic promises, we would be more accurate to call this God's covenantal obligations and promises to Abraham. The stories of Genesis 12–25 teach us about this covenant and show multiple examples of God demonstrating loyalty to Abraham. Furthermore, we observe in these stories Abraham's on-going development as a faithful servant of God. Abraham had to learn to trust God. Abraham had to learn to believe God. The only way for him, and for any of us, to learn that God will be true and faithful to His word is for God to give us trials and challenges where God's faithfulness is tested. Yes, we have to demonstrate our own faithfulness to God. But God wants us to see and experience His faithfulness to us. He wants us to know Him as the Almighty God. How can He do that if there are no circumstances in our lives for Him to display His almighty power? If His promises never came under threat, what opportunity would there be for God to show that He is loyal and faithful to us? What opportunity would He have to demonstrate His commitments to us by making those promises real? Just as we need opportunities to demonstrate our loyalty to God, He also makes use of opportunities to demonstrate his loyalty and faithfulness to us and His trustworthiness. God will show us, as He showed the patriarchs, that He is a rock that we can rely on.

We learn these lessons from the story of Abraham, and the stories of Isaac and Jacob follow the same pattern leading to the conclusion that ours is the God of Abraham, Isaac, and Jacob. In other words, that title for God, "the God of Abraham, Isaac, and Jacob," can rightly be translated as "the God who is faithful, trustworthy, willing, and capable to consistently fulfill the tremendous promises made to Father Abraham of property and posterity." Therefore, any loyal and faithful child of Abraham—and that includes you and includes me—can petition God to come to their aid when these promises are under threat. And He will. A careful study of the Biblical and Book of Mormon records will bear this out. Indeed, the scriptures have been written and preserved in part, to tell that very story, to give witness to the covenantal character of God's loyalty to us, just as He invites us to be loyal to Him. This divine and mutual loyalty is the essence of the covenant path.

# PART 2
## MOUNT SINAI AND THE COVENANT GOD OFFERED THE HOUSE OF ISRAEL

# CHAPTER 4

# GOD FULFILLS HIS COVENANT WITH ABRAHAM BY SAVING ISRAEL FROM EGYPT

The Book of Genesis is centered on God's unconditional covenant to Abraham (symbolized by Mount Moriah/Zion), while the Book of Exodus is centered on God's invitation through Moses to the House of Israel (as children of Abraham) to covenant to be His people (symbolized by Mount Sinai). Of the Five Books of Moses, also known as the Torah, (Genesis, Exodus, Leviticus, Numbers, and Deuteronomy) Genesis is thoroughly saturated and dominated by the covenant to Abraham while Exodus, Leviticus, Numbers, and Deuteronomy are thoroughly saturated and dominated by God's conditional covenant with the Israelites at Sinai. In some ways, the Mosaic or Sinai covenant is more influential and better known throughout recorded scripture than is God's covenant with Abraham, not because people are especially familiar with the covenant. Rather they are familiar with elements that support the Sinai covenant. Most people know that God made promises to Abraham, but few people realize that only God Himself is under covenant to bring those promises to reality.

On the other hand, most of us know about Moses encountering God at the burning bush, God's wondrous acts of salvation bringing the Israelites out of bondage, and His seeking to be in covenantal relationship with them. God sought to enact that covenantal relationship by delivering the Ten Commandments, by establishing priestly protocols for ritual and atonement, and by constructing a mobile temple in the wilderness with gradations of sanctity later to be replaced by the immovable Temple of Solomon at Jerusalem. Much of the Torah (the Five Books of Moses) and the narrative sections of the Old Testament and many of the Old Testament prophets are focused on the conditional covenant God made with His people at Sinai. And most of us know that there are many obligations we, as God's people, must live by to have His blessings and presence in our lives. We generally understand that is the essence of what the scriptures seek to convey.

What I'm trying to demonstrate in this book that the Sinai covenant is what instructs us on our covenantal obligations and duties (the commandments and so forth), while the Abrahamic promises record what God has to offer us. To truly understand the Bible, Biblical history, and the history of the House of Israel, we must understand these covenants, especially the conditional covenant at Sinai. In fact, many of the books in the Old Testament were written with one or the other covenant serving as the foundational orienting theme. The table below provides a grouping of the Old Testament books whose main theme is either the Abrahamic covenant or the Mosaic covenant.

| Old Testament Books Centered on the Theme of the Abrahamic (and Davidic) Covenant | Old Testament Books Centered on the Theme of the Sinai or Mosaic Covenant |
| --- | --- |
| Genesis<br>1 Chronicles<br>2 Chronicles<br>Ezra<br>Nehemiah<br>Haggai<br>Zechariah<br>Isaiah (portions)<br>Psalms (portions) | Exodus<br>Leviticus<br>Numbers<br>Deuteronomy<br>Joshua<br>Judges<br>1 Samuel<br>2 Samuel<br>1 Kings<br>2 Kings<br>Wisdom literature (Proverbs, etc.)<br>Hosea<br>Jeremiah |

## Why Did the Israelites Need God and Salvation?

The Book of Exodus opens with a list of the twelve tribes of Israel. The patriarchs have all passed on. But God has been true to His promise to multiply Abraham's posterity and to make his name great: "And the children of Israel were fruitful, and increased abundantly, and multiplied, and waxed exceeding mighty; and the land was filled with them" (Exodus 1:7). However, not all of God's promises were being met. God's people were not in the promised land.

Exodus lays out the tension clearly:

> Now there arose up a new king over Egypt, which knew not Joseph. And he said unto his people [the Egyptians], Behold, the people of the children of Israel are more and mightier than we: Come on, let us deal wisely with them; lest they multiply, and it come to pass, that, when there falleth out any war, they join also unto our enemies, and fight against us, and so get them up out of the land. Therefore they did set over them taskmasters to afflict them with their burdens. And they built for Pharaoh treasure cities, Pithom and Raamses. But the more they afflicted them, the more they multiplied and

grew. And they were grieved because of the children of Israel. And the Egyptians made the children of Israel to serve with rigour: And they made their lives bitter with hard bondage, in morter, and in brick, and in all manner of service in the field: all their service, wherein they made them serve, was with rigour. (Exodus 1:8–14)

The Israelites continued to suffer in bondage and God continued to bless them. As God blessed them, Pharaoh continued to stiffen the oppression, leading God to further strengthen and empower the Israelites. Still, the Israelites were slaves in a foreign land. They had few, if any rights. They were mistreated, misunderstood, feared, scorned, and taken advantage of. God watched on.

The tides changed in Exodus 2. Pay attention to how Exodus narrates that God remembered His covenantal duties.

> And it came to pass in process of time, that the king of Egypt died: and the children of Israel sighed by reason of the bondage, and they cried, and their cry came up unto God by reason of the bondage. And God heard their groaning, and **God remembered his covenant with Abraham, with Isaac, and with Jacob**. And God looked upon the children of Israel, and God had respect unto them [i.e., He knew and recognized their suffering and their need for salvation]. (Exodus 2:23–25; emphasis added)

Though Exodus will introduce us to a new covenant, the Abrahamic covenant is still in full force. God's covenant path includes Him remembering the promises made to the fathers. Exodus lays out the covenantal logic. The children of Abraham, specifically those of the House of Israel, were suffering in a foreign land. God was duty-bound to bring them to the land of promise, as He had promised to Abraham, Isaac, and Jacob.

## Did the Israelites Know God before Moses Revealed Him?

We should acknowledge here that the Israelites likely *had little to no idea who God was at this point!* The Israelites had not been faithful to any commandments. They didn't know the commandments. The Israelites had not been righteous or faithful. There was no expectation that they had received from God. They had not called upon God. Yes, their cry had come up unto God. But this only indicated that God heard them and knew of their suffering. There is no evidence that the Israelites were actively praying to God, petitioning God, or making sacrifices to God to get His attention. For all they knew, they were alone in the world with no Greater Power to save them. They were living in ignorance and in bondage temporal and spiritual.

Why do I make this point that the Israelites were seemingly ignorant of God? To underscore that God acted *on behalf of His covenant to Abraham, Isaac, and Jacob.* We'll see additional evidence momentarily that the Israelites had no idea who God was and that He would and could save them. Exodus 1–2 sets up the scenario to show us that God acts out of covenantal duty, loyalty, and love. God covenanted by passing through the cut-up animals of Genesis 15 to fulfill His vows or cease to be God. But God is the everlasting God. He will not cease to be God. Therefore, we can have ultimate, preserving, and thoroughgoing faith and trust that He will bring about the purposes He promised to the patriarchs.

## God Is Covenantally Bound to Save the Israelites from Egypt

As Exodus continues to narrate the drama-filled story, Moses enters. After he fled from Egypt, he found his way to Midian, becoming a shepherd and Jethro's son-in-law. The story is well known. One day while out with his flocks, Moses had an unexpected, life-changing, divine encounter.

And the angel of the LORD [i.e., God Himself / Jehovah] appeared unto [Moses] in a flame of fire out of the midst of a bush: and he looked, and, behold, the bush burned with fire, and the bush was not consumed. . . . Moreover [Jehovah] said, I am the God of thy father, the God of Abraham, the God of Isaac, and the God of Jacob. And Moses hid his face; for he was afraid to look upon God. And the LORD said, I have surely seen the affliction of my people which are in Egypt, and have heard their cry by reason of their taskmasters; for I know their sorrows; And **I am come down to deliver them out of the hand of the Egyptians, and to bring them up out of that land unto a good land** and a large, unto a land flowing with milk and honey; unto the place of the Canaanites, and the Hittites, and the Amorites, and the Perizzites, and the Hivites, and the Jebusites. (Exodus 3:2, 6–8; emphasis added)

In the quote above, I've highlighted two of the major reasons that God gave for why He was going to save the Israelites: (1) to deliver them from the hand of the Egyptians and (2) to bring the Israelites up out of that land (of Egypt) unto a good land, that is, the promised land. God's rationale for acting was motivated by commitment to His covenantal promises to the patriarchs. Yes, God loved His people. Yes, He did not want them to suffer longer. All of these things are true. But what we must not miss is the covenant path God was, and is, on. He is a God of covenants. He is a God of commitments. He is honor and duty bound to keep His covenants and His commitments. That is what it means to be on the covenant path, to make sacred oaths and promises to do certain things and then when the opportunity for action arises, to act faithfully in accordance with declared promises.

These later Israelites had sure knowledge that the God of Abraham, Isaac, and Jacob would deliver them in their afflictions because of what God eventually did for the Israelites in Egypt and the wilderness. God was and is the God of deliverance. Later we'll see why Nephi acted with so much faith and tenacity when faced with the seemingly impossible task to confront murderous Laban. Nephi knew that God would deliver the faithful.

## Did Moses Know God Before the Burning Bush?

Returning to Moses' encounter with God, we have to take the perspective that knowledge of the Ten Commandments and of the atoning sacrifice of Jesus Christ were all in the future. At the moment that Moses first encountered God, he was as innocent as a babe in terms of His knowledge and awareness of the God of the fathers. Notice how Moses responded when God told him to return to Egypt to deliver the people out of bondage, "When I come unto the children of Israel, and shall say unto them, The God of your fathers hath sent me unto you; and they shall say to me, What is his name? what shall I say unto them?" (Exodus 3:13).

Isn't that a fair question from Moses? We can hear him saying "God, you've sent me on an errand. We've just met. I don't even know who you are. Do you have a name? How am I to introduce you to the teeming masses of Israelites? What am I to tell them about You, especially so that I can convince them that I am not crazy, that You are real, and that they can trust You?"

God's everlasting reply to Moses still echoes across the generations for its sublimity and mysterious truth, "I Am That I Am: and he said, Thus shalt thou say unto the children of Israel, I Am hath sent me unto you" (Exodus 3:14).

## God Is the Self-Existing One—and the Reason that All Things Are!

If we looked at the original Hebrew of "I Am That I Am" we'd read *ehyeh asher ehyeh*. The verb *ehyeh* is the basis for the name *Yahweh*, the Hebrew name for God that has come down to us through some mangled transliteration as Jehovah. So "I Am That I Am" is God saying "I am Jehovah!" Or more beautifully:

The word Yahweh is the present tense of the Hebrew verb "to be." Other English translations of Yahweh's name could include "The Self-Existing One," "The Being," or simply "Is." Significantly, and distinct from many languages that I have studied, the present tense of the verb "to be" in Hebrew is reserved wholly and singularly for Yahweh. If I want to say in Hebrew, "I am a man," I simply say, "I a man" and readers and listeners fill in the context of the missing verb "to be" (in this case, the present tense form "am").

That sounds silly, of course, in English to say phrases without the verb "to be" such as "She a girl," "That a dog," "He a boy," or "You a friend." Instead, we appropriately expect to hear "She is a girl," "That is a dog," "He is a boy," or "You are a friend." You'll often notice in our English versions of the Old Testament italicized present tense forms of the verb "to be" because the words do not appear in the Hebrew so the translators supplied them for us, indicated by italics in print editions. See for example Genesis 1:29 where the present tense verb "is" is italicized: "And God said, Behold, I have given you every herb bearing seed, which is upon the face of all the earth, and every tree, in the which is the fruit of a tree yielding seed; to you it shall be for meat."

Think of the stunning symbolism and awesome reality that an entire language reserves the utterance of any present tense form of "to be" to God Himself whose name is "the Self-Existing One": Yahweh.

So, the next time you read the Old Testament and see the word "God" know that way back when in ancient Hebrew this read as "Gods." When you see the word LORD in all caps, know that the translators reverently did not say the name Yahweh. And when you remember that LORD = Yahweh you can also remember that He, the Self-Existing One, is the reason that all things ARE. ("How the Hebrew Translations of God and Jehovah Might Change Your Understanding of Deity" *LDS Living*, October 9, 2017, Taylor Halverson.)

Before the burning bush, Moses seems to have had no idea who God was, that He existed, or even something as simple as what to call Him. We, on the other hand, are awash in scripture, in revelation, and in Restoration truths so that it is difficult to imagine that a stalwart like Moses, or even all the children of Israel living in Egyptian bondage, had little to no idea who God was and had had no interaction with God prior to Moses's first encounter at Sinai. This is why we cannot argue that God acted to save the Israelites due to some righteousness or faithfulness on their part. They were in ignorance. Even Adam and Eve in all their innocence may have had more knowledge about God than the Israelites who were in Egypt. All that was about to change.

## God Declares His Why of Salvation, His Why for Saving the Israelites

> And God said moreover unto Moses, Thus shalt thou say unto the children of Israel, the LORD God of your fathers, **the God of Abraham, the God of Isaac, and the God of Jacob**, hath sent me unto you: this is my name for ever [Yahweh/Jehovah/I Am That I Am], and this is my memorial unto all generations. Go, and gather the elders of Israel together, and say unto them, The LORD God of your fathers, the God of Abraham, of Isaac, and of Jacob, appeared unto me, saying, I have surely visited you, and seen that which is done to you in Egypt: And I have said, I will bring you up out of the affliction of Egypt unto the land of the Canaanites, and the Hittites, and the Amorites, and the Perizzites, and the Hivites, and the Jebusites, unto a land flowing with milk and honey. (Exodus 3:15–17; emphasis added)

Notice again that God consistently gives Himself the title of "the God of Abraham, the God of Isaac, and the God of Jacob." The Israelites probably had heard some family stories of the great deeds God had done for their forefathers. They probably had some faint inkling of the trust their patriarchal ancestors exhibited. They may have known that their ancestors worshipped someone. But it appears, based on the narrative in Exodus, that the children of Israel knew very little about who God was, His character, His attributes, and, importantly, His covenantal nature and obligations. When God told Moses to introduce Him as the God of the Fathers, God wanted the Israelites to know Him as a covenantal God, a God who keeps His promises, a God that can be trusted, a God who will deliver His people. All of these meanings are bound up in the phrase "the God of Abraham, the God of Isaac, and the God of Jacob."

Moses did as he was commanded. He left Midian and returned to Egypt. He used his brother Aaron as a spokesperson, because Moses had a severe enough speech impediment that he had demanded of God someone to speak on his behalf. Aaron and Moses performed signs and wonders to convince the Israelites that they were legitimate representatives of God and they believed and worshipped God (see Exodus 4:31).

## Why Does God Want Us in the Wilderness?

There still was the matter of leaving Egypt. God had given Moses these instructions: "Ye shall say unto [Pharaoh], The LORD God of the Hebrews hath met with us: and now let us go, we beseech thee, three days' journey into the wilderness, that we may sacrifice to the LORD our God" (Exodus 3:18).

Let's reflect on these instructions. Why was it so important to God that the Israelites leave Egypt and journey several days into the wilderness to worship God? Can't we pray to God anywhere? Can't we show our devotions to Him in all places and at all times? Why didn't God simply ask the Israelites to throw a festival in His honor in Egypt? What was so special about the wilderness?

Though God is the God of the whole world, the wilderness holds a special place in His heart. Why? Because in the wilderness God is more easily found. When God seeks to build a people, He pulls them out of cities, He takes them from civilization, and He plants them in the wild places of the earth (the word "wilderness" literally means the "more wild parts"). Why? Because in the wilderness we are nothing. In the wilderness we are fully and entirely dependent upon God. In the city, we can pay for our time and resources for others to take care of all our needs.

Only in the wilderness will God meet all of our needs because only there are we truly back in our natural state of dependence. Consider that when God wanted to build a new people with Lehi's tribe He had them flee from civilization, from the city of Jerusalem, and enter the wilderness. After Jesus was baptized and acknowledged by God as His Beloved Son, Jesus headed out into the wilderness to be with God. Jesus did not go to the city. He did not immerse himself in human civilization. Jesus found God in the wilderness. Remember the story of the tower of Babel. God threw down the tower and the designs that these humans had contrived to build for themselves a city and civilization that they might make their name great. God scattered the people of Babel and sowed their languages with confusion. It was then that Jared and his brother fled into the wilderness there to find God, there to be with God, there to be guided by God to a promised land. God invites His people into the wilderness so that they can be in full communion and relationship with Him without the noise and distractions and allures of human-built salvation that will all pass away.

## God Showed Off His Mighty Powers to Save

Returning to God's call to Moses to draw the people out into the wilderness, God knew in advance that Pharaoh would utterly refuse to let the people go, saying, "And I am sure that the king of Egypt will not let you go, no, not by a mighty hand. And I will stretch out my hand, and smite Egypt with all my wonders which I will do in the midst thereof: and after that he will let you go" (Exodus 3:19–20).

Why didn't God simply allow the Israelites to remain in Egypt to worship Him? I shared some ideas above about the revealing power of wilderness to find God. Furthermore, God had promised Abraham and His posterity a promised land. Egypt was not the promised land for these people. Finally, and significantly, God wanted to take advantage of the circumstances of Pharaoh's hard heart to demonstrate His character, His power, His wisdom, His nature, His wonders. God wanted the Israelites to know Him, that He had the power to save His people, that He was true to His promises. By means of the obstacle of Pharaoh's pride, God had a pathway to display His power and His abilities. He wanted the Israelites to have a testimony of who He is.

The Book of Exodus deftly crafts narrative tension as a way to reveal the true nature of God, that He is a God of covenant making and covenant keeping. He is the God who is under covenant to bring His people into the promised land. The more spectacular the wondrous acts of salvation, the more long-lasting the convincing power He hoped He would have in the hearts and minds of His people.

What follows in Exodus 4–15 are a series of mighty acts of salvation God enacted against Egypt on behalf of His people.

- The plague of blood (Exodus 7:14–24).
- The plague of frogs (Exodus 7:25–8:15).
- The plague of lice and gnats (Exodus 8:16–19).
- The plague of wild animals or flies (Exodus 8:20–32).
- The plague afflicting livestock (Exodus 9:1–7).
- The plague of boils (Exodus 9:8–12).
- The plague of thunderstorm of hail and fire (Exodus 9:13–35).
- The plague of locusts (Exodus 10:1–20).
- The plague of darkness for three days (Exodus 10:21–29).
- The plague of the death of all firstborn not protected by the blood of the Atonement (Exodus 11:1–12:36).

We should add to this list the wondrous pillar of fire by night and cloud by day of God's presence that led the Israelites through the wilderness. And the most wondrous act of salvation occurred at the Red Sea where God smashed the Egyptian army and led the Israelites through dry ground: "Thus the LORD saved Israel that day out of the hand of the Egyptians; and Israel saw the Egyptians dead upon the sea shore. And Israel saw that great work which the

LORD did upon the Egyptians: and the people feared the Lord, and believed the Lord, and his servant Moses" (Exodus 14:30–31).

## Israelites Gained a Testimony of God's All-Powerful Salvation

After the final act that confirmed the physical salvation of the Israelites—the opening and closing of the Red Sea—the Israelites had no doubt about who God was. They shouted grateful praises to Him, asking these rhetorical questions, "Who is like unto thee, O LORD, among the gods? who is like thee, glorious in holiness, fearful in praises, doing wonders?" (Exodus 15:11). The obvious answer is that *no one* is like God. The Hebrew name *Michael* is itself a combination of three Hebrew words put together in interrogatory format ("Who is like God?"), much like we find in Exodus 15:11, with the unmistakable answer of "no one is like God!" God was preparing the Israelites to covenant with Him by revealing to them His character, powers, salvations, wonders, miracles, purposes, and nature.

Once in the wilderness, God continued to bare His arm in strength and salvation unto the Israelites, providing them manna or daily bread (note that the Liahona functioned like spiritual manna for the people of Lehi in the Book of Mormon), bringing fresh water forth from a rock, saving them from enemies, and giving them justice and judgment. What is the purpose of all these stories recorded in the Bible? To give overwhelming evidence, demonstrations, and support that the Israelites could trust God. He was like none other. He had all power, all majesty, all possibilities. God had labored diligently for the benefit of the people of Israel. After these mighty acts of salvation, He revealed why He had done all this:

> Ye have seen what I did unto the Egyptians, and how I bare you on eagles' wings, and brought you unto myself. Now therefore, **if** ye will obey my voice indeed, and keep my covenant, then ye shall be a peculiar treasure unto me above all people: for all the earth is mine: And ye shall be unto me

a kingdom of priests, and an holy nation. These are the words which thou shalt speak unto the children of Israel. (Exodus 19:4–6; emphasis added)

## God Makes Covenants With and in Order to Create a Treasured People

God wanted a special people, a covenant people, a treasured people who would be in covenantal relationship with Him. God had been true and faithful to His covenant to Abraham (providing property and posterity). God now wanted this contingent of Abraham's posterity to covenant with Him, to pledge their faith, devotion, and loyalty to God. He had demonstrated His trustworthiness, His power, His magnificent ability to save. He did all this to invite and encourage the Israelites that they too could become a covenant people as He was a covenant God.

Notice that I highlighted the word "if" in the scripture quoted above. That word, one of the smallest in the English language, is one of the most significant words in the covenant presented by God to the Israelites in Exodus (and throughout other portions of scripture). There is no *if* in the Abrahamic covenant. As long as God is God, He is duty and covenantally bound to fulfill His promise to Abraham to make his name great, and to grant him posterity and property.

However, when it comes to the covenant at Mount Sinai, there is a big *if*. That "if" signals a conditionality within the covenant. That "if" has nothing to do with God. In other words, the covenant is *not* about what God will or will not do. Rather, that "if" is directed to the Israelites and their heirs (all of us). That "if" is about whether we will be true and faithful to God. That "if" is about whether we will commit to keeping the commandments and then follow through with our commitment, or, at the very least have the righteous desire and intent to show loyalty to God. This covenant that God presents to the Israelites in Exodus puts the agency in their hands. Anyone who makes the covenantal commitment to God but has no desire to live the covenant is taking the Lord's name in vain. They are covenanting with no purpose, or with empty purpose, the key meaning of the word "vain." As long as we do not covenant in vain, we are within the bounds of covenantal loyalty. As long as our righteous intent is to strive to be faithful followers of God, we will not have compromised our position in the covenant.

# CHAPTER 5

# THE SECOND COVENANT OF THE COVENANT PATH REVEALED AT MOUNT SINAI

And this is where Exodus 20 reveals the second great covenant of the covenant path: the conditional covenant at Sinai. This covenant has been hiding in plain sight (the chapter with the Ten Commandments), but most of us have missed it. We cannot be on the covenant path if we cannot see the path. To see the path we need to see the covenants. The conditional covenant at Mount Sinai is one of the foundational covenants to see and understand of the covenant path. This covenant originated at Mount Sinai and is found peppered through the structure and language of the scriptures. I hope that what I share here will reveal and make plain the covenant path that permeates the Old Testament, the New Testament, the Book of Mormon, and even the Doctrine and Covenants and the Restoration.

I hope as you see what this covenant is, how it is described, and the words that mark the covenant, that you will see this covenant marking the path of the gospel throughout your scripture and gospel study.

The covenant at Sinai follows a simple, powerful structure that is found repeated throughout scripture, usually following this format below, though sometimes the order is found in a different sequence or with emphasis placed on different sections of the covenant.

1. God introduces Himself.
2. God reviews the great deeds that He has done for the people to encourage their loyalty, devotion, gratitude, and allegiance to Him.
3. God provides instructions on how to show Him covenantal love and loyalty. These stipulations are often in the form of commandments, stipulations, or divine statutes.
4. Witnesses certify or ratify the covenant.
5. God explains the blessings and curses associated with the covenant that are conditioned on one's covenantal loyalty and devotion to Him.
6. God ensures that the covenant is recorded and preserved in sacred location (like the Ark of the Covenant, or the temple).

The order, or number, of the covenantal elements is not what is significant. What does matter is that God, as the Supreme Power in the universe, invites His people to enter into a covenant. They are agents unto themselves. He does not force them. He gives them choice. The covenant is conditional. If they keep the commandments and divine statutes that He reveals, they will be blessed with a fullness of the promises made to Abraham. Those who fail to show devoted loyalty to God lose their access to the blessings of Abraham.

Let's now look closely at Exodus 20 and see how these scriptures fit the pattern of the covenant God offered His people at Sinai with its attendant promises and blessings conditioned on faithful devotion to God. Just as God had been faithful to the patriarchs and their descendants, God invited the people to follow His example and commit to be devoted covenant partakers with Him.

## Part 1 of the Covenant: God Introduces Himself (Exodus 20:1–2)

And God spake all these words, saying, I am the LORD thy God.

Earlier we discussed that when we encounter the word LORD in all capitals in the Old Testament, that is the English translation for rendering the Hebrew word for Jehovah. We also discussed that the word Jehovah is more accurately rendered Yahweh, or I Am That I Am. So the phrase "I am the Lord thy God" would more precisely be expressed as "I am Jehovah/ I Am That I Am/ Yahweh thy God." This is the very name that God used to reveal Himself to Moses and the name that He commanded Moses to reveal to the people in their salvation from Egypt. When God initiated the covenant at Mount Sinai, He began by introduction Himself to the people. He declared His identity. The people needed to know Who they were entering into covenant with.

## Part 2 of the Covenant: God Reviews His Great Deeds to Encourage Loyalty (Exodus 20:2)

> I am the LORD thy God, which have brought thee out of the land of Egypt, out of the house of bondage.

Before inviting the people to enter into covenantal relationship with Him, God briefly summarized the great deeds He had done for them so that they would remember His love for and loyalty to them. God wanted to sear into their minds that He was a God that could be trusted. That He Himself was a God of covenant. Remember, based on their own efforts or their own actions, they did not deserve to be saved. There was nothing that the Israelites had done, said, believed, acted upon, or planned to deserve salvation. The salvation that God gave them was a free gift. God had acted on and had given them grace. He saved them because of love. He didn't save them because they deserved it. He did not save them because they had been righteous. He did not save them because they had been faithful. They had little to no idea who God was before Moses revealed Him to them. God acted to save them because He loved their forefathers. And he loved (i.e., was loyal to) Abraham, Isaac, and Jacob and was devoted to the covenant He had made to them. God presented such an indomitable position of strength, how could the people have felt anything but devotion, gratitude, and loyalty to God? When they remembered what great things God had done for them, they would have felt an overwhelming sense of "This is the God that I want to be in covenantal relationship with!"

The word "remember" is one of the most important covenantal terms in all of scripture found in phrases like "Remember what great things God has done. The word does not appear in the verse above, but is implicit in the covenantal relationship. When you remember what great things God has done, you'll remember His undying love and devotion to you and to the Abrahamic Covenant. You'll remember His grace. And then you'll remember to follow His lead to enter into a covenant relationship with Him and like Him, stay loyal and committed to that covenant.

To remember means to put members back together again. The scriptures are full of stories of God's saving acts, mercy, and love. But these stories get scattered across the books of scripture and fall to pieces in our own memories when we don't regularly review them. God has asked us to put the pieces back together in a coherent order, that we can make sense of His wondrous acts and see and feel, as did the Israelites at Mount Sinai, His indomitable power, His thorough loyalty to His covenantal obligations, and His love for us. When we put the pieces back together, we are re-membering. And in remembering, we see the whole picture of God's plan of salvation and our place in it. If we fail to remember, we will fail to see God's purpose, fail to understand His plan, fail to see the need for covenants and covenantal loyalty, which will lead us to fail to be in a covenantal relationship with God. Ultimately we will fail to experience the joys and blessings of this life and in the life to come. In essence, the covenant God made to Abraham and the covenant God invited the Israelites to enter into at Sinai are the boundary stones marking the path—the covenant path—that lead us into His presence. When we remember, we acknowledge the boundaries, we see the stepping stones along the pathway. Forget, or fail to remember, and then we fail to see the way, we fail to put the steps of the path in their proper place and we find ourselves wandering lost, off in forbidden paths into the wastes of nothingness.

On the topic of remember, think of how often that word appears in scripture. The entire point of the yearly Passover meal that the Israelites celebrated was to remember the great deeds God had done for them in saving them from hard bondage. That remembering was updated at the last Passover supper Jesus participated in when He revealed that He was the Passover Lamb, slaughtered to save the Israelites from bondage. Note how seamlessly and beautifully the covenant path unfolds to our very day. When we partake of the sacrament each week, we are re-enacting the Passover meal God revealed to the Israelites as a means for them to remember the covenant path. And like the Israelites, we are asked to remember. And what are we to remember? We are to "always remember" Jesus and remember to "keep his commandments" (see for example Moroni 4:3). By so doing, we will have put the members of the covenant path in their proper place so that we do not stumble as we make our return journey to the presence of God.

We also see the theme of remembering in the final promise of the Book of Mormon. We so often focus on the need to pray to ask God if the Book of Mormon is true that we entirely miss Moroni's exhortation for us to do the hard work first of remembering.

> Behold, I would exhort you that when ye shall read these things, if it be wisdom in God that ye should read them, that ye would **remember how merciful the Lord hath been unto the children of men, from the creation of Adam even down until the time that ye shall receive these things**, and ponder it in your hearts. (Moroni 10:3; emphasis added)

We also see Lehi in offering his final counsel to his family pleading with them to remember the great things the Lord had done for them and their forefathers:

And I desire that ye should remember to observe the statutes and the judgments of the Lord; behold, this hath been the anxiety of my soul from the beginning. (2 Nephi 1:16)

All of this remembering is Mount Sinai covenantal language. It is the language of our duties in the covenant to show loyalty to God. If we do not remember, we cannot show loyalty. Just as God remembered His covenant to Abraham, Isaac, and Jacob, and He therefore acted to save the Israelites from the Egyptian misery, we too must remember so that we act on our covenantal obligations. The call to "remember to observe the statutes and the judgments of the Lord" is the call to remember the stipulations for covenantal loyalty that God has revealed. When we partake of the sacrament each week, we are renewing the covenant path expressed at Sinai that we commit to be devoted to God. And as we share our love and devotion to God, we can have full access to the promises God covenanted to give to Abraham.

In Exodus 20:3, God reminded the people what great deeds He had done on their behalf, therefore they should give Him their unswerving loyalty by entering into a covenant with Him.

## Part 3 of the Covenant: God Provides Instructions on How to Show Him Covenantal Love and Loyalty (Exodus 20–23, especially 20:3–17)

We have discussed the power of memory and remembering and why God reminded the Israelites of His great deeds; we are ready to learn about the next element of the covenant. Since the people saw their need for loyalty to God because He had been loyal to them, we should expect to hear instructions and stipulations from God about how to show covenantal loyalty to Him. These stipulations are often in the form of commandments or divine statutes. So what do we see next in Exodus 20:3–17? God's covenantal stipulations and conditions for showing faithful devotion to Him. And what do we call these stipulations and conditions? *The Ten Commandments!*

That's right! *The Ten Commandments are the very essence of the Sinai covenant.* The Ten Commandments are the very heart of the covenant God invited His people to make with Him in the wilderness. If we love God, if we are grateful to God for the free gift of our salvation, we would be wise to carefully remember and live the expressions of covenantal love and loyalty God outlined by means of the Ten Commandments. And in case anyone is worried we'll need to start raising lambs for sacrificial slaughter, God has continuously sent prophets, and eventually His own Beloved Son, to provide clarifications, updates, and enhancing revelation on the conditions God expects us to live by to show Him devoted loyalty.

Let's review each of the Ten Commandments and think deeply about why God would ask us to show loyalty by means of each commandment.

## First Commandment / First Way to Show Covenantal Love and Loyalty

Thou shalt have no other gods before me. (Exodus 20:3)

Why is this the first of the Ten Commandments? Simple. God wants to be in covenantal relationship with us. He wants our exclusive loyalty and commitment. Imagine this to be an enduring marriage. There is to be no other. We are to have eyes for no other god. Only the God of the fathers is the God we worship and are in league with. If we put other gods in place of God, if we make commitments to other gods other than God, if we covenantally obligate ourselves to other gods besides God, then God can no longer be our God. He cannot deliver His promises to Abraham to us. If we make a covenantal commitment to some other god or gods, we would have to petition those other gods for protection, salvation, property, posterity, and prosperity (good luck with that experiment!). But in truth, there is no other way, because there are no other gods. This is an all or nothing enterprise. Either we have God 100% or not at all. He is absolutely unwilling to share us with any other gods. Therefore, the first commandment for demonstrating covenantal fidelity and loyalty to God is to choose Him and none other, to be firm and steadfast in regularly renewing those vows of commitment. How do we do that? One step on the covenant path is baptism. Another step along the covenant path (of renewal of vows of loyalty to God alone) is the weekly promise we make at sacrament. It's that simple. God wants to be our God. He wants us to be His people. Is it really that hard to put Him first, front, and always? Is there any other fake god that can give us anything of greater value than what the God of the Universe has already delivered to us and has in store for us throughout the eternities?

## Second Commandment / Second Way to Show Covenantal Love and Loyalty

> Thou shalt not make unto thee any graven image, or any likeness of any thing that is in heaven above, or that is in the earth beneath, or that is in the water under the earth. Thou shalt not bow down thyself to them, nor serve them: for I the LORD thy God am a jealous God, visiting the iniquity of the fathers upon the children unto the third and fourth generation of them that hate me. And shewing mercy unto thousands of them that love me, and keep my commandments. (Exodus 20:4–6)

This commandment or these stipulations are related to the first commandment, or first stipulation for how to show devoted faithfulness and loyalty to God. Put God first and everything else falls into place. More importantly, only God truly can grant you the blessings you dream of. If you put yourself into commitment with any other god, that god will not and cannot deliver. You will fail. You will be damned (stopped in your onward progress).

Because of the Restoration and the revelation received by Joseph Smith, we know that we are only responsible for the sins we commit and not for the sins of our fathers (or mothers). So why, then, does God seem to be so unjust as to bring "the iniquity of the fathers upon the children unto the third and fourth generation"? It turns out we've lost something in translation. The phrase "third and fourth generation" had a specific meaning in ancient Israelite times. Families units were typically multi-generational. That is, more than one generation lived in the family tent (or home). In the modern west we do the opposite. Once the kids reach the magical age of adulthood (that age has been a moving target in recent years!) they are supposed to leave the home and create their own home. Not so in ancient Israel. A man would have children. The males would marry and stay within the tent of their father. The females would marry and, with their husbands, join the tent of their father-in-laws. That is the source of the phrase "enlarge thy tent" and "strengthen thy stakes." As the family grew, the tent had to be enlarged. And the larger the tent, the stronger the cords and stakes must have been to hold up the tent.

In the scenario I've described there were two generations living within the tent. When the children had children, grandchildren were then within the family unit, living in the tent. That was the third generation. If the patriarch, or head of the household, was still alive when the male grandsons married, those family units also joined the tent. And if the grandsons had children while the patriarch was alive, there were four generations living in the enlarged tent. Ultimately the patriarch was responsible to teach the truth of God's law (i.e., the Ten Commandments) to his family and to model for his family covenantal fidelity to God by living all the commandments. If the patriarch failed to teach or live this covenantal fidelity, the blessings of the Sinai covenant were no longer available to that man or to those within his tent, that is, to those of the first, second, third, and fourth generations (if there were grandchildren and great grandchildren living in the tent). That is the ancient Israelite context of the phrase "unto the third and fourth generation": Tenting culture and multigenera-tional family units living in one tent.

Notice also the use of the word "hate" in these verses. That is a strong word. That is not a word that creates fluffy, feel-good feelings in our hearts. We should remember this crucial context.

In scripture, the word "hate" does not mean odious loathing. Hate in these scriptural contexts is a covenantal term meaning "not in the covenant." If you hate God, you demonstrate that by either not being willing to be in a committed, faithful covenantal relationship with Him or by making the covenant to have Him as your God but then failing to be loyal by taking other gods to be your god.

See the conditionality of the Sinai Covenant? God has already saved us from Egyptian bondage and He has so much more to offer us if we show covenantal loyalty in return. His mercy has been freely given and is freely available (because of His covenant to Abraham). He simply and only wants our love and loyalty, as expressed through the Sinai covenant. That is the covenant path.

## Third Commandment / Third Way to Show Covenantal Love and Loyalty

> Thou shalt not take the name of the LORD thy God in vain; for the LORD will not hold him guiltless that taketh his name in vain. (Exodus 20:7)

Many of us think that saying some version of "Oh my [fill in any version of God's name]" is taking the Lord's name in vain. Certainly the Lord is not pleased when we speak His name flippantly, or in anger, or without thought. God's name should not be used as an exclamation point, or for emphasis in speaking. God is not trivial and we should not treat Him or His name as trivial. But this is not what this commandment is speaking of. There is something far more serious and significant that God wants us to avoid, and for good, covenantal reasons.

What we typical miss in this commandment is that God asks us to not make covenants without real intent or without real purpose to fulfill the covenant. God essentially said here in this third commandment or stipulation, "Do not make a covenant in the name of the Lord without real purpose and real intent." We should never proclaim in the name of God that we are going to make a covenant while secretly in our hearts we are already plotting ways to not keep the agreement. We should not verbalize commitment to God if we harbor no interest in fulfilling the obligations. If we have empty purpose (or zero purpose or no purpose) in our agreements with God, we have taken His name in vain. The word "vain" means empty, lacking purpose. It is therefore far more serious to make an agreement in the name of God to keep a commitment or a covenant when you have no intention to do so.

Remember and never forget. If there is any message I could write on your heart as you read: God is not expecting perfection the way we conceptualize perfection. He wants our devoted loyalty and love. My wife, though she would love to be married to a perfect man (and I'm pretty close except for that pesky humility thing!), is far more interested in being in a relationship with a loving and devoted husband. That I can do. Am I perfect? No. Am I committed, loving, devoted? Yes. Do I make mistakes? Not that I'd like to talk about. But we are in a committed relationship where we recognize we are growing as we are committed.

God wants the same with us. He does not want our perfection, as we so often and erroneously describe the term. He wants us committed and devoted to Him. He understands that in our fallen natures we trip up at times. We fail to always be successful in our intentions to honor our commitments to God. The point is not that we are always successful in honoring our commitments. Rather, God wants us intentionally committed to Him. Mess up? Get up and try again. Make a mistake? That is expected. Give it another shot. Your heart is committed to God even if your flesh sometimes derails you. The point of this command is that God does not want duplicitous people, enemies in the camp who can recite the holy words but secretly intend to purposely not walk in God's paths.

Want to show loving loyalty to God? Then start with your heart and have pure motives and intentions when making promises and commitments in the name of God.

## Fourth Commandment / Fourth Way to Show Covenantal Love and Loyalty

> Remember the sabbath day, to keep it holy. Six days shalt thou labour, and do all thy work: But the seventh day is the sabbath of the LORD thy God: in it thou shalt not do any work, thou, nor thy son, nor thy daughter, thy manservant, nor thy maidservant, nor thy cattle, nor thy stranger [i.e., foreign-born person, non-Israelite] that is within thy gates: For in six days the LORD made heaven and earth, the sea, and all that in them is, and rested the seventh day: wherefore the LORD blessed the sabbath day, and hallowed it. (Exodus 20:8–11)

God recognizes that we must work and labor to survive. We are no longer in the Garden of Eden where our needs are met with little to no effort on our part. We deal with the noxious weeds of life that encumber our time and purposes. Some think that they can get further ahead by never taking a rest, working at every waking hour. Science has demonstrated repeatedly the revivifying power of sleep, rest, vacation, down-time, diversions, and recreation. Still we struggle, especially in modern western society. We feel like we always have to be "on" and available 24/7. Of course, we don't need science to tell us what God has taught for millennia. Make sacred time to rest. There is covenantal power in demonstrating love to God (and ultimately that is love to self, too) by resting from the cares of the world at appointed times. Let yourself be refreshed and refocused. Resting in the Lord on a weekly basis allows us to recalibrate our priorities, remember our commitments and covenants, and feel the renewal that comes from the mutuality of love found in covenantal relationships.

What is often missed in this command—or stipulation or way for showing covenantal love to God—is that not only should we rest from worldly cares, we should establish the conditions so that those within our sphere of responsibility also are able to rest. When God first established the Sabbath as a day of rest, it was to follow His example of resting after creation. God had done these incredible deeds of creating and organizing the order of the universe, and then He rested. Later, after God had done great deeds to save the Israelites from bondage, God changed the purpose of Sabbath from remembering His great deeds at creation (see Exodus 20:11) to remembering His great deeds of salvation on behalf of the Israelites (see Deuteronomy 15:5). God instituted the yearly Passover meal so that Israelites would remember what He had done for them so that they would pledge to remain faithful to Him. Later after the resurrection of Jesus, the day and memory of the Sabbath was changed yet again. The Sabbath is now celebrated on Sunday (instead of Saturday) to remember the great deeds God has done (as Jesus Christ) to save the world (see Acts 20:7). The Sabbath is now a day where we remember God's loyalty to us and where we have an opportunity to show our loyalty back to Him by partaking of the new Passover meal of Jesus's body called the sacrament.

So far we've reviewed four of the Ten Commandments. The first four commandments are how we show loyalty to God by loving Him. The final six commandments are how we show loyalty to God by loving others. Those two categories are neatly summed up later in the New Testament as "love God and love thy neighbor" (Matthew 22:36–40). That is the essence of the Ten Commandments. And that love of God and neighbor is how to show covenantal commitment to God. That well-known phrase to "love god and love thy neighbor" is fundamentally covenantal in terminology, nature, and purpose. The next time you hear that phrase, you can pause and ask yourself, "How well am I doing at showing my covenantal loyalty to God by loving Him and loving my neighbor?"

## *Fifth Commandment / Fifth Way to Show Covenantal Love and Loyalty*

> Honour thy father and thy mother: that thy days may be long upon the land which the LORD thy God giveth thee. (Exodus 20:12)

In this Sinai covenant stipulation to love father and mother, we see echoes of the Abrahamic covenant. Why does God command this? Why does He ask His people to demonstrate covenantal loyalty by honoring parents? Because God promised the promised land to Abraham and his posterity. What good would that promise be if those who could inherit the promise die before they have fully realized and appreciated the promised blessings? God did not simply set aside a promised land as though it were some never-to-be-used space. God intended the land to be used, lived upon, appreciated, and sustained. We are to find joy and happiness in the land of promise, but not simply by living on the land. That joy and satisfaction comes through lovely and harmonious family relationships. See the mutuality? The land makes possible a peaceful family life. And a peaceful family life makes the blessings of the land that much more pronounced. Where there is no land, or no inheritance, it is more difficult for a family to flourish. Bringing peace to parents is one way that the blessings of the promised land flow and are fulfilled. No one can argue that dishonored parents would feel that God's blessings have been entirely fulfilled.

## *Sixth Commandment / Sixth Way to Show Covenantal Love and Loyalty*

Thou shalt not kill. (Exodus 20:13)

This command is so obvious and so universal that there seems to be no need to explicate further. But for the sake of revealing the covenant more clearly, let us consider why God would include living this stipulation as a way for us to demonstrate love to Him. Remember that God introduced Himself to the Israelites at the beginning of this covenant, reminding them of the great deeds He had done for them in saving them from Egyptian bondage. He had saved them from death on multiple occasions in Exodus, such as when the atoning blood of the Passover lamb was applied to the door lintels of Israelite homes to protect the Israelite firstborn from the destroying angel and then spectacularly at the Red Sea where the Egyptian armies were drowned.

If God had labored so diligently to *save the Israelites because of His covenantal responsibilities to Abraham*, who are we to reverse God's labor? To stand in the way of God's work? To deny His promises or the possibility of His promises being fulfilled in our lives or other's lives? Do we see, through a covenantal lens, the seriousness of killing? That act disallows God to fulfill His covenantal responsibilities to make the promises to Abraham available to the children and inheritors of Abraham. Would we really want to stand in the way of God fulfilling His covenantal duties? Anyone engaged in murder is essentially saying to God, "I will not allow you, God, to make the promises of Abraham available to this person. I will remove them from the promised land and from life so that they no longer have access to those promised blessings you covenanted to Abraham to provide." There are, of course, many other reasons killing and murder are such grievous sins. We know and understand those reasons so I have no need to recount them here. But most of us have likely never thought about the covenantal context and consequences for God including this command among His stipulations for us to show devoted loyalty to Him.

When we consider the case of Alma the Younger being harrowed up for his sins, one of the things that racked his soul with eternal torment was the memory that he had spiritually murdered many of God's children. Just as physical murder puts the murder squarely as an obstacle on God's covenant path, spiritual murder is the same. Would any one of us want to stand as a wall on God's covenant path, blocking Him from being loyal to His covenants or blocking others from showing their covenantal love and loyalty to God? Any act of murder, whether physical or spiritual, is an act against God because it compromises God's covenantal obligations. Ultimately, since God is God and will always remain God, He has plans for how to fulfill His covenants no matter the circumstances. Those who stand in His way, blocking His path of salvation, will find themselves swept aside and cast into the oblivion of weeping and wailing.

## Seventh Commandment / Seventh Way to Show Covenantal Love and Loyalty

Thou shalt not commit adultery. (Exodus 20:14)

Children deserve committed, covenantal, and loyal parents. What happens when the wild seeds have been sown in all directions, when spouses have not been faithful to each other? Metaphorically, who lives in which tent? Who belongs to which family? Who has access to the promised blessings? The Abrahamic promises become entangled or may be lost when family structures and parent-child relationships are severed, confused, or disordered.

Those entering into covenant with God show their faithful commitment to Him by not violating a neighbor's peace and prosperity, by not stealing virtue from others, by not bringing children into this world without covenantal protection and family support.

## Eighth Commandment / Eighth Way to Show Covenantal Love and Loyalty

Thou shalt not steal. (Exodus 20:15)

God has all things, knows all things, is able to provide all things. God grants to us, through Abraham, the blessings of posterity, property, protection, and a great name. God will do these things for us if we show covenantal devotion and loyalty to Him (which is the purpose of the Sinai covenant we are reviewing here via the Ten Commandments). If it is true that God can give us all good things, what is the logic of taking from anyone? The very act of stealing would communicate, "I don't believe God is capable or willing to fulfill the Abrahamic promises to me." Isn't the act of stealing an act of not having faith in God's promises? And then, from this covenantal context, isn't the act of stealing

## The Covenant Path in the Bible and the Book of Mormon 87

an act of trying to replace God? The thief is saying, in essence, to God, "Your plan for distributing your good gifts to your children is insufficient or flawed. I am going to take your place and make the distributions the way I see fit." A thief who steals has now denied God, denied God's role in blessing us, denied the power of covenants, and denied God's purposes. An act of stealing is an act of faithlessness. It is an act of defiance against God. It is an act against both the Abrahamic covenant God made and the Sinai covenant we are invited to make and keep.

### Ninth Commandment / Ninth Way to Show Covenantal Love and Loyalty

> Thou shalt not bear false witness against thy neighbour. (Exodus 20:16)

In a world that seems to thrive on gossip, innuendo, fake news and false stories, and weaponized ignorance, this commandment God delivered to His people is especially pertinent. God is a God of truth. To be like Him we must also act on truth, share truth, and deny falsehoods and lies. Can the purposes of God be fulfilled if we lie about others, obfuscating their true nature? Yes, God can do His work, but how many lives will be hurt by not telling the truth? How much longer will we have delayed salvation because of supporting falsehoods or supporting those who create and teach lies, especially about others?

We are all children of God. Would we stand in the way of God's covenant path to say otherwise about anyone? How is it covenantally loyal to God to spread falsehood and rumors about another person? Does God run the plan of salvation according to what is printed in tabloid magazines or what appears to be trending on Twitter? Is God a god of twitchy fingers, always aching to press "like" on any gossip that comes His way? Or to rage whenever He is triggered by blazing headlines?

As a note of connection to the Book of Mormon, Laban bore false witness against Laman, claiming "thou art a robber and

I will slay thee" (1 Nephi 3:13). Unfortunately for Laban, but significant for the Book of Mormon, Nephi records this detail as evidence that Laban was *not* covenantally loyal to God and therefore he no longer qualified for the blessings of life in the promised land. That is especially true because Laban made a rash vow, based on a false witness, to kill Laman. According to the covenantal law at Mount Sinai we've been reviewing, anyone bearing lying or false witness against a neighbor, and threaten-ing punishment against that neighbor based on the false report, would be punished with the same punishment they had devised to be inflicted upon their neighbor. Therefore, Laban's own con-demnation to death was already signaled by his own mouth in 1 Nephi 3:13 when he falsely accused Laman and vowed that Laman would die.

## Tenth Commandment / Tenth Way to Show Covenantal Love and Loyalty

> Thou shalt not covet thy neighbour's house, thou shalt not covet thy neighbor's wife, nor his manservant, nor his maidservant, nor his ox, nor his ass, nor any thing that is thy neighbour's. (Exodus 20:17)

Similar to the invitation to show covenantal love to God by not taking from anyone, this command paves the covenant path by expecting us to not even harbor feelings of wanting to steal from others. God is everything. He can and will give us all that He has, if we are true and faithful to the Sinai covenant and any subsequent revelatory updates to the covenant path God discloses (i.e., in the New Testament, the Book of Mormon, the Doctrine & Covenants, and ongoing Restoration). Why would we ever want such a small and fleeting prize of what limited resources we could snatch from a neighbor when the God of the universe promises that we can be as He is? Furthermore, the peace and prosperity intended for the promised land will be compro-mised when the inhabitants of the land are raging in their hearts against their neighbors, conspiring to deprive their neighbors of God's covenanted blessings. For those who feel that the blessings of the promised land are insufficient, God has an answer: "I will send you to another land" (see Jeremiah 16:13). In fact, that is exactly what has happened throughout Israelite history. When the people failed to live in peace and tranquility in the promised land, when the Israelites continually and continuously showed covenantal *infidelity* by coveting, stealing, murdering, committing adultery, and loving other gods, God left them to their own devices and kicked them out of the promised land.

Those who want the promises of the promised land must be willing to live the covenant path marked for the land. That path is marked by the Ten Commandments. Break those Ten Commandments enough and you forfeit the promised land. This is no different than a renter breaking an agreement with a landlord. Eventually the landlord will throw the renter out. Or a mortgage holder of a home. If the mortgage holder consistently breaks the agreement with the bank, eventually the bank will repossess the home and throw out the occupants. Does that make the landlord or the bank the bad guys? No, the landlord or the bank are covenantally obligated to remove unfaithful tenants. God is in the same circumstance. He lovingly prepared the promised land for His people. He told them in words of plainness that this land was theirs as long as they showed covenantal fidelity. He gave them ten specific and clear ways to show that covenantal love (actually, there are other stipulations, but these are primary and we are trying to keep this book shorter than your bookshelf). If they consistently did not live up to their commitments, God was covenantally obligated to remove them from the land as noxious weeds that destroy the growth of trees of life.

At this point we've reviewed the Ten Commandments as covenantal stipulations given by God to the children of Israel for them to show devoted love to God. So the next time you hear about, talk about, or think about the Ten Commandments, remember that these are all covenantal statements. We should no longer talk about these commandments without their covenant context. By so doing, we miss the very heart of God's invitation to be in covenantal relationship with Him! The Ten Commandments are the God-established expectations for us to show love to God. The Ten Commandments are the guide posts on the covenant path for us to show loyalty to the loyal God who has saved us from the terrors of Egypt.

Now that we have reviewed the conditions God established for covenantal fidelity, let's continue to the next stages of the Sinai covenant.

## Part 4 of the Covenant: Witnesses Certify or Ratify the Covenant (Exodus 24:3)

> And Moses came and told the people all the words of the LORD, and all the judgments: and all the people answered with one voice, and said, All the words which the LORD hath said will we do.

Covenants are agreements. Because of their significance, they are not done in the dark, or in whispers, or in a corner. The covenantal agreement has binding expectations and promises that must be publicly declared and assented to. Therefore, such an agreement requires ratifying witnesses who can truly attest that the parties willingly entered into the agreement. Furthermore, especially in ancient societies, the witnesses were obligated to bear witness for or against the covenant-making individuals according to their faithful adherence to the agreement. Just as in modern times we sign our names to documents of agreement, anciently the people would speak in the affirmative if they had willingly joined the covenant. By so doing, they became witnesses of the covenant. They took upon themselves the added responsibility to witness to each other about their covenantal faithfulness. If they saw a neighbor struggling to keep the agreement, they could be supportive and helpful. If the neighbor persisted in breaking the covenant, the witnesses could bring that neighbor to the judge who would pronounce a sentence against a faithless covenant breaker. In addition to the covenant makers being witnesses to the covenant, sometimes angels are called as witnesses. What is implicit in the text, and not explicitly mentioned, is that God Himself is also a witness in the Sinai covenant.

## Part 5 of the Covenant: God Explains the Conditions and Expectations of the Covenant (Exodus 23:20–33)

> Behold, I send an Angel before thee, to keep thee in the way, and to bring thee into the place which I have prepared. Beware of him, and obey his voice, provoke him not; for he will not pardon your transgressions: for my name is in him. But if thou shalt indeed obey his voice, and do all that I speak; then I will be an enemy unto thine enemies, and an adversary unto thine adversaries. For mine Angel shall go before thee, and bring thee in unto the Amorites, and the Hittites, and the Perizzites, and the Canaanites, the Hivites, and the Jebusites: and I will cut them off. Thou shalt not bow down to their gods, nor serve them, nor do after their works: but thou shalt utterly overthrow them, and quite break down their images. And ye shall serve the LORD your God, and he shall bless thy bread, and thy water; and I will take sickness away from the midst of thee. There shall nothing cast their young, nor be barren, in thy land: the number of thy days I will fulfil. I will send my fear before thee, and will destroy all the people to whom thou shalt come, and I will make all thine enemies turn their backs unto thee. And I will send hornets before thee, which shall drive out the Hivite, the Canaanite, and the Hittite, from before thee. I will not drive them out from before thee in one year; lest the land become desolate, and the beast of the field multiply against thee. By little and little I will drive them out from before thee, until thou be increased, and inherit the land. And I will set thy bounds from the Red sea even unto the sea of the Philistines, and from the desert unto the river: for I will deliver the inhabitants of the land into your hand; and thou shalt drive them out before thee. Thou

> shalt make no covenant with them, nor with their gods. They shall not dwell in thy land, lest they make thee sin against me: for if thou serve their gods, it will surely be a snare unto thee.

Though this is a long quote, it's useful to see how God clearly laid out for the Israelites the associated blessings or curses they would experience *conditioned on their faithfulness to the covenant entered into at Sinai*. Remember, God *unconditionally bound Himself to the promises of Abraham*. By His grace He makes those promises available to the children of Israel, including us. However, our access to those covenantal blessings is *conditioned on our righteousness* to the Sinai covenant as memorialized by the Ten Commandments and the other Five Books of Moses (and any revealed updates to the covenant, as found in other books of scripture and in the living prophets). Keep the commandments and the blessings flow. Don't keep the commandments and the spigot of divine influence is turned off. It's our choice. And in covenantal context, God clearly instructs and teaches His people the consequences of righteousness (covenantal loyalty) or wickedness (covenantal disloyalty).

## Part 6 of the Covenant: The Covenant Is Recorded and Preserved in a Sacred Location (Exodus 24:7)

> And he took the book of the covenant, and read in the audience of the people: and they said, All that the LORD hath said will we do, and be obedient.

Though we have new technologies and inventions far different than the ancient Israelites, our mode for making and keeping agreements is not much different from theirs. Even today when we make agreements we record the agreement and preserve it in a safe location. We expect, actually we demand, that the agreement never be altered unless the parties agree to the updates. So too in the ancient Israelite world. God wrote the agreement down. He carved, with His finger, the covenant onto stone tablets. So when we think of the Ten Commandments as carved on stone, we now

*The Covenant Path in the Bible and the Book of Mormon* 93

realize that this was simply the way of preserving the covenantal text of the agreement the Israelites entered into with God. Once the agreement was written down, God ordered it to be securely preserved in a safe location: the Ark of the Covenant! During the Israelite sojourn in the wilderness, and until the time of King Solomon, the Ark of the Covenant remained in the mobile temple known as the tabernacle, which essentially was a holy tent. Later, when the temple of Jerusalem was built, the Ark of the Covenant transferred into the temple. The Ark of the Covenant was placed in the holiest spot of the tabernacle (or temple). Once a year on the holy day remembering God saving His people from Egypt, the Day of Atonement, the Israelite high priest would enter into the Holy of Holies and place the atoning blood of the sacrificial lamb on the Ark of the Covenant. This symbolized the covering, empowering, and vivifying strength of the blood of the Atonement to keep the Sinai covenant alive.

The Ark of the Covenant and the tablets with the inscribed agreement of the Sinai covenant were lost when the Babylonians conquered Jerusalem a few years after Lehi and his party fled Jerusalem. We've never recovered the tablets, though a really popular Hollywood movie hints that the Ark of the Covenant is lost somewhere in the bureaucratic nightmare of a huge U.S. government warehouse. (Compelling story, but not true.) It is only fitting that the tablets of the covenantal agreement went missing. The people of Israel had consistently shown *infidelity* to the covenant made with God at Sinai. After so many years of such lack of faith and love shown to God, God removed the people from the promised land, as He had said He would do if the people broke the covenant. Since the covenant was broken, there was no need for the text of the agreement to remain. The agreement was null and void. We do hear, however, prophecies from Isaiah and other prophets that God would eventually find a remnant of the children of Abraham and renew His covenant with them (see Isaiah 11:11–16), bringing them again to the promised land for another try (such as when the Jews returned from Babylonian captivity) or leading them to new promised lands (such as is represented by the Book of Mormon).

Let's consider a modern-day analogy. Imagine you made a written agreement with a bank to buy a home. The bank provides an agreement for you to enter into in order to access such vast sums of money so that you can acquire the property. That agreement has expectations that you must follow in order to obtain and retain the money and the land. You and the bank agree to a certain set of commitments regarding the payment of the home, how the property will be cared for, etc. The bank agrees to keep the agreement document, which both of you have signed, in a safe and secure place. Now, imagine that a few months into the agreement, you decide you don't like the agreement the bank gave you. So you create your own agreement and live by that agreement. What would happen? The bank eventually would throw you out of the house.

Or imagine that there is a portion of the agreement you don't like and so you sneak into the bank, find the master copy of the agreement, and add words, delete others, and otherwise modify the agreement, without authorization. When you get thrown out of your house, you shouldn't be surprised.

Or imagine that the bank sends a representative to you and lets you know that the bank has offered some new terms, or made some modifications to the agreement. The bank representative explains all these things to you, representing truthfully that the essence of the agreement between you and the bank is still valid, that is, that you continue to remain in the house so long as you pay the mortgage and stay committed to the expectations of the agreement. If you signed on to these updates to the agreement, you would continue to enjoy the peace and prosperity of living in your home. But what would happen if when the bank representative came to your home and you were unwilling to listen to them? What if you maltreated them? What if you beat the bank representative? Killed them? What would the bank do? Throw you out of the house.

All these scenarios are relevant to the conditions of the Sinai covenant. God is like the bank who is willing to give us land to live on if we abide by certain agreed to stipulations. It is not our right to change the stipulations of the agreement. We are not to add to or take away from the agreement. That would make the agreement null and void. We hear that same language both in the Old Testament and the New Testament.

> Ye shall not add unto the word which I command you, neither shall ye diminish ought from it, that ye may keep the commandments of the LORD your God which I command you. (Deuteronomy 4:2)

> What thing soever I command you, observe to do it: thou shall not add thereto, nor diminish from it. (Deuteronomy 12:32)

> For I testify unto every man that heareth the words of the prophecy of this book, If any man shall add unto these things, God shall add unto him the plagues that are written in this book. (Revelation 22:18)

These are covenantal passages. These passages *do not* mean God will never speak again. These passages *do not* mean that more revelation cannot be received. These passages *do not* mean that no more scripture will be added to the canon. If that were the case then God would have stopped talking at Deuteronomy 4:2 and there never would have been a Revelation 22!

These are covenantal phrases impressing upon the minds of those entering into the covenant with God that *they* are not supposed to change the conditions of the covenant. God offered the covenant. God owns the covenant. The Israelites do not own the covenant. Therefore they cannot and should not try to change the covenant. To do so would be to break the covenant. God, as the owner of the covenant, can change or update the covenant. He will never do so without first telling us about proposed changes. That is the purpose of prophets and ongoing revelation. That is the core meaning of Amos 3:7, which affirms that "Surely the

Sovereign Lord does nothing without revealing His plan to his servants the prophets" (NIV translation).

These specific verses are directly giving command to the Israelites, as the tenants on the land and God is the bank, that they are not to modify the covenant at Sinai. Yet God being God, He can update the stipulations and expectations of the agreement. He will never do so without notifying the people of the land who have covenanted with Him. He will send His representatives (the prophets) to explain and clarify the existing agreement (the covenantal obligations the people signed on to at Sinai) and any updates or proposed changes in the expected conditions for showing loyalty.

But what did the Israelites do at times (and this also happened in the Book of Mormon)? They wouldn't listen to the authorized representatives (i.e., the prophets) and sometimes they killed God's representatives. What is God left to do with such unruly tenants on the land, when in good faith He intended to help them stay true and faithful to Him? He throws them out. That is why the ten northern tribes were led into Assyrian captivity and are lost to human history. And that is why the Jews were taken into Babylonian captivity.

We have prophets today asking us to stay on the covenant path. They plead with us to be faithful and loyal to God. And yet don't we hear people clamoring for the modern-day prophets to reveal a different agreement, a different covenant? Don't we see people today ignoring the prophets? Don't we see people who think that the prophets are too boring because they keep talking about the basics of the gospel (which are the very fundamentals of the covenant God made with His people at Sinai)? Don't we see people wishing that the prophets would reveal so-called mysteries instead of talking about the covenant path? What good would any of those revelations be if we can't be committed, true, and faithful to fundamental and basic stipulations of covenantal loyalty? If we first demonstrated thorough fidelity, wouldn't God then have more to share?

If we have not mastered, lived, and taught what has already been given, what good would it be to receive more? And what more do we need beyond faith, repentance, baptism, Holy Ghost, and enduring to the end? Are we seeking for a new gospel? A new covenant path? An alternate gospel? An alternate covenant path to the presence of God than what has already been revealed? Different gods to talk about and worship? If we persist in resisting the prophets, we will be like the ancient Israelites who ignored, broke, or tried to change the covenantal agreement. Their prize was to lose the covenant of Sinai and get kicked off the land.

If we want to be disciples of God, we need discipline. We need constraints and boundaries. The covenant path provides discipline, boundaries, and guidance. If we want to be a disciple, we need to get on the covenant path and hold to the rod!

## Summary of the Sinai Covenant

As an act of fidelity to His covenant to Abraham, Isaac, and Jacob, God saved the Israelites from Egyptian bondage. He led them into the wilderness where He invited the Israelites to covenant with Him to be His people. If they showed covenantal loyalty, He would be their God and lead them to peace and prosperity in a land of promise. When God initiated the covenant He

1. Introduced Himself to the people.
2. Reminded them of His loyalty to them in doing great deeds of salvation for them to encourage them to be loyal to Him.
3. Instructed the people to show loving faithfulness in the covenant to God. These expectations for showing faithfulness are the Ten Commandments.
4. Received the ratification of covenantal witnesses (the people themselves).
5. Detailed the blessings and curses associated with the conditional covenant.
6. Ensured that the covenant was recorded and preserved in a safe or sacred location.

The basic idea of the Sinai covenant can be summarized by this oft-repeated scriptural phrase, "If ye keep my commandments, ye shall prosper in the land." You can see how in-depth this conditional covenant at Sinai really is. There is much to be said about it. If you were an ancient prophetic writer, would you want to repeat everything God had already said about the Sinai covenant before you encouraged people to be faithful? Or would you use a readily understandable shorthand covenantal phrase to summarize the covenant and encourage fidelity? Whenever you see the phrase "If ye keep my commandments, ye shall prosper in the land" anywhere in scripture, you now know the following things. The Sinai covenant is being referenced. The conditions of the Sinai covenant are in force. The covenant is meant for us, as children of the promise, to demonstrate our covenantal love and loyalty to God just as He has done for us. That based on expressed and lived covenantal loyalty, the children of Abraham and their descendants will experience the blessings and promises associated with the conditional covenant at Sinai.

The covenant path is marked, or bounded with borders, by these two covenantal mountains: Mount Moriah in Jerusalem (also known as Mount Zion) and Mount Sinai. Mount Moriah represents the unconditional covenant God made to Abraham to give Him posterity, property, and prosperity. The conditional covenant at Sinai invites the children of the promise to show their covenantal love to God. If they are true and faithful to God, as He had been to their fathers and has been to them, then they will live in peace and prosperity in the land. If they fail to be faithful to God (if they invent their own gods, or if they do not love their neighbors, or if they consistently fail to show love to God by keeping the commandments), then eventually they will lose their access to the Abrahamic promises to have progeny and prosperity in the land of promise.

## The Torah Is Covenantal Instruction Inviting and Reminding the People to Be Faithful to God

What happens if God reveals a covenant but then never teaches people about it? Eventually everyone forgets. If we don't know what the covenant is, can we live it? If we forget the stipulations for covenantal loyalty, can we be faithful? Because God will never cease to be God, He is covenantally obligated to reveal His covenant and to instruct His people on the covenant. That is why God continues to send prophets to teach us. That is why over the generations God has asked the prophets to teach and record these covenants. That is why God commanded Lehi to have his sons retrieve the covenantal instructions (the scriptures) held by Laban.

God knew that human memory has a short shelf-life. He also knew that as the generations progressed after Sinai, the incredible signs and wonders He had enacted on behalf of the Israelites would be lost or forgotten. He knew that the feeling of immediacy and power of His saving acts would not be felt by later generations, unless He preserved these stories and had each generation share and remember these stories. God knew that each generation would need to be instructed in the covenant. God knew that He needed to leave instructions that marked the covenant path. The word "instruction" comes from the word "structure," which is a system of interlocking parts that provides a supporting framework and enduring stability. The covenant path is a supporting framework that offers us enduring stability if we stay on it. And an instructor is someone who puts structure and a supporting framework into something. God is our Divine Instructor. Another word associated with instruction and structure is "instrument," which means tool. Tools are devices that allow us to accomplish far more than we could do on our own. For us to succeed in our return journey to God, we need tools of support. The covenant path is a tool, an instrument that provides supporting structure for our progress to God's presence.

What are the instructions that God has provided? What supporting framework or tools has He revealed so that we are empowered to be like Him? Those instructions are the Torah, also known as the Five Books of Moses: Genesis, Exodus, Leviticus, Numbers, and Deuteronomy. There is a long-standing association between the word "law" and "Torah." That is an appropriate association since the Torah contains God's laws, or rather, His covenants with His people. However, more precise than the word "law," the literal Hebrew meaning of the word "Torah" is "instruction."

Why are the Five Books of Moses called the Torah or "The Instruction"? Because God wanted to preserve an instructional record that provided guided structure and tools for His people along the covenant path.

What is the instruction about? God's covenants. First His covenant to Abraham at Moriah (Zion) and second the covenant at Sinai when He invited the Israelites to live in committed relationship with Him.

For whom are these instructions, this Torah? For us. For anyone wanting to know the great deeds that our faithful God has displayed to His people. And for anyone wanting to know how to show loving gratitude to God through covenantal loyalty.

God wanted to provide plenty of support and guidance for His people to stay on the covenant path. He did so by giving them an instruction manual for how to live covenantally faithful to Him. That is, in part, the purpose of the Five Books of Moses. When we carefully read the Five Books of Moses, we read about the commandments God has given to His people, the rituals He has revealed associated with remembering the covenant, and stories that document the consequences of when the Israelites were faithful or not to the covenant God offered them. These stories provide a structured framework and enduring support as instruction to mark the covenant path.

When you read from the Torah, remember that you are reading God's revealed covenantal instruction manual!

## Where Else in Scripture Do We See the Structure of the Conditional Sinai Covenant?

God's conditional covenant initiated at Mount Sinai is found throughout scripture. The table below summarizes some of the scriptural locations where the conditional covenant pattern is repeated. Significant for us to see is that the *entire Book of Deuteronomy* is structured on the conditional covenant at Sinai! Before Moses died, and before the second generation of Israelites entered into the promised land, God commanded Moses to instruct (Torah) the Israelites in the conditional covenant. Deuteronomy literally means "second telling of the law" or the second time that Moses instructed the people on the covenant. The Israelites needed to know what the expectations of loyalty were for them to successfully occupy and prosper in the promised land. Later prophets, especially in the Book of Mormon, in order to economize in their preaching and teaching, summarized the entire Book of Deuteronomy and the entire Sinai covenant with the phrase, "If ye keep my commandments, ye shall prosper in the land." Remember, whenever you see that phrase in scripture, or a phrase like it, you can immediately know that it summarizes the entire Book of Deuteronomy and represents the Sinai covenant.

Whenever God has a promised land to deliver to His people, He delivers to them this conditional covenant. Notice that the pattern of the Sinai covenant appears repeatedly throughout the Book of Mormon record. Why? Because God had granted Lehi's people a new promised land. To retain the land, they needed to show loyalty to the God of the land. The Sinai covenant was the instruction book for how to show loving faithfulness to God. Notably King Benjamin's speech in the book of Mosiah is actually a modified version of the covenant God gave to the children of Israel at Sinai (see Mosiah 1–6). And then notice that this same covenantal pattern appears in the latter days, in the Restoration scripture of Doctrine and Covenants. Soon after the

Church was restored in this dispensation in April 1830, God told Joseph Smith that He would reveal where the promised land was to be, where Zion would be established.

In August 1831 Joseph Smith and a small contingent of Saints arrived in Jackson County, Missouri. The first three revelations received in Jackson County (D&C 57 on July 20, 1831, D&C 58 on August 1, 1831, and D&C 59 on August 7, 1831) all focus on revealing the land of Zion, the new promised land, and the covenant associated with the promised land. What do we see? These sections follow the same covenant path revealed at Sinai. Why would that be? God is the same today, yesterday, and forever. What we think of as ancient covenants are actually enduring covenants of God's love and grace. These covenants still matter today. Whenever God wants to create a people and plant them in a promised land, He reveals to them the instructions of a covenant conditioned on their faithfulness to Him. Why are the modern-day Saints not gathered in Jackson County? Because they were not fully true and faithful to the covenant God delivered to them in D&C 58–59 and so He removed them to other lands where He tried anew to covenant with them.

|   | Exodus | Deut. | Joshua | Mosiah | D&C 58–59 |
|---|---|---|---|---|---|
| Introduction of Covenant Parties | Ex. 20:1–2 | Deut. 1:1–5 | Joshua 24:1–2 | Mosiah 1:1–2:9 | D&C 59:24 |
| Historical Review of Great Deeds | Ex. 20:2 | Deut. 1:6–3:29 | Joshua 24:2–13, 16–18 | Mosiah 2:9–21, 23–30 | D&C 58 |
| Stipulations and Instructions for Showing Loyalty in the Covenant | Ex. 20–23 (especially 20:3–17) | Deut. 1:1–5 | Joshua 24:14, 18, 23 | Mosiah 2:22, 24, 31–41; 4:6–30 | D&C 59:5–15, 21–23 |
| Witnesses | Ex. 24:3 | Deut. 31:19–32:45 | Joshua 24:16, 19, 21–23 | Mosiah 5:2–8 | D&C 59:24 |

| Blessings and Curses | Ex. 23:20–33 | Deut. 27–28 | Joshua 24:19–20 | Mosiah 5:9–15 (see also 3:24–27) | D&C 59:24 |
|---|---|---|---|---|---|
| Record the Covenant and Store it in a Sacred Location | Ex. 24:7 | Deut. 31:1–9 | Joshua 24:25–27 | Mosiah 2:8–9; 6:1–3, 6 | D&C 59:1–4, 16–20, 23 |

(Modified from "The Treaty / Covenant Pattern in King Benjamin's Address (Mosiah 1–6)" by Stephen D. Ricks, BYU Studies Vol. 24, No. 2 (Spring 1984), pp. 151–162.)

## Conclusion

We've reviewed the two significant mountain covenant traditions in the Bible: The unconditional covenant that God made with Abraham at Mount Moriah in Jerusalem (also known as Mount Zion or Zion's Mount), and the conditional covenant to the children of Israel at Mount Sinai. The Abrahamic covenant protects the rights of the children of Abraham. The Sinai covenant protects the rights of God. The Abrahamic covenant is a reward for past loyalty. The Sinai covenant is encouragement for future loyalty. These two covenants provide the foundation and structure for the rest of the Old Testament and for the New Testament. Significantly, these two covenants (especially the Sinai covenant) deeply influence the structure, narrative themes, and doctrinal discourses in the Book of Mormon. In the next section of the book, we'll look at how these covenants played out in the Old and New Testament.

# PART 3

# THE COVENANT PATH BETWEEN MOUNT MORIAH AND MOUNT SINAI IN SELECT OLD TESTAMENT AND NEW TESTAMENT PASSAGES

In this portion of the book, we'll review key features of the Old Testament and the New Testament and demonstrate that the Bible makes much more sense, and is more relevant to us today, when we read through the lens of these two covenants. The titles "Old Testament" and "New Testament" would be better translated and expressed as "Old or Former Covenant" and "New Covenant." What were the former or old covenants found in the Old Testament? As we have explored at length earlier in this book, there are two covenantal mountains that mark the covenant path: Mount Moriah (or Zion) in Jerusalem represents God's unconditional covenant to Abraham and his posterity while Mount Sinai represents the conditional covenant God invites His people to live by. Jesus is the "New Covenant" or "New Testament". We'll explore further in this part of the book how Jesus updated the expectations for covenantal loyalty. But first, we'll review how the two covenant mountains played out in key Old Testament texts.

# CHAPTER 6

# THE OLD TESTAMENT IS STRUCTURED ON AND PRESERVES THE INTERACTIONS OF THE TWO MOUNTAIN COVENANTS

The Old Testament is full of stories representing how God was faithful to the Abrahamic covenant and stories about the causes and consequences of when Israelites were or were not faithful to the covenant at Sinai. Old Testament biblical books are saturated with these covenants and can even be categorized by the covenant on which they focus, represented in a table format earlier in this book.

**After the Israelites Received the Promised Land, They Rejected the King of the Land (Jehovah)**

After the Israelites entered the promised land and began to occupy it (see the Book of Joshua), they had alternating episodes of faithfulness to God where they prospered, or periods where they forgot to keep the covenant at Sinai and were oppressed by their neighbors. The Israelites would then remember to call upon God for deliverance and He would send a judge to deliver them back into covenantal freedom. This pride cycle is one of the major themes of the Book of Judges. Eventually, the Israelites clamored

## The Covenant Path in the Bible and the Book of Mormon 107

for God to give them a king. What was the Israelite reasoning for wanting a king? One of the key reasons was that they wanted to be like all the other nations of the earth: "Now make us a king to judge us like all the nations" (1 Samuel 8:5).

As this statement indicates, the people of Israel no longer wanted to be unique. They did not want to be God's special treasure as He had desired when He stated, "Now therefore, if ye will obey my voice indeed, and keep my covenant, then ye shall be a peculiar treasure unto me above all people: for all the earth is mine: And ye shall be unto me a kingdom of priests, and an holy nation" (Exodus 19:5–6). It was as though the Israelites were saying they no longer wanted the divine protection offered by the Divine King who owned the promised land, but that they would rather try their luck with the arm of flesh, that is, with a human king. The children of Israel no longer wanted their special status as God's people. They wanted to follow in the footsteps of all other nations. They wanted to be like everyone else. They gave in to peer pressure. And like the phrase "When in Rome, do as the Romans do," they effectively said to God "We are in the world and we want to be of the world." God was grieved at this turn of events, as was His servant prophet-judge Samuel. Notice how in His response to their faithless demand, God reminded the people of His covenantal loyalty to them:

> But the thing displeased Samuel, when they said, Give us a king to judge us. And Samuel prayed unto the Lord. And the LORD said unto Samuel, Hearken unto the voice of the people in all that they say unto thee: for they have not rejected thee, but they have rejected me, that I should not reign over them. According to all the works which they have done since the day that I brought them up out of Egypt even unto this day, wherewith they have forsaken me, and served other gods, so do they also unto thee. (1 Samuel 8:6–8)

Who is the real king of the promised land? Only God. For the people to acquire and experience the blessings of the Sinai covenant and the promised land, they needed to accept Jehovah as their God and King. Replacing the Heavenly King with a human king could only lead to disaster.

Doesn't the Book of Mormon make this point repeatedly? In fact, the great prophet Jacob in the Book of Mormon correctly taught the people that the only real king to whom the people should have total allegiance was God Himself: "For he that raiseth up a king against me shall perish, for I, the Lord, the king of heaven, will be their king, and I will be a light unto them forever, that hear my words" (2 Nephi 10:14). Notice the covenantal language God used to express His kingship, that those who will hear His words will have His light in their lives. Hearing the word of God is one of the core covenantal duties and expectations expressed in the Sinai covenant, "Hear, O Israel" (Deuteronomy 6:4).

God respected the agency of the Israelite people to reject Him as king in favor of a human king with these instructions to Samuel: "Now therefore hearken unto their voice: howbeit yet protest solemnly unto them, and shew them the manner of the king that shall reign over them" (1 Samuel 8:9). The remainder of 1 Samuel 8 details the way that a human king who does not stay firm in the Sinai covenant would cause significant problems for the people of Israel. The king would take the resources of the land to protect and enrich himself. The king would set up an army to fight battles with the strength of his own arm instead of relying on the arm of Jehovah. The king would require the people to work on his projects and on his behalf. The king would ultimately lead the people into apostasy.

Despite this detailed report of the disasters that a king could bring upon the nation, the Israelites persisted in their insistence on having a human king, "Nevertheless the people refused to obey the voice of Samuel; and they said, Nay; but we will have a king over us; That we also may be like all the nations; and that our king may judge us, and go out before us, and fight our battles." (1 Samuel 8:19–20.) They did not want to be judged by the creator of heaven and earth. They did not want the Lord of

Hosts to fight their battles! The word "hosts" means heavenly army. When you have the Divine Warrior (God) and all of His heavenly hosts available to fight on your behalf, why would you reject that tremendous show of support and force? We see the peoples of the Book of Mormon falling into the same thinking that they can fight their own battles without the presence of God. The consequences were typically disastrous. Sometimes we have to wonder about the decision making of humans.

The Israelite choice of a human king led to a long series of bad kings, the breaking up of the house of Israel into two separate and warring kingdoms (the Kingdom of Israel in the north and the Kingdom of Judah in the south), the fall into apostasy, the breakdown of the kingdoms, and their eventual destruction and subsequent captivity of the people. All the traps that God warned the people about, they fell into. They failed to stay covenantally loyal to God and He therefore removed the availability and accessibility of His saving grace—the Abrahamic covenant—from their lives, until they repented or until their descendants were ready to be in a covenantal relationship and follow the covenant path.

## God's Divine Expectations of a Human King or Leader

God had foreseen that the Israelites had the potential to turn away from His covenant. Back in the Book of Deuteronomy when Moses laid out the stipulations for covenantal faithfulness to God, he revealed these words of God to the Israelites about kings and kingship:

> When thou art come unto the land which the LORD thy God giveth thee, and shalt possess it, and shalt dwell therein, and shalt say, I will set a king over me, like as all the nations that are about me; Thou shalt in any wise set him king over thee, whom the LORD thy God shall choose: one from among thy brethren shalt thou set king over thee: thou mayest not set a stranger over thee, which is not thy brother. But he shall not multiply horses to himself, nor cause the people to return to

Egypt, to the end that he should multiply horses: forasmuch as the LORD hath said unto you, Ye shall henceforth return no more that way. Neither shall he multiply wives to himself, that his heart turn not away: neither shall he greatly multiply to himself silver and gold. And it shall be, when he sitteth upon the throne of his kingdom, that he shall write him a copy of this law in a book out of that which is before the priests the Levites: And it shall be with him, and he shall read therein all the days of his life: that he may learn to fear the LORD his God, to keep all the words of this law and these statutes, to do them: That his heart be not lifted up above his brethren, and that he turn not aside from the commandment, to the right hand, or to the left: to the end that he may prolong his days in his kingdom, he, and his children, in the midst of Israel. (Deuteronomy 17:14–20)

These verses are the most significant passages in the entire Bible for understanding God's view on kings and kingship. God is theoretically open to allowing a human king serve in His stead, but only under very limited conditions of fidelity and faithfulness. The human king, if there is to be one, should be the paradigmatic example of faithful devotion to God as instructed in the Sinai covenant. In summary, God established the following conditions for kingship.

| Covenantal Kings Should NOT Do These Things | Covenantal Kings Should Do These Things |
|---|---|
| 1. Don't acquire many horses (don't raise a military) (v. 16).<br>2. Don't return the people to Egypt (don't return people to the house of bondage/apostasy) (v. 16).<br>3. Don't acquire many wives (v. 17).<br>4. Don't seek after silver and gold (v. 17). | 5. Have a copy of the scriptures (v. 18).<br>6. Read the scriptures every day (v. 19).<br>7. Teach the scriptures; instruct the people about the covenant path and its obligations (vs. 19–20).<br>8. Do not lift himself up above his brethren (v. 20). |

Unfortunately, throughout most of human history, far too many people in power have done the exact opposite of what God expects. We regularly see leaders and people in positions of power abusing the sacred trust that has been given them. They use the resources of the land to build up armies and navies to glorify themselves. They do not live the stipulations of covenantal fidelity God has established and they do not teach people to live in covenantal faithfulness to God. They acquire many wives and lose themselves to such extravagances that include the seeking and hoarding of wealth. What does God want from a true leader? Teach the Torah. That is, get a copy of the covenantal instructions found in scripture. Teach that to everyone within your realm of responsibility. And model covenantal fidelity to everyone.

## What Does the Bible Narrate to Us about the Consequences of Kingship for the Israelites?

All the kings of the Northern Kingdom of Israel failed to be covenantally loyal to God and thus the ten northern tribes were taken into captivity.

| Kings of Northern Israel | Scriptural Passage Summarizing Their Covenantal Fidelity to God and Their Modeling to the People of Living the Sinai Covenantal Expectations |
|---|---|
| Jeroboam | Thou hast not been as my servant David, who kept my commandments, and who followed me with all his heart, to do **that only which was** right in mine eyes; **But hast done evil above all that were before thee: for thou hast gone and made thee other gods**, and molten images, to provoke me to anger, and hast cast me behind thy back. (1 Kings 14:8–9; emphasis added) |
| Asa | And he did evil in the sight of the LORD, and walked in the way of his father, and in his sin wherewith **he made Israel to sin**. (1 Kings 15:26; emphasis added) |
| Baasha | And he did evil in the sight of the LORD, and walked in the way of Jeroboam, and in his sin wherewith **he made Israel to sin**. (1 Kings 15:34; emphasis added) |
| Elah | Elah his son, by which they sinned, and by which they **made Israel to sin**, in provoking the LORD God of Israel to anger with their vanities. (1 Kings 16:13; emphasis added) |

| | |
|---|---|
| Zimri | For his sins which he sinned in doing evil in the sight of the LORD, in walking in the way of Jeroboam, and in his sin which he did, to **make Israel to sin**. (1 Kings 16:19; emphasis added) |
| Omri | But Omri wrought evil in the eyes of the LORD, and did worse than all that *were* before him. For he walked in all the way of Jeroboam the son of Nebat, and in his sin wherewith **he made Israel to sin**, to provoke the LORD God of Israel to anger with their vanities. (1 Kings 16:25–26; emphasis added) |
| Ahab | And Ahab the son of Omri did evil in the sight of the LORD above all that *were* before him. And it came to pass, as if it had been a light thing for him to walk in the sins of Jeroboam the son of Nebat, that he took to wife Jezebel the daughter of Ethbaal king of the Zidonians, and **went and served Baal, and worshipped him**. (1 Kings 16:30–31; emphasis added) |
| Ahaziah | And he did evil in the sight of the LORD, and walked in the way of his father, and in the way of his mother, and in the way of Jeroboam the son of Nebat, who **made Israel to sin**: For he served Baal, and worshipped him, and provoked to anger the LORD God of Israel, according to all that his father had done. (1 Kings 22:52–53; emphasis added) |

The Southern Kingdom of Judah had a mix of faithful and faithless kings. Unfortunately, enough of these faithless kings infected the populace with infidelity to God so that they apostatized and God was required, because of covenantal commitments, to throw them out of the land and leave them to be put into captivity.

| Kings of Judah | Scriptural Passage Summarizing Their Covenantal Fidelity to God and Their Modeling to the People of Living the Sinai Covenantal Expectations |
|---|---|
| Saul | It repenteth me that I have set up Saul to be king: for he is turned back from following me, and hath **not performed my commandments**. (1 Samuel 15:11; emphasis added) |
| David | **David did that which was right in the eyes of the LORD**, and turned not aside from any thing that he commanded him all the days of his life, save only in the matter of Uriah the Hittite. (1 Kings 15:5; emphasis added) |

| Solomon | And Solomon **loved the LORD**, walking in the statutes of David his father: **only he sacrificed and burnt incense in high places**. (1 Kings 3:3; emphasis added) |
|---|---|
| Abijam | And he walked in all the sins of his father, which he had done before him: and **his heart was not perfect with the LORD his God**, as the heart of David his father. (1 Kings 15:3; emphasis added) |
| Asa | And Asa **did that which was right in the eyes of the LORD, as did David his father**. . . . But **the high places were not removed**: nevertheless Asa's heart was perfect with the LORD all his days. (1 Kings 15:11–14; emphasis added) |
| Hezekiah | And he **did that which was right in the sight of the LORD, according to all that David his father did**. . . . For he clave to the LORD, and departed not from following him, but kept his commandments, which the LORD commanded Moses. And the LORD was with him; and he prospered whithersoever he went forth: and he rebelled against the king of Assyria, and served him not. (2 Kings 18:3, 6–7; emphasis added) |
| Josiah | And **he did that which was right in the sight of the LORD**, and walked in all the way of David his father, and turned not aside to the right hand or to the left. (2 Kings 22:2; emphasis added) |
| Jehoiachin | And **he did that which was evil in the sight of the LORD**, according to all that his father had done. (2 Kings 24:9; emphasis added) |

## The Rise of Kings in Israel and the Davidic Covenant Modeled on the Abrahamic Covenant

We might rightly ask, "Who made these evaluations of the kings of Israel and Judah and what criteria did they use to make these judgments?" To answer that question we need to review a little bit of Israelite history. You might think at this point, how does this all relate to the covenants of Mount Moriah and Mount Sinai? We'll tie all that together through this historical review.

We return to the story of Samuel, the last Israelite judge. God commanded him to find and anoint a king over Israel. Samuel was led to Saul. However, after some time, Saul sought His own will and His own aggrandizement, such as building a monument to himself after winning a battle where he explicitly disobeyed the orders of God (see 1 Samuel 15, especially vv. 12–13, 19). Because of these and other faithless acts, God appointed another king—David.

David was a loyal and faithful servant of God who brought peace and prosperity to the land. Because of David's utter loyalty to God, God gave a special unconditional covenant to David that was very much like the unconditional covenant God gave to Abraham. For our purposes in this book, we can group the Davidic or messianic (i.e., anointed king) covenant in the same category with the Abrahamic covenant. Both of these covenants were given to God's appointed servants who had been unswervingly faithful to Him. The covenants were delivered in Jerusalem, the location of Mount Moriah and Mount Zion. These covenants were unconditional. That means that God is the one responsible for fulfilling the covenant.

Listen to God's unconditional messianic covenant to David and hear how it echoes the unconditional promises God granted to Abraham:

> Now then, tell my servant David, "This is what the LORD Almighty says: I took you from the pasture, from tending the flock, and appointed you ruler over my people Israel. I have been with you wherever you have gone, and I have cut off all your enemies from before you. **Now I will make your name great**, like the names of the greatest men on earth. And **I will provide a place for my people Israel** and will plant them so that they can have a home of their own and no longer be disturbed. Wicked people will not oppress them anymore, as they did at the beginning and have done ever since the time I appointed leaders over my people Israel. I will also give you rest from all your enemies. The LORD declares to you that *the* **LORD himself will establish a house [a dynasty and posterity] for you**: When your days are over and you rest with your ancestors, I will raise up your offspring to succeed you, your own flesh and blood, and I will establish his kingdom [Solomon]. He is the one who will build a house

[temple] for my Name, and I will establish the throne of his kingdom forever. I will be his father, and he will be my son. When he does wrong, I will punish him with a rod wielded by men, with floggings inflicted by human hands. **But my love will never be taken away from him**, as I took it away from Saul, whom I removed from before you. **Your house and your kingdom will endure forever before me; your throne will be established forever**." (2 Samuel 7:8–16; emphasis added, NIV Translation)

The main idea of the Davidic covenant is that God would establish a Davidic dynasty, that the throne of David would endure forever, and that God's love (a code word for covenantal faithfulness) would always remain with David. Jesus is the ultimate fulfillment of this grand promise. God still expected David and his royal descendants to demonstrate loyalty in return to Him in the form of living the conditions detailed at Sinai. As the ultimate messianic fulfillment of the Davidic covenant, Jesus was the most fully loyal of all God's servants; He is therefore called the Beloved Son.

David ruled over united Israel and then bequeathed the kingdom to his son Solomon. After Solomon's death, the people asked for taxes and other burdens to be lightened. Solomon's son Rehoboam refused but instead raised taxes and oppression. The ten northern tribes of Israel rebelled against Rehoboam and started their own separate kingdom under the leadership of Jeroboam. From that time forward, the two split kingdoms (the Kingdom of Israel in the north and the Kingdom of Judah in the south) would never be reunited. One of the purposes of the Restoration is to gather scattered Israel and to unite the separated kingdoms into one whole under God.

## The Kings of Israel Led the People into Sinning against God and Breaking the Sinai Covenant

Jeroboam established alternative worship in the Northern Kingdom at Dan and Bethel, building golden calves for the people to worship. In that way, he led the Israelites into sin and apostasy.

All the kings of the Northern Kingdom of Israel maintained those false idols as national icons of religious worship. Instead of turning to God, the landlord of the promised land to whom they owed fealty and allegiance, the kings of the Northern Kingdom of Israel turned the hearts of the Israelites to make league with false gods. The kings (like we see later in the Book of Mormon with King Noah) modeled apostasy for the people and the people followed, losing access to the protecting power and prosperity that comes from God. In turning the people away from covenantal fidelity to God, the kings "made Israel to sin," as the scriptural record so often reports. Reviewing the list above of "Kings of Northern Israel" we see that all of them continued the practices that "made Israel to sin." For some two hundred years Northern Israel persisted in being disloyal to the covenant at Sinai, despite many prophets calling the people to repentance (Elijah, Elisha, Amos, and others). Because of these ongoing years of spiritual rebellion and abandoning God, led by apostate Israelite kings, God abandoned the Northern Kingdom to their enemies. The ten northern tribes were conquered by the Assyrians (around 722 BC), taken into captivity, and lost to history.

At the time of the Assyrian invasion of Northern Israel, some Israelites fled south to the safety of Jerusalem (as evidenced by a new wall built around Jerusalem at this time to accommodate and protect the immigrants), which was led by righteous King Hezekiah and the prophet Isaiah who were faithful to God's covenants and instructed everyone on their covenantal duties. Nephi's ancestors from the tribe of Manasseh were among those who fled south to the protection of Hezekiah and Jerusalem. There was a crush of immigrants coming into the Southern Kingdom of Judah, camping outside the walls of Jerusalem. Hezekiah realized that these fellow brethren from the Northern Kingdom of Israel would be unprotected outside the city walls. But there was no space inside the city. So what did Hezekiah do? He did as Isaiah urged, "Enlarge the place of thy tent, and let them stretch forth the curtains of thine habitations: spare not, lengthen thy cords, and strengthen thy stakes" (Isaiah 54:2). Hezekiah enlarged the "tent" of Jerusalem by building a new wall that encompassed and protected these refugees. He didn't build a wall to exclude them. He built a wall to include them. By so doing, he strengthened his society tremendously and fulfilled His covenantal obligations to demonstrate loyalty to God by loving his neighbors as himself. Lehi and his family would have had their home not far from where that new wall was built. In recent years, archaeologists in Jerusalem have found that wall. For the interested pilgrim, you can visit that wall in Jerusalem and know that you are not far from where Lehi and Nephi used to live in Jerusalem.

About a century after the Assyrian invasion, King Josiah came to the throne of Judah. Like good and righteous kings before him who wanted to show love for God by building, or refurbishing, a temple in His honor, Josiah commanded a thorough repair and update to the Jerusalem temple (not unlike efforts by the Church beginning in 2020 to refurbish the Salt Lake City Temple). In the process of those extensive efforts, the Book of the Law was discovered.

## What Was the Book of the Law?

Remember that in our earlier discussion of the Sinai covenant one key aspect of the covenant was the need to document the covenant, and the associated instructions for the covenant, and then store the written covenant and instructions in a sacred location. What better place to store this sacred record and sacred instructions than somewhere inside the temple? The Book of the Law was likely some version of the Torah (Genesis, Exodus, Leviticus, Numbers, and Deuteronomy) or simply the Book of Deuteronomy, which itself is the fullest expression of the covenant God offered the Israelites at Sinai and by which they were to order their lives and community. When we read in 2 Kings 22:8 about the discovery of the Book of the Law during repairs to the Jerusalem temple, "list" most likely meant the Book of Deuteronomy. "And Hilkiah the high priest said unto Shaphan the scribe, I have found the book of the law [that is the Book of Deuteronomy] in the house of the Lord."

The temple workers brought the Book of the Law before King Josiah and read it to him. Why didn't Josiah read to himself? Because most people in the ancient world were illiterate, including the king. The very few people who took the many long years to gain literacy were typically governmental scribes. For those not fully in tune with God's divine instructions for kingship in Deuteronomy 17:14–20, they saw the king's role as physically protecting the kingdom. In such a scenario, the king had little to no need to spend his time learning to read, especially when he had trained government bureaucrats who could handle document production, organization, and interpretation. This is not unlike many modern companies that are dependent upon software for success but the CEO may have little to no capacity for creating or interpreting computer code. Of course, if we reflect on what God expected of a fully righteous king, it was to spend his days reading and teaching the law, or covenant, revealed at Sinai. Josiah was not doing those things. His illiteracy was part of the problem.

What happened next is curious to the modern reader: "And it came to pass, when the king had heard the words of the book of the law, that he [ripped] his clothes" (2 Kings 22:11). How many people do you know who rip their clothes to shreds while reading, especially scripture (okay, maybe a seminary student) or when someone else is reading to them (besides students cramming for final exams)? In the ancient world, ripping one's clothes was a sign of extreme penance, humility, and mourning. Why was Josiah feeling such great grief and penance?

The reason was simple. *Josiah immediately understood that he and the people had not been faithful to the Sinai covenant and were prone to experience all the curses associated with covenantal infidelity.* He asked the chief priest to inquire about the mind and will of God. Would the people be destroyed? Would they have an opportunity to repair the covenantal breach and show their committed faith and love to God? "Go ye, enquire of the LORD for me, and for the people, and for all Judah, concerning the words of this book that is found: for great is the wrath of the LORD that is kindled against us, because our fathers have not hearkened unto the words of this book, to do according unto all that which is written concerning us" (2 Kings 22:13).

Why hadn't the people of Judah hearkened to the words of "this book"? Had they been lazy? Had they forgotten to attend early morning seminary? To read their scriptures thirty minutes each day on their smart phones? The alert reader will immediately recognize that the ancient Israelites didn't have early morning seminary or smart devices. But did they have scriptures?

No.

Remember that nearly everyone was illiterate in ancient societies such as ancient Israel. People depended on a few, well-trained, literate individuals who were educated in the skills and arts of reading and writing. These individuals would copy and preserve the word of God. And they would read the word of God, containing the instructions regarding His covenants, to their people and interpret it for them. Remarkably, Nephi fits into this picture in very important ways. He was literate in reading and writing. He used those skills throughout his life to make the written word of God accessible, comprehensible, and defensible to as many people as possible. In fact, Laman and Lemuel seem to have been illiterate like King Josiah. In 1 Nephi 22, after Nephi had read the words of Isaiah to his brothers, they asked him to interpret for them the things that he had read to them.

> And now it came to pass that after I, Nephi, had read these things which were engraven upon the plates of brass, my brethren came unto me and said unto me: What meaneth these things **which ye [not us] have read**? (1 Nephi 22:1; emphasis added)

Notice that Laman and Lemuel did not request, "Nephi, explain the things that *we* read together," but rather "explain what *you, Nephi, have read to us.*" Without literacy, knowledge of and faithfulness to God in the covenant is very difficult. Without the scriptures, Lehi, Nephi, and their people would not have known of God's covenants. That is why it was essential for the salvation of Lehi's tribe to retrieve a copy from Laban of the Brass Plates (Torah, the instruction manual of God's covenants containing the Five Book of Moses and other revealed scripture).

Returning to the Old Testament, we understand that Josiah was so distraught because he realized that his people had not been faithful to the covenant. Why had the people not been faithful to the covenant? Because the one copy of the Book of the Law had been inadvertently lost somewhere in the temple for generations. Totally unlike our day and time when we are awash in access to the written (and spoken) word of God, in the ancient world, hard copies of the word of God were few and far between. The few copies, if multiple copies existed, were often carefully stored away in safe and sacred locations that few people had access to. So for the space of a number of generations, active knowledge about God's covenant with His people at Sinai was effectively forgotten. Had the leaders done their job to yearly read and renew the covenant with the people, this ignorance would have not descended upon the kingdom. In such ignorance, the people could not demonstrate covenantal fidelity. Josiah immediately recognized the serious threat he and the people were under and that it was his role as the leader to rectify the situation. Here they were living in the promised land, but they had failed to renew or enliven the agreement that allowed them to live on the land.

## Josiah Launched a Religious Reformation throughout Jerusalem and Judah

In the year 622 BC when the Book of the Law was discovered after having been lost for who knows how many generations, Josiah immediately started a religious reformation throughout the land (see 2 Kings 23), inviting everyone to know and take seriously the covenantal obligations detailed in the Book of the Law (likely the

Book of Deuteronomy as we mentioned earlier). But it may have been too late for the people of Judah at this point for God said, "Because they have forsaken me, and have burned incense unto other gods [remember that according to the Ten Commandments the first way to show covenantal loyalty was to worship God first and only], that they might provoke me to anger with all the works of their hands; therefore my wrath shall be kindled against this place, and shall not be quenched" (2 Kings 22:17).

About this same time, Josiah and others encouraged an effort to gather together the history and sacred writings about the people of Israel from the time of Moses to their day. These scribes were deeply influenced by the values, virtues, and covenantal ideology presented in the Book of Deuteronomy. They began writing a narrative history of the Israelites describing and explaining the causes and consequences of Israelite history through the lens of the Sinai covenant. These scribes helped to edit or produce the Biblical books of Joshua, Judges, 1 Samuel, 2 Samuel, 1 Kings, and 2 Kings. Modern-day scholars call these narrative books of the Bible the Deuteronomistic history compiled by the Deuteronomistic historians. The fancy terms "Deuteronomist" and "Deuteronomistic" refer to the deep influence that the Book of Deuteronomy—and the Sinai covenant—had on the thinking, compiling, and writing that these scribes undertook. These scribes appear to have started the work at the invitation of King Josiah during his religious reformation.

## Bible Narrative Likely Written by Covenantally Loyal Scribes Influenced by Deuteronomy; Nephi and Jeremiah Likely Part of this Group

Earlier we asked this question, "Who made these evaluations of the kings of Israel and Judah and what criteria did they use to make these judgments?" Based on the discussion presented here, the likely group who evaluated Israelite and Judean kings and then documented those evaluations in their narrative history of

Israel was the group of Deuteronomy-influenced scribes and writers in Jerusalem during and after the reign of Josiah.

This is where we make strong connections to the Book of Mormon (which we will continue to explore in the latter half of this book). If Lehi's party left Jerusalem in 600 BC and if Nephi was about 15 years of age when they left, we could estimate that Lehi was about 20 years old when Josiah started the Book of the Law religious reformation in Judah and Jerusalem. He would have been a young man, perhaps still forming his faith. Perhaps he was deeply impacted by the religious fervor of his day. Perhaps he embraced whole-heartedly the revelations delivered through the Book of the Law and taught them to his family throughout the remainder of his life. When receiving the call to flee from Jerusalem, Lehi may have been around 42 years old while Laman may have been 21; Lemuel, 19; Sam, 17; and Nephi, 15.

Note: The ages of these Book of Mormon individuals are my guesstimates. We are never told the specific dates of these individuals births and so we are left to piece together clues to arrive at plausible estimates, as I have presented here. The intent here is not focus us on their potential ages, but rather to call attention to the reality of their lives and how they would have grown up in the midst of this religious fervor for people everywhere in the kingdom to recommit their lives to God demonstrated by covenantal fidelity to the stipulations laid out in the Sinai covenant. We can imagine how inspiring and transformative such religious fervor and actions may have been for Lehi. In fact, we can see in the preaching of Lehi that his words, phraseology, and doctrines align significantly with the covenant of Sinai, which was likely at the core of the rediscovered Book of the Law.

Another individual in Jerusalem who seems to have been deeply and intimately involved in the Deuteronomistic reforms was the prophet Jeremiah. A careful review of the covenantal themes, language, imagery, and phraseology in Deuteronomy and the Book of Jeremiah demonstrates many close and intriguing connections. One powerful example from Jeremiah of his deep connection to the Sinai covenant is his recording of this revelation from God: "But this shall be the covenant that I will make with the house of Israel; After those days, saith the Lord, I will put my law in their inward parts, and write it on their hearts; and will be their God, and they shall be my people" (Jeremiah 31:33). The major take-away from this verse is that God no longer cares about rock tablets that have a record of His covenant with the people. God cares more that the people have the covenant written in their hearts and that they live it. What good is a written covenant that no one reads, or that is forgotten in some corner or foundation stone of the temple? If the covenant is unavailable to influence God's people to remember His loving kindness and goodness, then that covenant is as good as nonexistent. But more importantly, the covenant is intended to lead people on the path of salvation. When they have that covenant written in their hearts, when they let that covenant guide their thoughts and actions, when what is written in their hearts leads them to be faithful and loyal to God at all times, in all things, in all places, then God truly will be their God and they will be His people, just as He has desired since the beginning.

The fact that Jeremiah's writings are saturated with Sinai covenant language leads us to conclude that Jeremiah may have been a member of the scribal group composing the narrative review of Israelite history through the lens of the Book of the Law. If that was the case, we should take seriously the detail that Jeremiah was named early in the Book of Mormon. Though Nephi indicates that there were many prophets active in Jerusalem, that fact that a Deuteronomistic scribe and prophet was the only Jerusalem prophet that Nephi named may suggest several things: That Nephi, Lehi, and their family were personally and intimately connected to Jeremiah. That Nephi and Lehi knew how to write. That Nephi likely was actively being trained as a scribe when they fled from Jerusalem. That the scribal class in Jerusalem seemed to encompass Jeremiah. And that the scribal class seemed to be deeply influenced by the Deuteronomistic worldview. If these statements are valid, we can make a tentative but deeply significant and intriguing conclusion.

## Nephi Was Trained as a Mount Sinai Covenant Scribe

We can conclude that Nephi was trained as a Deuteronomistic scribal historian. That is, Nephi was thoroughly versed and committed to the Sinai covenant.

If this was the case, we can test the authenticity of the Book of Mormon. If Nephi was a scribe, we can test his writings in the Book of Mormon. Do his writings follow the literary conventions scribes were trained in around Jerusalem near the year 600 BC? The answer is yes. Do the themes, ideas, perspectives, and worldview that Nephi brought to his writing reflect a Deuteronomistic worldview? Yes. Nephi fits comfortably into the very context he describes. And that 600 BC context has been thoroughly verified by modern-day scholars who have paid the price to learn the languages, histories, cultures, writings, covenants, literary works, political structures, and religious institutions of ancient Israel.

What does this mean for the Book of Mormon? The first writer in the Book of Mormon, Nephi, was deeply influenced by the Sinai covenant. If Nephi had been trained as a Deuteronomistic historian and scribe, as likely he was, then he had been trained to write narrative history through the lens of "How well did the people of God adhere to the covenant at Sinai? How well did the people of God show loyal fidelity to God by living the stipulations of the covenant made in the wilderness?" If Nephi was influenced by this Deuteronomistic perspective, we should expect to see the covenantal structures, symbols, ideas, language, phraseology, and ideology of the Sinai covenant throughout Nephi's writings. And indeed we do! If Nephi was embedded in the ideological and literary Mount Sinai covenant traditions, we should expect him to value and declare the ideals of kingship and leadership God revealed in Deuteronomy 17:14–20. And indeed that is the case. Nephi sought to avoid kingship while he ended up living the very life that God expected of a human king: total dedication to preserving and teaching the law of God and His covenants. The Book of Mormon is a covenantal text! And as a covenant text, the Book of Mormon beautifully traces the path of God's covenant path between Mount Moriah/Zion and Mount Sinai.

## Conclusion

This review has demonstrated that the covenant path of the Abrahamic covenant and the Sinai covenant influenced the structure, production, memory, and telling of the Israelite and Biblical story. We learned that God gave a version of the Abrahamic covenant to David, unconditionally promising that his throne would last forever. We know that Jesus is the fulfillment of that unconditional promise. We also saw the pattern of the Sinai covenant woven throughout many of the Biblical narratives. We discussed the discovery of the Book of the Law (likely the Book of Deuteronomy) around 622 BC by King Josiah's temple workers as the impetus for the Deuteronomistic reforms and history writing. We learned that a group of scribal historians devoted to God's covenant at Sinai compiled the Biblical record and evaluated the merits of each king of Israel through the lens of covenant fidelity. Finally, we laid out a strong case that Nephi, the scribal progenitor of all subsequent prophetic writers in the Book of Mormon, was likely trained in the Deuteronomistic worldview. That is, Nephi shares his religious perspective through the lens of how groups and individuals demonstrated loyalty to God through their commitment to keeping the commands He gave them at Sinai.

With this tremendous Old Testament background (laying out the two major covenant traditions of the Bible that mark the covenant path) we are ready to explore the Book of Mormon from the covenant path perspective. But before jumping into the Book of Mormon, let's briefly investigate significant ways these two covenant traditions play out in the New Testament.

# CHAPTER 7
## THE COVENANT PATH IN THE NEW TESTAMENT

In the New Testament, the unconditional covenant that God made to Abraham and His posterity was renewed, or fulfilled, through Jesus while He simultaneously updated the Sinai covenant. Jesus brought together the old into the new and in His person combines both the Abrahamic covenant and the Mosaic (Sinai) covenant.

We start with Matthew's Gospel. Matthew wrote his Gospel for a Jewish audience. He did so in a way that mirrored Moses and the Torah (the Five Books of Moses: Genesis, Exodus, Leviticus, Numbers, and Deuteronomy). Remember that we learned earlier that the Torah contains the instructions for the covenant path.

**Matthew 1 Is Like Genesis**

Just as Genesis is the opening of the Bible, so too is Matthew 1 the opening of the Gospel. Just as Genesis is full of genealogies and introduces the main characters and themes in the story, so too, Matthew 1 begins with an introduction to the main characters and themes of the Gospels. One of the first words that Matthew uses is "genesis." Matthew 1:1 reads "The book of the generation [Greek = genesis] of Jesus Christ, the son of David, the son of Abraham," clearly calling to mind for readers the first book of the Old Testament.

Significant for our discussion of covenants is that Matthew explicitly connects Jesus to David and to Abraham. We remember that the primary purpose of the Book of Genesis in the Old Testament is to show that God is a God of covenant making and covenant keeping. He had promised Abraham property, posterity, and prosperity. Then the Abraham cycle (Genesis 12–25) preserved a variety of stories. In some of the stories God demonstrated to Abraham His trustworthiness to keep His promises. Other stories showed God testing Abraham with challenging circumstances that invited Abraham to show trust and faith in God. Other stories focused on God making an unconditional covenant to Abraham to fulfill His promises. The unconditional promises given to Abraham animate and influence the majority of the Book of Genesis. It is only proper that Jesus is directly linked to Abraham because Jesus is the ultimate fulfillment of the promises to Abraham. Through Jesus we will all have never-ending property, posterity, and prosperity as we will become co-inheritors with Him.

We also learned earlier that the Davidic covenant is modeled on the Abrahamic covenant. God covenanted and promised to David that he would have an enduring throne. Again, Jesus as the real Messianic King is the fulfillment of the Davidic promise. It is only natural that Matthew's Gospel begins by linking Jesus to David. So just as the Torah begins with Genesis, which is focused on unconditional covenants, so, too, does the Gospel of Matthew begin like the Torah, focusing on the characters in the Old Testament associated with unconditional covenants.

## Matthew 2 Is Like Exodus

Matthew 2 corresponds to Exodus. In the Book of Exodus, there was a miraculous birth of a prophetic figure who was pursued by a king wishing to kill the prophet. So too, in Matthew 2, Jesus, the new prophet, was miraculously born and then pursued by a king who wished to kill him. In Exodus God brought His chosen people out of Egypt and led them to the promised land. In Matthew 2, Jesus was God's Chosen Son who was led out of Egypt to the promised land of Israel.

## Matthew 3 Is Like Leviticus

The third Book of Moses is Leviticus, which focused on the priesthood ordinances necessary for salvation. In Matthew 3, Jesus fulfilled the laws, rites, and ordinances of salvation by being baptized by John the Baptist.

## Matthew 4 Is Like Numbers

The Book of Numbers in the Old Testament detailed the Israelite nation wandering in the wilderness for forty years, suffering from thirst and hunger, and experiencing all sorts of temptations. Matthew 4 was patterned on the Book of Numbers. In Matthew 4, Jesus wandered in the in the wilderness for forty days, suffering thirst, hunger, and temptation.

## Matthew 5 Is Like Deuteronomy

In the Book of Deuteronomy Moses ascends a mountain and delivers God's laws to the Israelite people before they entered into the promised land. Deuteronomy literally means "Second Law" or "the second time that the instructions of the law were given to the people." What happens in Matthew 5? Jesus, as the new Moses, ascended a mountain and delivered the "second" or "higher law" and instructed us on all what we must do to enter the promised land of God's salvation. Matthew wrote his Gospel to reveal that Jesus Christ is the New Moses, sent by God to live and reveal the laws that lead to salvation. Anyone with ears to hear and eyes to see would rejoice in Matthew's powerfully designed Gospel.

[Author's note: This section above on Matthew 1–5 is modified from "How Matthew Is Like Moses and What that Reveals about Jesus" published at taylorhalverson.com on January 14, 2019.]

## The Sermon on the Mount as the New Sinai Covenant

We'll dwell on the Sermon on the Mount / Book of Deuteronomy connection for a moment because of its thorough significance to declaring, highlighting, and teaching the covenant path. We discussed earlier that the key selections of the Book of Exodus are structured on the conditional covenant God gave to the Israelites, through Moses, at Mount Sinai. Where the Book of Exodus is partially structured on the Sinai covenant, the *entire* Book of Deuteronomy is structured on the Sinai covenant. That covenant structure has six parts.

1. God introduced Himself.
2. God reminded the people what great deeds He had done on their behalf, therefore they should give Him their unswerving loyalty.
3. God instructed the people on how to show loyalty. These statements are called The Ten Commandments.
4. God received the people's witness that they had accepted the covenant.
5. God explained the conditional curses and blessings associated with the covenant. Those who are faithful receive the blessings. Those who are not faithful do not receive the blessings but instead receive curses.
6. God directed the recording of the covenant and its preservation in a sacred location (the Ark of the Covenant).

God delivered the Sinai covenant to Moses on a mountaintop, who then shared it with the Israelites. What do we see Jesus doing? He is the new Moses, just as the Sinai covenant had promised God would provide:

> The LORD thy God will raise up unto thee a Prophet from
> the midst of thee, of thy brethren, like unto me; unto him

ye shall hearken.... I will raise them up a Prophet from among their brethren, like unto thee, and will put my words in his mouth; and he shall speak unto them all that I shall command him. And it shall come to pass, that whosoever will not hearken unto my words which he shall speak in my name, I will require it of him. (Deuteronomy 18:15, 18–19)

Who is the prophet that God promised to raise up? Jesus. And Jesus demonstrated that truth by getting to a mountain to deliver an update to the stipulations God asks His people to live by in order to demonstrate their covenantal faithfulness. Just as the Sinai covenant was conditioned on people's faithfulness, so too is the Higher Law (or update to the original Sinai Covenant) as delivered at the Sermon on the Mount) conditioned on people's righteousness. If we live what Jesus taught, we will find peace and happiness. Reject the teachings of Jesus and lose the promised blessings.

The format that Jesus used to show fulfillment and updating of the covenantal stipulations in the Sermon on the Mount often followed this formula: "Ye have heard that it was said of them of old time [in the older covenantal instructions from the time of Moses], but I say unto you [these are the updated covenantal instructions for how to show loving faithfulness and loyalty to God]."

As you review the Sermon on the Mount in Matthew 5–7, you can note how Jesus made adjustments and clarifications about what God's expectations for loyalty had become. Of course, Jehovah of the Old Testament is Jesus, so Jesus is fully within His right to make these clarifications and updates to the covenantal instruction manual.

## Be Ye Therefore Perfect

Jesus closes Matthew 5 with a famous exhortation that has caused serious consternation, worry, and misunderstanding for generations of Christians and especially for perfectionist-prone members of The Church of Jesus Christ of Latter-day Saints. Why? Because we never talk about the covenantal context or significance of Jesus's invitation to be perfect. He said, "Be ye therefore perfect, even as your Father which is in heaven is perfect" (Matthew 5:48).

In order to put into context the covenantal meaning of this phrase, let's wind back the clock to the time of Abraham. Let's return to the Old Testament where a similar phrase is used by God when talking to Abraham. In Genesis 17, God appeared again to Abraham to renew His unconditional covenant with Him, "And when Abram was ninety years old and nine, the LORD appeared to Abram, and said unto him, I am the Almighty God; walk before me, **and be thou perfect**. And I will make my covenant between me and thee, and will multiply thee exceedingly" (Genesis 17:1–2; emphasis added).

Most readers of the scripture forget that long before Jesus exhorted all of us at the Sermon on the Mount to be perfect, God had commanded His friend Abraham to be perfect. What was God thinking? Doesn't He know that *we are all fallen*? It is programmed into our very natures to sin. No one will make it out of this life without sinning, or missing the mark of perfection. Does God really intend to create never-ending angst and depression by requiring the impossible? Is that the type of God He is? Or might we have misunderstood His meaning because we haven't listened with covenantal-context intent? Have we been too busy listening with modern ears rather than covenantal ears?

When God commanded Abraham to be perfect, what God intended was for Abraham to be covenantally loyal to God. Yes, that's right! Earlier in this book we learned how the word "perfect" in the Bible is a covenantal word that is best translated as loyal or faithful. Perfect in the covenantal context does not mean "without sin" or "without blemish" or "without error." The word "perfect" describes the focus on our orientation. Are we oriented toward God or facing away from Him? Are our hearts pointed to serving and loving God, even if we get distracted at times and our attention is pulled away? Is our intention to be God's servant, even if we fail or stumble at times?

## What Does it Really Mean to Be Perfect? Be Loyal

God is not expecting us to save ourselves by perfection in the modern sense that we understand the word. God only wants to know that it is our commitment and intention to be loyal to Him, through thick and thin. That when we fail, we turn to Him. When we hurt, we let Him heal us. When we are lonely, we let Him in. When we are less than what we have promised, we are willing to let Him show us a better way. To be perfect is simply to be a dedicated, loyal, faithful, if fallen, follower of God. To be perfect is to willingly enter into a covenant relationship with God. Perfection is contrasted with imperfection, which is someone who purposely chooses not to covenant with God, chooses not to want God's presence in their life, or, if having made a covenant with God, does so in vain with the intentionality of not keeping the covenant. Those are examples of imperfection. With such clarity, can we see now that perfection is far more attainable right now than we ever imagined? *In fact, you are already perfect!* Your desire to learn more about God and be faithful to him is you showing perfection on the covenant path! You simply choosing to willingly enter into a covenant with God, to strive with your best efforts (even though you fail to always succeed), and to be faithful and loyal to God, *that is perfection.*

With this covenantal context in mind, let us retranslate what Jesus said, "Be ye therefore loyal, even as your Father which is in Heaven is loyal" or "Be ye therefore wholly devoted [loyal], even as your Father which is in Heaven is devoted [to the covenant that He has bound Himself to in perpetuity]."

Wow. That is a bold strike of revelation that Jesus delivered, full of covenantal love and significance!

Let's dig deeper. Jesus asks us to be loyal. What is the covenant that we willingly enter into to show loyalty? The Sinai covenant. Or, more precisely, the Higher Law revealed through Jesus at the Sermon on the Mount and His other revelations. What is the perfection or loyalty of Father in Heaven that Jesus refers to? That the God of Abraham, Isaac, and Jacob has *always* been loyal to His covenant with the patriarchs. God has modeled covenant fidelity to us throughout the generations. Let us therefore be like God. Let us be loyal as He is loyal. Let us no longer let our hearts linger with other gods or other distractions. Let us no longer let our hearts dwell in anger. Let us turn and heal our relationships with family, friends, neighbors, and enemies. In so doing we show our love to them *and to God*. We demonstrate covenantal loyalty. By so doing, we become perfect as God is perfect. That is, we have become faithful, true, and loyal to the covenants we have willingly entered into.

The covenant path of God is so beautiful, so pure, so compelling, so inviting, and so eminently walkable! As we walk with God (as Abraham did) we will have Him by our side in a mutuality of covenantal strength and love. That is the promise and prosperity of the covenant path.

In summary, when Jesus concluded this portion of the Sermon on the Mount, He said in essence "Be ye therefore loyal [to the Sinai covenant, now updated via the Sermon on the Mount], even as your Father which is in Heaven is loyal [to the Abrahamic covenant]."

# CHAPTER 8

## EXPRESSIONS OF THE TWO MOUNTAIN COVENANTS ELSEWHERE IN THE NEW TESTAMENT

The purpose of this book is not to provide an exhaustive account for all the ways that the themes, structures, ideas, words, and phraseology of the Abrahamic covenant and Sinai covenant appear throughout scripture. As I've said elsewhere, a careful review of much of the Bible will demonstrate that typically one or both of these covenants is just under the surface, providing contextual clues for understanding the scriptures. We've seen above that the Sermon on the Mount is profitably read through the frame of Jesus as the new Moses on a new Mount Sinai inviting Israel to covenant fidelity. But where do we see the Abrahamic covenant perspective in the New Testament?

Hiding in plain sight!

### Paul: Covenantal Faith is Grace

Anyone who has spent time with the writings of Paul knows of his total devotion to faith as the saving element in salvation. So forceful and stirring are Paul's words concerning faith that Martin Luther's reading of Paul led to earth-shattering religious reformation. Paul's most sophisticated and complex expression of

*The Covenant Path in the Bible and the Book of Mormon* 135

the gospel, founded on faith, is found in the last writings we have from him, Paul's epistle to the Romans. This very same letter is what so deeply stirred Martin Luther to focus the rest of his life preaching that we are saved by faith, saved by grace, a concept that seems to have been lost over the centuries since the time of Paul and Christ.

Early in the Romans, Paul declared the central intent of his letter. We could call this his thesis statement:

> I am ready to preach the gospel to you that are at Rome also. For I am not ashamed of the gospel of Christ: for it is the power of God unto salvation to every one that believeth; to the Jew first, and also to the Greek. For therein [that is, in the gospel message] is the righteousness of God revealed from faith to faith: as it is written, **The just shall live by faith**. (Romans 1:15–17; emphasis added)

Diligent Biblical scholars have determined Paul quoted this phrase "*The just shall live by faith*" from the Old Testament prophet Habakkuk. Though Paul correctly quotes from the Greek translation of the Hebrew Old Testament, the Greek translation slightly garbles the real meaning of Habakkuk's original Hebrew. Let's go back into the Old Testament and see what Habakkuk had to say. You can already guess that Habakkuk made a powerful covenantal statement.

If we turn to Habakkuk 2:4, we find the source of Paul's thesis statement, "The just shall live by his faith." We immediately see the difference between Paul's quote and what is in Habakkuk: "the just shall live by faith" (Paul) versus "the just shall live by **his** faith" (Habakkuk; emphasis added). So who is the "his" of Habakkuk 2:4? Turns out that the text is a bit ambiguous. However, if we carefully read the context, we see that it references the Lord Jehovah. The faith that will cause the just to live is therefore the faith of Jehovah!

But there is more to unpack here. The word for "just" is better translated as "righteous." A better translation would render Habakkuk 2:4 as "The righteous will live because of the faith of

Jehovah." The underlying word for "faith" in this verse is from the Hebrew word *aman* from whence our word "amen" derives. Remember earlier in this book we explored Genesis 15:6 and its covenantal significance? I think it worthwhile to repeat a portion of that discussion again because the gospel is tied together here between Old Testament and New Testament within the thesis statement of Paul's most powerful written work about faith and grace. Here is what we discussed earlier in the book.

**Genesis 15:6.** *And he believed in the LORD; and he counted it to him for righteousness.*

> Abraham was a good learner. He believed God. He knew that God would not lie. What we usually miss in this verse is the covenantally significant word "believe." It comes from the Hebrew word *aman*, as does the word "amen" that we use at the end of blessings, prayers, or whenever we assent our agreement to something. *Aman* means to be covenantally faithful, which demonstrates belief. So our word "amen" literally means "faithful," that is, I concur that what I just heard was faithfully and truthfully stated, therefore I agree. So Abraham was not simply believing God. Abraham was demonstrating faithfulness and truthful commitment to God—righteousness. Furthermore, the word "righteous," or "righteousness," is a covenantal term. It does not simply mean "not committing sin" or "keeping the commandments." In the Bible, the word "righteous" is best understood as faithful commitment to a covenant or trusting dedication or loyal allegiance. Abraham trusted God. Abraham demonstrated loyal allegiance. Abraham was faithfully committed to God. These descriptors are the essence of righteousness. And this is the righteousness of Abraham so succinctly expressed in Genesis 15:6.

The Hebrew word *aman*, which means faith or faithful, is a covenantal code word signaling fidelity and loyalty to the covenant as well as trustworthiness to do all that has been promised in the covenant. The word "righteousness" is also another covenantal code word that also conveys the idea of being determined to be loyal and faithful to the covenant, or rather, to those within the covenant, such as God being loyal to us and us being loyal to God.

So let's rewind Habakkuk 2:4 yet again and fully translate what this crucially fundamental verse in scripture really means.

> **"The faithful and loyal covenant makers and keepers [of the Mount Sinai covenant] will be made to live [forever] because of Jehovah's covenantal trustworthiness and loyalty to Abraham, Isaac, and Jacob [as expressed via the Mount Moriah covenant]."**

When Paul imports Habakkuk into Romans 1 as his foundational statement and message, he brings along the entire covenant path that we've been discussing throughout this book!

What I'm saying here is that Paul has been not fully understood by Christian thinkers across the centuries. We have been too blithe, reading his words at face value, importing our own present meanings into later translations. We have missed the searing beauty of the covenantal significance that Paul packs into a few spare phrases. (I know that Paul has never been accused of being spare with his words.) The faith that Paul talks about throughout his letters is not the simple faith of shouting "I believe in Jesus!" which is too often simplistically preached among Christians worldwide (as if declaring Jesus's name is *all* that is required in the act of covenantal salvation). Salvation requires both the faith and action of God, which He promised to the patriarchs, as well as the faith and action of each of God's children.

When Paul preached that we are saved by grace, he was absolutely correct! We are saved by the grace, or rather by the covenantal faithfulness of God as expressed in His covenant to Abraham. Do we have any obligations? Yes. We must return God's loyalty back to Him in the form of living the stipulations revealed at the Sermon on the Mount and through other prophets, which represent an update to the Mount Sinai covenantal stipulations.

Remember that Jesus is the fulfillment of the Abrahamic promise. His death vivifies and makes certain all of the Godly acts of faith recorded in the Old Testament. And we must not forget that Jesus is the Jehovah of the Old Testament who made the promises to Abraham, covenants to give Abraham enduring posterity and property. Too often we think that those promises end when this life ends. But God has greater plans. Jesus wants us to be as He is. To inherit all that He has. That is the true fulfillment of the Abrahamic promises and covenant. There is nothing we have done or can do to qualify for God to offer those blessings to us. That is a free gift. That is grace. God freely makes the Abrahamic gifts available. In this regard, Paul is absolutely right. There are no works, no acts of faith, no righteousness of our own, none of our own merits that have or will make the Abrahamic promises available. All those promises are already there, waiting for us to claim them. That is grace.

We should be careful to not fall into the trap that too many Pauline commentators have fallen into. They have forgotten, or not been aware, that the covenant path involves both the unconditional covenant to Abraham and the conditions set forth in the covenant at Sinai. Paul's thesis statement in Romans quietly imports both those covenants into his message. But without someone putting the brakes on reading, without pausing to dig deeper into what Paul was messaging, we'll miss, as many have, that though the Abrahamic promises are an expression of God's grace, our faithless actions can block our access to them.

Therefore, the intent of Paul's writings was to invite his readers to recognize that salvation has already been offered to them by God, who is trustworthy because He covenanted to be so. No one need think that they have to earn salvation. Still, if we wish to experience the salvation God offers, we must be covenant makers and keepers as He is. We must be willing to show our faith by entering into a covenant to live the teachings delivered to us by Jehovah in the flesh. That covenant path is to demonstrate faith that Jesus is our Savior by getting on the covenant path (repenting), which is at the gate of symbolically entering the grave through baptism, receiving the gift of the Holy Ghost so that a member of the Godhead may be with us at all times and in all things (if we are faithful), and be trustworthy and loyal as we endure on the covenant path until the end when we are fully received into the presence of God.

## Part 3 Conclusion

We've reviewed how the covenant path of the Abrahamic covenant and the Sinai covenant are at the core of the most significant turning points in Israelite history and scripture, both in the Old and New Testament. My hope is that at this point you are thoroughly convinced that the faithful Bible writers intentionally preserved, recorded, and shared these covenants for later generations to benefit. God invites us, by means of the Bible, to trust Him to fulfill His obligations. He also invites us to be as the children of Israel at Sinai, to willingly assent to join Him in a covenant. What he most desires is that we are as loyal to Him as He has been to us and as have been our spiritual forebearers. Many of their stories have been preserved in scripture. We demonstrate that loyalty by living according to the stipulations He has revealed. Without revelation, without prophets sharing the expectations God has for us, without prophets explaining what God desires of us in a covenant relationship, we would not be able to demonstrate our covenantal fidelity. The purpose of the scriptures and of prophets is to bring forth and preserve those revelations so that we might clearly see the covenant path and faithfully walk it.

If, as I hope, I've made a convincing case that the Old and New Testament are profitably, beautifully, and meaningfully revealed through the lens of covenant making and keeping—the covenant path—I hope to convince you that the Book of Mormon is also best read as a covenantal text.

# PART 4

## THE COVENANT PATH IN THE BOOK OF MORMON

# CHAPTER 9
# BOOK OF MORMON TITLE PAGE: THE BOOK OF MORMON RESTORED THE COVENANT PATH

God launched the Restoration with the Book of Mormon. The Book of Mormon laid the foundation for the Restoration of the priesthood, the Restoration of the Church, the Restoration of ongoing revelation, and the Restoration of God's covenants and knowledge of His covenants. The coming forth of the Book of Mormon reignited God's covenantal relationships with His people. The Book of Mormon is a covenantal text, as so boldly declared in D&C 84:57, "Remember the new covenant, even the Book of Mormon." Reviewing that verse's context, we find that D&C 84:43–59 is drenched in covenantal terminology and significance. God operates by means of covenants. The God of Abraham, Isaac, and Jacob is the same yesterday, today, and forever. If He is to have a covenant people, He will reveal His covenants to them. We see this in the Book of Mormon.

The Book of Mormon was created and preserved for our day, so that now, in the latter days, we can be like God, making and keeping covenants. The Book of Mormon starts with God creating a new covenant people (the people of Lehi) after the prophesied destruction of a people who failed to keep their covenantal loyalty to God (the Israelites). The Book of Mormon concludes at the destruction of a significant portion of Lehi's people who, like the Israelites, had failed to stay on the covenant path, who failed to show enduring covenantal fidelity. As the Israelites before them, they were removed from the land like so many encumbering weeds. This covenant book has come forth in our day as a witness and a warning. The Book of Mormon witnesses to us of God's loving graciousness in preserving His covenant people who are faithful to Him. And the Book of Mormon warns us of the consequences of breaking the covenants God has established for those who wish to live in peace and prosperity upon His promised lands (wherever He has designated those lands to be).

The Book of Mormon signals its covenantal foundation and purpose loud and clear at the beginning via the Title Page. The message is consistent and constant throughout the text of the Book of Mormon. And the book concludes with a challenge, like no other book ever produced, that is grounded entirely in covenantal thinking.

## Book of Mormon Title Page

Let's carefully review a few select phrases from the Title Page of what Moroni teaches us about the purpose of the Book of Mormon, about covenants, and how the Book of Mormon both instructs us on covenants and fulfills God's covenants.

*"Written to the Lamanites, who are a remnant of the house of Israel"*

Moroni first addresses this record to the Lamanites, who he correctly identifies as a remnant of the house of Israel. Because they are part of Abraham's tribe, the Lamanites are inheritors of the Abrahamic promises. God made a covenant to make those promises available to his descendants. The Book of Mormon is one of the means by which God fulfills the Abrahamic promise, by making known the covenants of the fathers to the children!

## "Written . . . also to Jew and Gentile"

This book is for *everyone*. For the children of Abraham, whether Jew or Lamanite, or of any other tribe of Israel. The Book of Mormon is also written to all Gentiles. Anyone who covenantally joins the people of God are adopted into Abraham's family. They are welcomed into the tent. This concept can be elucidated by the traditional Arabic greeting of welcome: *ahlan wa sahlan*. This phrase literally translated means, "tents and families." The essence of the phrase is that "you are welcome to join our tribe. And as you do, our tent and our family expands and multiplies." This is the covenantal message of God found in the Book of Mormon. We are all invited to join God's tent and family whether we were born into the covenant or adopted in. God lengthens the cords of His sacred tent and strengthens the stakes so that a larger family of covenant people are invited in and protected within His tent. Once we are in the tent, God is under obligation to preserve us and maintain us and to protect us. If we leave the tent, we lose His protecting presence. If we consistently act against the covenant of the tent, compromising the peace and prosperity of those within it, God will remove us from the tent. The spreading of the gospel is God's way of extending His tent to encompass more people in the grace of His salvation and promises as expressed in the phrase "lengthening the cords and strengthen the stakes."

## "Written by way of commandment"

Remember that commandments are ways or instructional guidance for us to show our devotion to God. Moroni, and the other writers, compilers, and preservers of the Book of Mormon, demonstrated their covenantal love for God by fulfilling His command to create these records. If the Book of Mormon was written under covenant, shouldn't we read it and live it under covenant?

### "Which is to show unto the remnant of the house of Israel what great things the Lord hath done for their fathers"

Earlier we learned that the Ten Commandments are simply the stipulations for faithful loyalty within the covenantal agreement between the Israelites and God, inaugurated at Mount Sinai. And we remember that before inviting the Israelites' devoted loyalty, He reminded them of the great deeds of salvation He had done on their behalf. We remember that He did those deeds because He is the God of Abraham, the God of Isaac, and the God of Jacob and He was fulfilling His promises to the patriarchs. He promised to be loyal. And He has been. The Mount Sinai covenant was the means He created for the Israelites and their descendants to show loyalty to Him in return. As a way to encourage ongoing loyalty and love from His people, God preserves and shares the stories of His saving acts. God ensures that the stories demonstrating His trustworthiness as a covenant keeper are recorded and divulged. That is the covenantal purpose of scripture. Moroni understood that covenantal purpose, which is why he so clearly messages to us in the Book of Mormon Title Page, in essence, "Read this book as a covenantal treasure trove and instruction manual."

### "That they may know the covenants of the Lord"

Again, Moroni speaks as plain as words can be that the Book of Mormon is a covenantal book. God has made covenants. How would we know unless someone told us? How would we know unless the stories of God's covenant making were recorded and transmitted? How would we know that God invites us to covenant with Him unless the memories and instructions for those covenants were preserved? How would we know the consequences of faithfulness if those stories had not been kept to be shared with us? The Book of Mormon was compiled and preserved, in part, to reveal the covenants of the Lord.

### "That they are not cast off forever"

This is a very curious purpose for a book. Do you know of any other book whose promise to the reader is, "Once you have read this book, you will know that you are not cast off forever"? This is a bold and encouraging promise! The essence of this promise is covenantal. As the God of Abraham, Isaac, and Jacob, God has made covenantal promises to make posterity and property available to the patriarchal descendants so that they might prosper. The Lamanites (a principle audience of the Book of Mormon) are not cast off forever, even if some of their ancestors were unfaithful. No one can destroy God's promises to Abraham. Sure, any one of us can act in an unfaithful way and block our access to those promises either temporarily or permanently. But there is nothing I or any other human can do to destroy God's promises to Abraham. God is covenantally bound to make those promises available to Abraham's descendants, which includes the Lamanites. In this regard, we see the context for the prayer of many Book of Mormon prophets that their covenantal words be preserved and brought forth to the salvation of Lamanites in the latter days. When God agreed to these prophetic prayers, He was doing no more than agreeing to what He had already covenanted with Abraham to do. The Book of Mormon is a witness that God has been true and faithful to Abraham. The coming forth of the Book of Mormon is a witness that the restoring of Abraham's children to their covenantal promises is beginning. And, the Book of Mormon reveals the means by which we show our covenantal loyalty back to God. And of course, we do all these things by and through Jesus Christ.

The promise, that they might know that they are not cast off forever, is not exclusive to the Lamanites. This is the promise to any of the children of Abraham. Or to any who choose to join the covenantal clan. They are then adopted into the family of Abraham.

## *"And also to the convincing of the Jew and Gentile that Jesus is the Christ, the Eternal God, manifesting himself unto all nations"*

The overarching covenantal purpose of the Book of Mormon is to instruct us on the nature, identity, and character of the covenant-making and covenant-keeping God: Jesus Christ, Jehovah of the Old Testament. It was Jehovah that promised to Abraham. It was Jehovah who saved the Israelites. It was Jehovah who offered the Sinai covenant of faithfulness and loyalty. It was Jehovah who, as Jesus Christ, became the Passover Lamb, the sacrificial victim to bridge the gap between us and incompleteness. Jesus Christ makes all things whole. We cannot do that on our own. We cannot save ourselves. We cannot be perfect on our own. We cannot be whole without Him. He invites us to be devoted to Him and He recognizes that we will fall far short of total perfection. So He fills the gap. He bridges the divide. In modern parlance, Jesus says to us, "Be whole in me and do so by regularly and consistently showing your love and devotion to me."

## *"And now, if there are faults they are the mistakes of men; wherefore, condemn not the things of God, that ye may be found spotless at the judgment-seat of Christ"*

Moroni concludes the Title Page, and his writing of the Book of Mormon, with this warning to not condemn or reject the things of God. What exactly would we be condemning if we rejected the Book of Mormon? God's covenants. God's covenant path. We cannot hope to arrive in the presence of God unspotted from the things of this world if we decided to create our own path, our own way. Jesus is the path and the way. The covenant path goes right through Jesus. That is the purpose of the Book of Mormon, to reveal the covenant path. If we reject the path, where will we go? Where will we end up? Will we find God through some other forbidden path? If we reject the covenantal instruction so plainly revealed through the Book of Mormon, will we be able to experience the enduring joy that God has designed for the covenantally faithful, as so well expressed in 2 Nephi 2:25, "[We are] that [we] might have joy."? The Book of Mormon is a pathway and a warning. The Book of Mormon lays out the covenant path while presenting a loving warning to all who may feel unwilling to embark on the pathway that returns us to the presence of God.

Moroni, the last prophetic writer of the Book of Mormon, made the covenantal purpose of the Book of Mormon unmistakably clear. The Book of Mormon is a covenant text. The Book of Mormon should be read as covenantal instruction. And we are invited to trust God's covenants while faithfully entering into covenantal relationship with Him. God restored His covenantal truth to the world so that He could create a people who are a peculiar treasure to Him, because of their covenants. Finally, Jesus Christ is at the center of all righteous covenants. His atoning sacrifice brings meaning, life, and vitality to the purposes of God's covenants with His children.

In the remainder of this portion of the book, we'll focus on identifying, highlighting, and elucidating elements of the covenant path found throughout the Book of Mormon. My purpose is not to be exhaustive but rather to provide sufficient guidance on how to look for and then follow the covenant path as expressed in the Book of Mormon. As you pursue your own personal searching of the covenant path in the Book of Mormon, I hope what you learn here will pay rich dividends.

# CHAPTER 10

# 1 NEPHI AS A RECORD OF THE COVENANT PATH

**1 Nephi 1: Nephi's Thesis Statement. Nephi's Testimony Was Grounded in the Two-Fold Covenant Path**

The Book of Mormon opens with intense drama. Packed into a single chapter is a beautifully succinct biographical introduction and a brief overview of the wickedness of Jerusalem, heavenly visions and prophetic revelation, fiery preaching and angry denunciations, that set the stage for fleeing the depravity of civilization to find God in the wilderness. Nephi concludes the opening chapter of the Book of Mormon with one of the most sublime testimonies ever uttered.

> I, Nephi, will show unto you that the tender mercies of the Lord are over **all those whom he hath chosen** [Abrahamic covenant], **because of their faith** [Mosaic covenant], to make them **mighty even unto the power of deliverance** [Abrahamic covenant]. (1 Nephi 1:20)

Do you see that Nephi's thesis statement or testimony of truth is based on the mutuality of the two covenants we've learned about in this book? The Abrahamic covenant is represented by God's tender mercies as well as God choosing His people. Then the Mosaic covenant is represented by the phrase that individuals agentively demonstrate their covenantal faith and fidelity. The verse concludes with the Abrahamic covenant being activated on a faithful person's behalf so that they are empowered through God to be delivered.

Nephi's thesis statement or testimony is an invitation for a revealing scripture study of Nephi's words. Reread 1 and 2 Nephi and ask this question, "How does what Nephi include show me that the tender mercies of the Lord are over all those whom he hath chosen, because of their faith, to make them mighty even unto the power of deliverance"?

Other aspects of 1 Nephi echo the interplay between the Abrahamic and Mosaic covenants, including the following: Lehi saw a pillar of fire. Remember that in the Book of Exodus God appeared as a pillar of fire to save and guide the Israelites away from danger? God also appeared in a flaming apparition to Moses, revealing many things to him. Lehi is like a new Moses. When Lehi attempted to preach to the people, as God's authorized representative, the people rejected him and thus rejected God and His covenant. The narrative demonstrates how the people were ready to lose their land of inheritance for lack of faithfulness to God's commands and authorized servants.

Other clues to the covenantal traditions influencing the structure, wording, phraseology, and recording of the Book of Mormon are the names of key characters. Consider the fact that Nephi's name likely is the Egyptian word for "good," and "good" is also a covenantal term representing one who is within the covenant relationship. Then contrast that with Laman, whose name may mean "not believing, not faithful" [La (not) aman (believing)]. On one side you have Nephi representing those who are true and faithful to God's covenants. On the other side you have Laman representing those who do not believe, those who are not faithful, those who are outside of God's covenant. The stark contrast between "in the covenant" and "out of the covenant" plays out throughout the Book of Mormon, first within Lehi's family (essentially Nephi vs. Laman) and then among the two warring tribes over 1000 years of history (the Nephites vs. the Lamanites). In other words, these two names represent one of the main themes of the Book of Mormon: who is in the covenant and who isn't. There seems to be a dividing line (though the rule doesn't always hold fast throughout the Book of Mormon) that have the faithful Nephites on one side. They were in the covenant with God. And then on the other side were the unfaithful Lamanites who were out of the covenant. By their choices, they closed off their access to the promises of the Mount Moriah covenant because they were not faithful to the Mount Sinai covenant.

## 1 Nephi 2: To Believe or Not to Believe

The Book of Mormon plays upon the meanings of these two names in interesting ways, subtly highlighting that the purpose of the Book of Mormon is to serve as an instruction manual for how to live in covenant fidelity to God while sharing examples of what happens when individuals, groups, and nations do or do not live faithfully within a covenant relationship with God. For example, in 1 Nephi 2, Nephi made a clear contrast between Laman (remember his name likely means "not believing, not faithful) and Lemuel who *do not believe* and himself who does believe. Nephi described Laman and Lemuel becoming angry with their father:

> They did murmur [like the faithless children of Israel in the wilderness] because they knew not the dealings of that God who had created them. **Neither did they believe** [La (not) aman (believing)] that Jerusalem, that great city, could be destroyed according to the words of the prophets. (1 Nephi 2:12–13; emphasis added).

Nephi then went on to describe how with humility of heart he developed his faith unto knowledge: "Having great desires to know of the mysteries of God, wherefore, I did cry unto the Lord; and behold he did visit me, and did soften my heart that I did believe all the words which had been spoken by my father; wherefore, I did not rebel against him like unto my brothers" (1 Nephi 2:16). Following in the Torah tradition, Nephi became a teacher of the faith he gained, teaching his brother Sam what he learned.

Later in this same chapter, Nephi received promises that sound reminiscent on what God granted to Abraham yet is full of Sinai covenant language:

> And inasmuch as ye shall keep my commandments [reminiscent of the Sinai covenant], ye shall prosper, and shall be led to a land of promise [reminiscent of the Moriah covenant]; yea, even a land which I have prepared for you; yea, a land which is choice above all other lands. And inasmuch as thy brethren shall rebel against thee, **they shall be cut off from the presence of the Lord** [Sinai covenant teaches that to prosper means to have the presence of the Lord]. And inasmuch as thou shalt keep my commandments, thou shalt be made a ruler and a **teacher over thy brethren** [like Moses, Nephi would instruct his brothers in the Torah or in the instructions of the covenant]. For behold, in that day that they shall rebel against me, I will curse them even with a sore curse, and they shall have no power over thy seed except they shall rebel against me also. [God promises to Nephi what He had promised Abraham. "And I will bless them that bless thee, and curse him that curseth thee" (Genesis 12:3).]. And if it so be that they rebel against me, they shall be a scourge unto thy seed, to stir them up in the ways of remembrance. (1 Nephi 2:20–24; emphasis added)

The promise at Mount Sinai is that if you keep the commandments of God, you will prosper in the land. We learned earlier that the word "prosper" means to have God's presence with you. How can you fail if you have God with you? There is nothing worthy or good you cannot accomplish with God's presence with you.

Already in the first several chapters of Nephi we can see the strong influence of the two covenantal mountains. We cannot meaningfully read even the first two chapters of 1 Nephi without seeing the two covenants of the Bible tied together seamlessly in Nephi's family story. Without our awareness, understanding, and appreciation of the two major covenants in the Old Testament, we would not be able to fully understand and embrace Nephi's covenantal message.

## 1 Nephi 3: Nephi Believed in the Lord Like Abraham and It Is Counted unto Him for Righteousness

After Nephi's expression of belief in and loyalty to God and his receipt from God an Abrahamic type promise of God's loyalty to Nephi, Lehi received a command to return to Jerusalem to obtain the plates of brass. Why did God require Lehi's party to travel with this record? Remember in the Sinai covenant, for people to be instructed in the covenantal expectations, a written record is required. Lehi had already spent most of his life in Jerusalem seeing the consequences in society of the people not having easy access to the covenantal record and the efforts King Josiah and others enacted to bring the people back into covenantal loyalty. Lehi had already seen the covenantal disobedience that was destroying the fabric of the society in Jerusalem. And Lehi knew that because the people had so long not lived in covenantal faithfulness (in part because the record of covenantal instructions had been lost in the temple for generations), they were ripe for destruction. Lehi knew that without the covenantal record, his people would suffer the same fate that would soon befall Jerusalem.

Lehi asked Nephi to return to Jerusalem to retrieve the plates, a task that was fraught with peril and danger. Laman and Lemuel denied their father's wishes saying it was a hard thing he had commanded of them. Lehi corrected them that God had commanded it. If God commands, we show our loyalty and love to Him by obeying. Yet again Laman and Lemuel demonstrated the meaning of Laman's name—not faithful—and provided an example of the actions and attitudes of a noncommitted and non-covenantal person. In contrast, we see covenantal fidelity from Nephi. He was totally loyal to God in His willingness to fulfill God's request. Why was Nephi so loyal? Because he totally and fully trusted God, just as Abraham did.

Listen to Nephi's testimony and compare that to Abraham's willingness to endure a difficult command from God to sacrifice Isaac. In each instance, the covenantally loyal servant of God had total trust that God would provide a path of salvation. Nephi may have had in mind Abraham's faithfulness in binding Isaac for sacrifice, with the hope and faith that God would provide a path of deliverance, when he said, "I will go and do the things which the Lord hath commanded, for I know that the Lord giveth no commandments unto the children of men, save he shall prepare a way for them that they may accomplish the thing which he commandeth them" (1 Nephi 3:7).

When God saved Isaac with a ram caught in the thicket, Abraham named the location *Jehovahjireh*. Translated from the Hebrew, that means, "Jehovah will see to it [that a path of salvation is provided]." And the mount where this occurred was Mount Moriah, or the mountain where Jehovah saw to it or provided a path of salvation. The word "Moriah" is distinctly significant. The name may mean "the place of Torah" or "the place of instruction" or "Jehovah sees to it [Jehovah prepares a way]." Was 1 Nephi 3:7 Nephi's agreement to experience a Mount Moriah moment where he knew that this hard errand to retrieve the plates from Laban would be a time for covenantal instruction from Jehovah, who would see to it that a way was prepared for the faithful to be delivered?

### 1 Nephi 4: Nephi's Mount Moriah Moment

Why does Nephi trust God so much? Likely because he knew the stories of God's great deeds of wondrous salvation leading the Israelites out of Egypt from Pharaoh. If God could destroy Pharaoh's army, God could definitely empower Nephi and his brothers to overcome Laban, who from a literary standpoint plays the role of a pharaoh who will not let God's people go out into the wilderness to worship God. Nephi uses such rousing reasoning with his brothers:

> And it came to pass that I spake unto my brethren, saying: Let us go up again unto Jerusalem, and let us **be faithful in keeping the commandments of the Lord**; for behold he is mightier than all the earth, then why not mightier than Laban and his fifty, yea, or even than his tens of thousands? Therefore let us go up; let us be strong like unto Moses; for he truly spake unto the waters of the Red Sea and they divided hither and thither, and our fathers came through, out of captivity, on dry ground, and the armies of Pharaoh did follow and were drowned in the waters of the Red Sea. (1 Nephi 4:1–2; emphasis added)

These very deeds of God's covenantal loyalty to Abraham's posterity (enacted through Moses) are the ones that, at Sinai, God called the Israelites to remember when He encouraged them to bind themselves in a loyal covenant of faithfulness to Him. And these great deeds are also what Nephi remembered, from a covenantal context, to give him the encouragement and faith that He could trust the God of Abraham, Isaac, and Jacob to deliver him from any difficulty.

As we explored briefly above, Nephi has a moment which parallels Abraham on Mount Moriah. Like Abraham, Nephi went up to Jerusalem (where Mount Moriah is located). Like Abraham, Nephi did not know beforehand what he was going to do. Like Abraham, Nephi trusted God. Nephi was led by the Spirit. We may be able to surmise that Abraham also had been led by the Spirit. Like in the Abraham story, the prophet-hero did not want to shed blood. Like in the Abraham story, God provided an unexpected path for salvation. Like in the Abraham story, a life is sacrificed for the salvation of the one and the many (the ram in the Abraham story and Laban in Nephi's story). Like Abraham, Nephi returned down the mountain with a lad (Isaac in the Abraham story and Zoram in Nephi's story).

Like Abraham, Nephi fully trusted God to provide a way. Like in the Abraham story, Nephi succeeded because of his faith to be delivered. For his loyalty, Abraham became an exalted father within the covenant (the meaning of his original name "Abram" in Hebrew, *ab* means "father" and *ram* means "exalted") and for his loyalty, Zoram also became exalted within the covenant that he co-inherited with Nephi (Zoram means "he who is exalted" in Hebrew, *zo* means "he who" and *ram* means "exalted"; see 2 Nephi 1:30–32 where Zoram is called "a true friend" to Nephi, which is covenantal language).

There are probably other connections between the Abraham at Mount Moriah story and Nephi and the Laban story that we can tease out. For our purposes, we have seen clear evidence that Nephi's story and story-telling is deeply enmeshed in the covenant traditions originating with Abraham and Moses, to the point that Nephi narrates his own life in the guise of these two prophetic covenant heroes.

## 1 Nephi 4 Reprised: Where Is King David in the Book of Mormon and in Nephi's Narrative?

Earlier in the book we explored how God made an unconditional covenant to David that his throne would endure forever. We discussed how the Davidic covenant was modeled on or was very similar to the Abraham covenant. And we concluded that the Abrahamic and Davidic covenants could be grouped under one heading. So far in our review of the Book of Mormon we've only seen examples of how the Abrahamic and Mosaic covenants are interwoven into the structure, language, phraseology, and ideology of the Book of Mormon. Should we expect to see the Davidic covenant in Nephi's writings or elsewhere in the Book of Mormon?

Curiously enough, King David is hiding right below the surface in 1 Nephi 4.

Some years ago—Tuesday July 3, 2007, to be exact—I woke up much earlier than normal. Now I'm one who loves to study Lehi's dream so I don't spend any more time being awake than absolutely necessary. My wife can attest that I don't practice Lehi's dream while I drive, though I've been known to make church meetings a bit more interesting for fellow saints when my snoring reverberates across a silent chapel. At that early hour when I habitually roll over and return to the bliss of slumber, I had to get up. I had awoken with this thought: "Nephi killed Laban with Laban's own sword and then kept the sword; David did the same to Goliath." Having spent several years being trained in ancient Near Eastern languages and literary skills (such as intertextuality), I wondered if Nephi had created literary echoes between his story confronting Laban and David's story confronting Goliath.

I got up, opened up the two stories, read them simultaneously, and made a chart of parallels. I found something like twenty-four parallels between the stories of Nephi and Laban and David and Goliath. There in front of me was a list unmistakably showing that these two stories were connected. In modern times we call that plagiarism. In ancient times, that is called intertextuality, a brilliant literary strategy of stories echoing each other. In Nephi's day, he would have been trained in his scribal school to share stories that provided echoes to other great stories from the past. The new story invites rereading the older story to compare and contrast the two for instructive benefit.

A year or two later I learned that my "discovery" had been seen by an earlier riser than me, and a more brilliant scholar. Beginning in the early 2000s, Ben McGuire began to study and present on this beautiful literary intertextuality between Nephi vs. Laban and David vs. Goliath, culminating in 2009 in his brilliant article entitled "Nephi and Goliath: A Case Study of a Literary Allusion in the Book of Mormon."

Some years later, I worked with Book of Mormon Central to write a short essay on this topic, working off my 2007 research, as well as Ben McGuire's presentations and publications over the years, and additional insights from other scholars and my colleagues at Book of Mormon Central. Below is our combined list of the thirty-eight (38) beautiful and stunning literary parallels between Nephi vs. Laban and David vs. Goliath.

| Nephi vs. Laban | David vs. Goliath |
|---|---|
| Nephi was chosen by God as a ruler before his conflict with Laban (see 1 Nephi 2:22; 3:29). | David was anointed as a king of Israel before his conflict with Goliath (1 Samuel 16:13). |
| Nephi was "exceedingly young" when he slew Laban (1 Nephi 2:16). | David was "but a youth" when he slew Goliath (1 Samuel 17:33). |
| Despite his youth, Nephi was "a man large in stature" and received "much strength of the Lord" (1 Nephi 2:16; 4:31). | Despite his youth, David was "a mighty valiant man" (1 Samuel 16:18), who had killed a lion and a bear (see 1 Samuel 17:34–37). |
| Nephi was sent by his father to obtain the plates of brass, which led to his confrontation with Laban (see 1 Nephi 3:3–4). | David was sent to the battlefront by his father, which led to his confrontation with Goliath (see 1 Samuel 17:17–18). |
| Nephi obeyed the commands of his father: "And it came to pass that I, Nephi, said unto my father: I will go and do the things which the Lord hath commanded" (1 Nephi 3:7). | David obeyed the commands of his father: "And David rose up early in the morning, and left the sheep with a keeper, and took, and went, as Jesse had commanded him" (1 Samuel 17:20). |
| Nephi received a blessing of divine favor from his father: "Therefore go, my son, and thou shalt be favored of the Lord, because thou hast not murmured" (1 Nephi 3:6). | David received a blessing that God would be with him from Saul: "And Saul said unto David, Go, and the LORD be with thee" (1 Samuel 17:37). |
| Nephi declared, "Let us be faithful" (1 Nephi 3:16; 4:1) and "Let us be strong" (1 Nephi 4:2). | David declared to Saul, "Let no man's heart fail because of [Goliath] (1 Samuel 17:32). |
| Nephi declared to his father that he would "go and do the things which the Lord hath commanded" (1 Nephi 3:7). | David declared to Saul, that he would "go and fight with this Philistine" (1 Samuel 17:32). |

| | |
|---|---|
| Laman said to Nephi, "How is it possible that the Lord will deliver Laban into our hands? Behold, he is a mighty man, and he can command fifty, yea, even he can slay fifty; then why not us?" (1 Nephi 3:31). | Saul said to David, "Thou art not able to go against this Philistine to fight with him: for thou art but a youth, and he a man of war from his youth" (1 Samuel 17:33) |
| In response to his brothers' doubts, Nephi cited two miracles related to the parting of the Red Sea—the deliverance of the Israelites and the destruction of the Egyptian army (see 1 Nephi 4:2). The Israelites were saved and the Egyptians were killed. | In response to the Saul's doubts, David reported two times when he was tending sheep and was miraculously delivered by the Lord—once from a lion and once from a bear (see 1 Samuel 17:34–37). The sheep were saved and the predators were killed. |
| Nephi then applied the two miraculous deliverances he had just cited to their own situation: "Let us go up; the Lord is able to deliver us, even as our fathers, and to destroy Laban, even as the Egyptians" (1 Nephi 4:3). | David then applied the two miraculous deliverances he had just cited to his current situation: "The LORD that delivered me out of the paw of the lion, and out of the paw of the bear, he will deliver me out of the hand of this Philistine" (1 Samuel 17:37). |
| Nephi's older brothers (and especially his eldest brother, Laman) were angry with him and "did speak many hard words" (1 Nephi 3:28). | David's oldest brother, Eliab, was angry with him and chastised him for his bold confidence that Goliath could be beaten (see 1 Samuel 17:28). |
| Nephi was the youngest son in his family, and he left his three older brothers behind when he went out on his own to confront Laban (see 1 Nephi Introduction; 4:5). | David was the youngest son in his family, and he left his "three eldest" brothers behind when he went out on his own to confront Goliath. (1 Samuel 17:14). |
| Laban was a "mighty man" who commanded many soldiers (1 Nephi 3:31). | Goliath was a "champion" soldier (1 Samuel 17:4, 23, 51). |
| An angel prophesied of Laban's death before Nephi slew him: "Behold ye shall go up to Jerusalem again, and the Lord will deliver Laban into your hands" (1 Nephi 3:29). Nephi then more directly predicted that Laban would be slain: "Lord is able to deliver us . . . and to destroy Laban" (1 Nephi 4:3). | When confronting Goliath, David prophesied of Goliath's death before he slew him: "This day will the LORD deliver thee into mine hand" (1 Samuel 17:46) and also "the battle is the LORD'S, and he will give you into our hands" (v. 47). |

| | |
|---|---|
| Nephi confidently proclaimed that they could conquer Laban even if he had "tens of thousands" of soldiers (1 Nephi 4:1), which was far more than the "fifty" soldiers that Laman was worried about (1 Nephi 3:31). | David was especially known for slaying "ten thousands" of enemy soldiers, whereas Saul only slew "thousands" (1 Samuel 18:7–8). |
| Nephi had never killed a man before he slew Laban: "And it came to pass that I was constrained by the Spirit that I should kill Laban; but I said in my heart: Never at any time have I shed the blood of man" (1 Nephi 4:10). | Because David only mentioned that he slew a lion and a bear, it suggests he had never killed a man or fought in battle before slaying Goliath (see 1 Samuel 17:33–37). |
| Unlike his older brothers, Nephi was not afraid of Laban (see 1 Nephi 3:31–4:3). | Unlike his older brothers and the rest of the Israelites, David was not afraid of Goliath (see 1 Samuel 17:26). |
| Nephi went to confront Laban without wearing armor or a sword (see 1 Nephi 4:18–19). | David went to confront Goliath without wearing armor or a sword (see 1 Samuel 17:38–39, 50). |
| Laban insulted one of Lehi's sons, bore false witness against him, and made a rash vow that he would slay him: "Wherefore, he said unto him: Behold thou art a robber, and I will slay thee" (1 Nephi 3:13). | Goliath insulted David, cursed him by false gods, and made a rash vow that he would slay him: "And the Philistine said unto David, Am I a dog, that thou comest to me with staves? And the Philistine cursed David by his gods. And the Philistine said to David, Come to me, and I will give thy flesh unto the fowls of the air, and to the beasts of the field" (1 Samuel 17:43–44). |
| Nephi confronted Laban in the name of the Lord (see 1 Nephi 3:15; 4:12). | David came against Goliath in the name of the Lord: "but I come to thee in the name of the LORD of hosts, the God of the armies of Israel" (1 Samuel 17:45). |
| Before Nephi smote off Laban's head, Laban had "fallen to the earth" in his drunkenness (1 Nephi 4:7). | Before David smote off Goliath's head, Goliath "fell upon his face to the earth" (1 Samuel 17:49). |

| | |
|---|---|
| When Nephi approached Laban's fallen body, he "beheld his sword, and [he] drew it forth from the sheath" and "took Laban by the hair of the head, and . . . smote off his head with his own sword" (1 Nephi 4:9, 18). | When David approached Goliath's fallen body, he "took his sword, and drew it out of the sheath thereof, and slew him, and cut off his head therewith" (1 Samuel 17:51). |
| The Spirit of the Lord made special mention of the significance of one man's death: "It is better that one man should perish than that a nation should dwindle and perish in unbelief" (1 Nephi 4:13). | Goliath's challenge placed the fate of their respective nations on the outcome of one man's death: "If [an Israelite warrior] be able to fight with me, and to kill me, then will we be your servants: but if I prevail against him, and kill him, then shall ye be our servants, and serve us" (1 Samuel 17:9). Jonathan later said that David "slew the Philistine, and the LORD wrought a great salvation for all Israel" (1 Samuel 19:5). |
| The Lord delivered Laban into Nephi's hands: "I knew that the Lord had delivered Laban into my hands for this cause—that I might obtain the records according to his commandments" (1 Nephi 4:17). | The Lord delivered Goliath in David's hands: "This day will the LORD deliver thee into mine hand; and I will smite thee, and take thine head from thee" (1 Samuel 17:46). |
| Nephi made a special mention of the good quality of Laban's sword: "the hilt thereof was of pure gold, and the workmanship thereof was exceedingly fine, and I saw that the blade thereof was of the most precious steel" (1 Nephi 4:9). | Goliath's sword is also mentioned as a unique and unprecedented blade. Speaking of the sword, David said, "There is none like that" (1 Samuel 21:9). |
| Nephi kept Laban's sword, and it was eventually stored with sacred Nephite relics, including the plates of brass, the interpreters, the breastplate, the Liahona, and the Book of Mormon itself (see Mosiah 1:16; Doctrine and Covenants 17:1). | David obtained Goliath's sword, which was apparently kept with sacred Israelite relics, seeing that it was "wrapped in a cloth behind the [high priestly] ephod" (2 Samuel 21:9). |

| | |
|---|---|
| When Nephi, after putting on Laban's clothes, approached his brothers, they were "exceedingly frightened" and "fled from before [his] presence; for they supposed it was Laban" (1 Nephi 4:28). | When Goliath confronted the Israelites, "all the men of Israel, when they saw the man, fled from him, and were sore afraid" (1 Samuel 17:24 [23–24]). |
| After Zoram discovered that Nephi was disguised in Laban's clothes, he may have rightly assumed that Laban had been killed. In response to this discovery, he "began to tremble, and was about to flee" (1 Nephi 4:30). | We learn in 1 Samuel 17:51 that "when the Philistines saw their champion was dead, they fled." |
| Nephi's explanation that Zoram would be a "free man" rather than retain his position as a "servant" suggests that Zoram would have expected to have to have to serve Nephi and his family (1 Nephi 4:33–38). | Goliath's terms of combat stipulated that if an Israelite "be able to fight with me, and to kill me, then will we be your servants: but if I prevail against him, and kill him, then shall ye be our servants, and serve us" (1 Samuel 17:9). |
| Nephi killed Laban and took the plates so that his nation wouldn't "dwindle and perish in unbelief" (1 Nephi 4:13). Lehi prophesied that the brass plates would eventually "go forth unto all nations, kindreds, tongues, and people who were his seed" (1 Nephi 5:18). | David killed Goliath so "that all the earth may know that there is a God in Israel" (1 Samuel 17:46). |
| After slaying Laban, Nephi said, "I took the garments of Laban and put them upon mine own body; yea, even every whit; and I did gird on his armor about my loins" (1 Nephi 4:19). | After slaying Goliath, David took Goliath's armor and put it in his own tent (see 1 Samuel 17:54). Also, Jonathan, Saul's heir to the throne, immediately "stripped himself of the robe that was upon him, and gave it to David, and his garments, even to his sword, and to his bow, and to his girdle" (1 Samuel 18:4). |
| After slaying Laban, Nephi took the plates of brass from Laban's treasury (see 1 Nephi 4:20–24). | After slaying Goliath, the Israelites "spoiled [the Philistines'] tents" (1 Samuel 17:53). |

## The Covenant Path in the Bible and the Book of Mormon 163

| | |
|---|---|
| After slaying Laban, Nephi made a solemn oath to Zoram that if he joined them, Zoram could be "a free man like unto us" (1 Nephi 4:33). Later, Lehi declared that Zoram had been "a true friend unto my son, Nephi, forever. Wherefore, because thou hast been faithful thy seed shall be blessed with his seed" (2 Nephi 1:30–31). | After slaying Goliath, "Jonathan and David made a covenant, because he loved him as his own soul" (1 Samuel 18:3). Later Jonathan declared that "we have sworn both of us in the name of the LORD, saying, The LORD be between me and thee, and between my seed and thy seed for ever" (1 Samuel 20:42). |
| After slaying Laban, Nephi returned to the tent of his father and showed him the plates of brass (see 1 Nephi 5:10). | After slaying Goliath, "David returned from the slaughter of the Philistine" and was brought "before Saul with the head of the Philistine in his hand" (1 Samuel 17:57). |
| After slaying Laban, Nephi returned to his father's tent and His parents' "joy was full" (1 Nephi 5:7). In particular, his mother, Sariah, was "exceedingly glad" (v. 1), and she verbally praised the Lord for delivering her sons (see vv. 7–8). | After slaying Goliath, David was immediately made a military leader in Saul's army. Upon returning from his first reported campaign, "the women came out of all cities of Israel, singing and dancing . . . with joy" and also verbally praising David (1 Samuel 18:6 [6–7]). |
| Jacob related that his people "loved Nephi exceedingly, he having been a great protector for them, having wielded the sword of Laban in their defence" (Jacob 1:10). | In 1 Samuel 18:16–17 we learn that "all Israel and Judah loved David, because he went out and came in before them" on his way to "fight the LORD'S battles." |
| Laman was the firstborn, became jealous of Nephi for his success, and repeatedly attempted to kill him. Nephi was chosen by the Lord to be a ruler over Laman and was eventually made a king by his people (see 2 Nephi 5:18–19). | Saul, the current king of Israel, became jealous of David's success and repeatedly attempted to kill him. David was chosen by the Lord to replace Saul and was eventually appointed to be a king by his people (see 1 Samuel and 2 Samuel 2:4; 5:3). |

(Adapted from Book of Mormon Central's KnoWhy #411, "Why Was the Sword of Laban So Important to Nephite Leaders?")

Having seen this extensive comparison, the big questions that need to be asked are these:

If Nephi so clearly narrated his interactions with Laban on the model of David and Goliath, why didn't he overtly clue us readers into that brilliant connection? Furthermore, why doesn't Nephi ever name David?

Nephi names Abraham eight times in his record. But he *never* names David. In fact, Abraham is mentioned twenty-nine times in the Book of Mormon. But David is *only* mentioned three times. And each of those mentions is negative. Only Jacob, the younger brother of Nephi, ever mentions King David by name and only to tell the people of Nephi, "Do not be like King David." The memories of David in the Book of Mormon are nearly non-existent. The limited memories of David that do appear are all negative.

The Book of Mormon is built on the base of the two core covenants of the Bible: The Abrahamic covenant at Mount Moriah and the Mosaic covenant at Mount Sinai. We learned earlier that the Davidic covenant can be grouped with the Abrahamic covenant. What does Nephi think of the Davidic covenant? Given the lack of discussion of David by Nephi or any other Book of Mormon writer, except in the negative, we can surmise the following.

## *Nephi Saw the Messiah, Not David, as the Ultimate Fulfillment of the Unconditional Covenant*

The main promise of the unconditional covenant God made with David was the promise of the Messiah. God promised to send the true anointed King to confirm and ratify His covenants through the Atonement. Nephi had no need of King David when he had the Messiah. Hence the only portion of the Davidic covenant that was retained among the Nephites was that God would send Jesus as the Messiah. In the Book of Mormon the concept of the Messiah is mentioned in twenty-five instances. Most of those mentions are in the record of Nephi. When Nephi thinks of the unconditional covenant God made to provide a King, a Messiah, who would rule and reign in righteousness forever, after having walked the covenant path Himself, Nephi thinks upon Jesus and *not* upon David. Once Nephi died and the records passed to other record keepers, they replaced the title Messiah with Jesus Christ. So after the time of Nephi we only see a few instances of the title Messiah appear in favor of the name Jesus Christ.

## Nephi Wanted to Be a Prophet Like Moses and Not a King Like David

Nephi was launching a new political order. Nephi, under the direction of God, was creating a new kingdom. Nephi was not of the line of Judah and Nephi was not within the Davidic covenant. Nephi was from the tribe of Manasseh. He therefore had no legal claim to the throne of David or to the Davidic covenant. Nephi needed none of these for his legitimacy to rule as king over the Nephites. Nephi had received his own legitimating call from God to lead and rule over the people that wasn't reliant on David (see 1 Nephi 2:22).

So why would Nephi narrate his incredible faith affirming story of confronting and overcoming Laban in the guise of David? King David was one of the great and memorable heroes of the Old Testament. There are more references to King David in the Old Testament than to any other human being except for Moses! The exploits of young David outmatching Goliath, through the power of God, would have been known to any young boy, like Nephi, growing up in Jerusalem. I can imagine that the story of David would have been remembered, told, and retold much like our superhero stories of the day.

If David's story would have been so well-known and so influential, why didn't Nephi make those connections explicit? There are several reasons. One is that the writing technique of intertextuality does not require that the literary echoes tying together two different stories be explicit and overt. The well-read reader should be able to pick up the clues and see the connections without the author doing what I'm doing right now—making the literary connection totally apparent.

Second, Nephi could have used the David and Goliath story as the framework to share his story of overcoming Laban as a way to tell his brothers, and others, "Look, I'm the legitimate king!

Just like David's brothers didn't think he should be king, you are treating me the same way. But God will do His work and will call and empower whomever He will to lead His people. He has called me to be a ruler and teacher to you. And there is nothing you can do to stop the work and will of God. So why not join me in acting with God instead of fighting against me and God?"

Third, I think that there is another, more powerful reason that Nephi never mentioned David. I think that Nephi didn't much like David as a king (though he does respect the shepherd boy David). I think that Nephi was far more interested in modeling his life after that of Moses, to demonstrate covenantal fidelity to God, then to become a king who hoarded wealth and women and who was so distracted that he failed to remember and teach the covenants to his people. If we look carefully at Nephi's younger brother Jacob's complaints against the men of the Nephites, he specifically calls out their seeking of wealth and women as causing destruction in the society. Jacob insisted that the Nephite men *not* look to King David as a model for how to be kings in their own homes. The men of the Nephites should *not* excuse their behavior because of the actions of King David. Where did Jacob derive his low opinion of King David? Likely from his older brother Nephi who had been trained in all the government records and covenantal obligations. Nephi likely would have known how the kings of Israel and Judah eventually led the people of God into apostasy for failing to stay focused on what God expected of king: Keep the covenantal instructional manual close at hand (the scriptures, the Law of Moses, the Torah), live the covenant, and teach the covenant to others (see Deuteronomy 17:14–20). That is all that God expected of a human king. That is how Nephi lived his life, as did Jacob. But we know that David did not always stay true to that simple command from God to live and teach the Torah to his people. That, I believe, is the fundamental reason that Nephi did *not* call out explicit attention to the parallels between his life and that of David. And that is the reason why David is so seldom remembered in the Book of

Mormon, and in the few limited places where he is remembered, he is seen as a bad example to never be followed.

What does all of this talk about David have to do with the covenant path? Remember that there are two foundational covenants in the covenant path: The Abrahamic covenant at Mount Moriah and the Mosaic covenant at Mount Sinai. We saw earlier that the Davidic covenant can be grouped with the Abrahamic covenant. What Nephi appears to be doing is ungrouping and unlinking the Davidic covenant from the Abrahamic covenant, *except* for the Messianic promise. Nephi retained and taught the truth that God had unconditionally promised to send an anointed King (the Messiah, Jesus Christ) who would save His people from their sins and lead them to victory into the kingdom of God.

What kind of literary brilliance does it take on the part of Nephi to write one story that intertextually echoes the two heroes of the two unconditional covenants of the Bible: Abraham and David? And then which one does Nephi embrace and which one does he reject? He accepts Abraham and rejects David. Not being of the Davidic line, Nephi has no need for the promises of the Davidic messianic throne, except for the true Messiah who is Jesus.

### *The Nephi and Laban Story as a Retelling of the Moses and Pharaoh Story*

In this chapter we've discussed how Nephi's story about confronting Laban can profitably be read through the lens of Abraham being commanded to sacrifice Isaac on Mount Moriah (thus representing the Abrahamic covenant), and can be read through the lens of David confronting Goliath (thus representing the Davidic covenant). We just discussed reasons why Nephi and other Book of Mormon writers preserved little of the Davidic covenant, except for the promise of the coming Messiah.

There is yet another powerful way to read the Nephi and Laban story that connects us to the covenant path. We can read through the lens of Moses confronting Pharaoh (thus representing the Mosaic covenant). Let's review more than twenty intriguing connections between the story of Nephi vs. Laban and the story of Moses vs. Pharaoh in Exodus.

| Nephi vs. Laban | Moses vs. Pharaoh |
|---|---|
| Nephi was in the wilderness having fled civilization. (see 1 Nephi 3) | Moses was in the wilderness having fled civilization. (see Exodus 3) |
| God reveals His will to Nephi (through a dream to his father Lehi). (see 1 Nephi 3:2–6) | God revealed His will to Moses through a direct encounter with God at the burning bush at Mount Sinai. (see Exodus 3:2–10) |
| God commanded a return to civilization that resulted in the salvation of a nation. (see 1 Nephi 3:2) | God commanded a return to civilization that resulted in the salvation of a nation. (see Exodus 3:10) |
| Nephi was accompanied by his brothers in this difficult task. (see 1 Nephi 3:2) | Moses was accompanied by his brother in this difficult task. (see Exodus 4:14–16) |
| Laman asked Laban to let go of the sacred covenantal records (i.e., the Brass plates). (see 1 Nephi 3:11–12) | Moses and Aaron asked Pharaoh to let the people go. (see Exodus 5:1) |
| Laban became angry and made the task more dangerous and difficult. (see 1 Nephi 3:13) | Pharaoh became angry and made the task more dangerous and difficult. (see Exodus 5:4–9) |
| They were "exceedingly sorrowful" because of Laban. (1 Nephi 3:14) | The people were exceedingly sorrowful because of Pharaoh. (see Exodus 5:15, 20–21) |
| Nephi reminded his brothers of God's covenantal nature, urging them to trust God. (see 1 Nephi 3:15–21) | God reminded Moses of His covenantal nature, urging Moses and the people to trust Him. (see Exodus 6:3–8) |
| Nephi and his brothers gathered treasures for Laban to release the records. (see 1 Nephi 3:22–26) | God described the treasures available to those who leave Egypt. (see Exodus 6:3–8) |
| Laman and Lemuel were angry with Nephi. (see 1 Nephi 3:28) | The people of Israel were angry with Moses (see Exodus 6:9) |
| God interrupted the angry brothers with revelation. (see 1 Nephi 3:29–30) | God interrupted the angry Israelites with revelation. (see Exodus 6:11) |
| Laman and Lemuel murmured that the task was not possible to complete. (see 1 Nephi 3:31) | Moses murmured that the task was not possible to complete. (Exodus 6:12) |

## The Covenant Path in the Bible and the Book of Mormon 169

| | |
|---|---|
| Nephi encouraged trust in the strength of the Lord. (see 1 Nephi 4:1–3) | The Lord encouraged Moses and Aaron in their task. (see Exodus 6:13) |
| Nephi's brothers did as he and the Lord commanded and returned to Jerusalem. (see 1 Nephi 4:4) | Moses and Aaron did as the Lord commanded and returned to Pharaoh. (see Exodus 7:6–7) |
| Nephi discovered Laban was drunk with wine. He may have been drunk with Passover wine (That time period may have been Passover based on work found in Don Bradley's book *The Lost 116 Pages: Reconstructing the Book of Mormon's Missing Stories*, 2019). (see 1 Nephi 4:7) | By tradition (but not recorded in Exodus), Israelites partook of wine as part of the Passover meal. (Note that Jesus's Last Supper was a Passover meal. In that meal He had His disciples eat bread and drink wine.) |
| God commanded the death of a victim. (see 1 Nephi 4:10) | God commanded the death of a victim. (see Exodus 12:5–6) |
| God explained why the death of this one victim must occur. (see 1 Nephi 4:11–13) | God explained why the death of this one victim must occur. (see Exodus 12:13) |
| If the time period was Passover, was Laban the substitute Passover lamb prepared by God? (see 1 Nephi 4:11) | A Passover lamb was prepared. (see Exodus 12:3) |
| Possibly Laban was the first born appointed to be slain (this is speculation as we have no confirming evidence). (see 1 Nephi 4:11) | God promised to pass through the land of Egypt and smite all the firstborn. (see Exodus 12:12) |
| Laban was slain at night (on Passover night?). (see 1 Nephi 4:5, 18) | First born in Egypt were slain at night of the Passover. (see Exodus 12:29–30) |
| Laban died that a nation might be preserved. (see 1 Nephi 4:13) | First born in Egypt died that a nation might be preserved. (see Exodus 12:31) |
| Nephi obtained the treasures of Laban. (see 1 Nephi 4:20, 24) | The Israelites obtained the treasures of the Egyptians. (see Exodus 12:35–36) |
| Zoram, a non-Lehite, joined the Lehites leaving Jerusalem. (see 1 Nephi 4:34–35) | Non-Israelites (a mixed multitude) joined the exiting Israelites leaving Egypt. (see Exodus 12:38) |
| Nephi, his brothers, and Zoram departed into the wilderness. (see 1 Nephi 4:38) | The Israelites departed into the wilderness. (see Exodus 12:51) |

The purpose of showing these literary connections is to demonstrate yet again that the Book of Mormon is clearly founded on and influenced by the two main covenants and covenantal characters found in the Old Testament: The Abrahamic covenant and the Mosaic covenant.

## Laban Story Conclusion: Nephi as Abraham, Moses, and David

What we are doing in this section of the book, where we focus on the Book of Mormon, is to (1) establish that Nephi brought together in his own person the two covenantal traditions of the Bible (Abraham and Moses), (2) that he taught the covenants to his people, (3) that later prophetic record keepers continued to preserve these two covenants of the covenant path, and (4) that we can see the influence of these covenants throughout the Book of Mormon. In fact, when we read the Book of Mormon through the lens of the covenant path, when we understand and look for the unconditional covenant to Abraham and the conditional promises offered through the covenant of Moses, we will see the path marked bright and clear and we will see God's hand throughout the Book of Mormon.

Nephi showed how he subsumed the Abrahamic covenant (he also told stories that align him with the character of Abraham), subsumed the Mosaic covenant (he told stories showing how he was a new Moses, or at least is influenced by Moses), and subsumed the Davidic covenant (but rejected it except for the promise of the Messiah).

All three major covenants of the bible are subsumed in Nephi in the Laban story.

We can read the Nephi and Laban story as

1. Abraham sacrificing Isaac at Mount Moriah and then receiving a fullness of the blessings of the Abrahamic covenant returned to him.
2. David killing Goliath and becoming the anointed king (messiah): the essence of the Davidic covenant.
3. Moses confronting Pharaoh to liberate God's people physically and spiritually and then leading them into the wilderness

and then into the promised land where they can demonstrate covenantal fidelity to God by living the Mosaic covenant.

Nephi packed into the narrative of his own life, and specifically into this scenario of seeking the covenantal records retained by Laban, a multitude of literary connections to the Biblical covenantal heroes of Abraham, Moses, and David. Why is the Laban story so crucial? These three covenants come together in the person of Nephi. And when Nephi came away unscathed, he had retained the Abrahamic and Mosaic covenants while letting go of the Davidic covenant (except for the promise of the Messiah).

## 1 Nephi 5: The Goodness of God Is an Expression of Covenantal Fidelity

Nephi and his group finally returned to Lehi and Sariah and the wilderness. Sariah had been awash in motherly fear that her sons would all die. Lehi had sought to speak soothing words to her, testifying of the covenantal character of God who would fulfill His promise to Lehi to deliver his family. In the quote below, look for the words "goodness," which describes a trustworthy individual within the covenant such as God, and "deliverance," which God offers those who put their faith and trust in Him,

> And it had come to pass that my father spake unto her, saying: I know that I am a visionary man; for if I had not seen the things of God in a vision I should not have known the **goodness of God**, but had tarried at Jerusalem, and had perished with my brethren. But behold, I have obtained a land of promise, in the which things I do rejoice; yea, and I know that the Lord will **deliver** my sons out of the hands of Laban, and bring them down again unto us in the wilderness. And after this manner of language did my father, Lehi, comfort my mother, Sariah, concerning us, while we journeyed in the wilderness up to the land of Jerusalem, to obtain the record of the Jews. (1 Nephi 5:4–6; emphasis added)

Sariah gained her own testimony of God's power of deliverance when her sons returned home safe and sound. Nephi only directly quotes Sariah twice in his record. This second direct quote appears to be formatted in a chiastic structure centered on the concepts and meaning of her name—Sariah means "Jehovah is Prince" or "Jehovah is a Commander." The middle of the chiasmus focuses on the three qualities the Lord possesses as a prince or commander—His power to protect, deliver, and empower the faithful.

> A Now I know of a surety that the **Lord** [*iah*] hath **commanded** [sar] my husband to flee into the wilderness
> > B yea, and I also know of a surety that the **Lord** [iah] hath protected my sons
> > B' and delivered them out of the hands of Laban, and given them power
>
> A' whereby they could accomplish the thing which the **Lord** [iah] hath **commanded** [sar] them.
>
> (1 Nephi 5:8; emphasis added)

Perhaps Sariah's testimony formed a foundation for Nephi's testimony, for when he spoke to Lehi about the call to return to Jerusalem to retrieve the brass plates, Nephi said the following, and notice how he seems to echo the Hebrew meaning of his mother's name.

> I will go and do the things which the **Lord** [*iah*] hath **commanded** [*sar*], for I know that the **Lord** [*iah*] giveth no **commandments** [*sar*] unto the children of men, save he shall prepare a way for them that they may accomplish the thing which **he** [Lord/*iah*] **commandeth** [*sar*] them. (1 Nephi 3:7; emphasis added)

My purposes in sharing these references are these. First, the Book of Mormon is literarily beautiful with the wordplays in Hebrew and Egyptian reinforcing the covenantal purposes and themes of the Book of Mormon. Second, I love the thought that Sariah's own name may contain her testimony. Third, I'm mesmerized by the possibility that her testimony may have influenced Nephi's own testimony. Finally, the testimony that Nephi and Sariah express in 1 Nephi 3 and 1 Nephi 5 respectively are filled with covenantal themes. God will deliver those who are faithful to Him. He has promised to make that deliverance available. Those who are covenantally aligned to Him have access to that power of deliverance. And Nephi delivered yet again on his thesis statement of 1 Nephi 1:20, "Behold, I, Nephi, will show unto you that the tender mercies of the Lord are over all those whom he hath chosen, because of their faith, to make them mighty even unto the power of deliverance."

## 1 Nephi 6: Why Did Nephi Write His Covenantal Text?

In 1 Nephi 6, Nephi paused his narrative to explain why he was writing. When we review his words, we see the intertwining threads of the Abrahamic and Mosaic covenants.

> For the fulness of mine intent is that I may persuade men to come unto **the God of Abraham, and the God of Isaac, and the God of Jacob,** and be saved. Wherefore, the things which are pleasing unto the world I do not write, but the things which are pleasing unto God and unto those who are not of the world. Wherefore, I shall give **commandment** unto my seed, that they shall not occupy these plates with things which are not of worth unto the children of men. (1 Nephi 6:4–6; emphasis added)

We've seen repeatedly that the phrase "the God of Abraham, and the God of Isaac, and the God of Jacob" specifically calls to mind the characteristics of God's trustworthy fidelity to fulfill His promises to deliver His faithful children into prosperity in their promised lands. Notice, however, that it is not enough for God to be willing to save us. We have to choose to come unto God by living the commandments. We must allow the pleasing word of God to work upon us to persuade us to trust in God's great deeds of salvation. If He can save others, He can save us.

Nephi did not fill his record with anything he believed would distract from his core message, whether it was genealogical records, wars and rumors of wars, or political wrangling. He occupied the precious and limited space on the plates with words that invited people to take seriously their covenantal commitments to God, thereby experiencing God's promised blessings.

## 1 Nephi 7: Acting for or against God's Covenant Path

Nephi returned to Jerusalem with his brothers to find wives among the daughters of Ishmael. I always smile at the fact that Laman and Lemuel complained when they had to get their scriptures but there were no complaints when they were asked to find women to marry.

Laman and Lemuel's alacrity and willingness soon wore off after they returned to the wilderness. They murmured their dissent, expressing the desire to return to Jerusalem. Nephi reminded his brothers that the people of Jerusalem would soon be left to fend for themselves without the protective power of God's presence because they had so consistently broken the Mosaic covenant.

> And if it so be that we are faithful to him [Mosaic covenant], we shall obtain the land of promise [Abrahamic promises]; and ye shall know at some future period that the word of the Lord shall be fulfilled concerning the destruction of Jerusalem; for all things which the Lord hath spoken concerning the destruction of Jerusalem must be fulfilled. For behold, **the Spirit of the Lord ceaseth soon to strive with them** [the faithless people have lost God's presence therefore they will not prosper, they are ripe for destruction]; for behold, **they have rejected the prophets** [who deliver the covenantal instructions], and **Jeremiah have they cast into prison** [examples of how the people broke the Mosaic covenant]. And they have sought to take away the life of my father, insomuch that they have driven him out of the land. Now behold, I say unto you that if ye will return unto Jerusalem **ye shall also perish with them** [if you break the Mosaic covenant, you

cannot have the blessings of the Abrahamic covenant]. And now, if ye have choice, go up to the land, and remember the words which I speak unto you, that if ye go ye will also perish; for thus the Spirit of the Lord constraineth me that I should speak. (1 Nephi 7:13–15; emphasis added)

Nephi even spoke to Laman and Lemuel as though he were Moses reminding the people of the great deeds of loyalty God had demonstrated in delivering them from danger and death. Shouldn't they then owe their full trust and allegiance to God? Could they expect to experience the blessings of the patriarchs if they failed to demonstrate the trust and belief of the patriarchs? "Yea, and how is it that ye have forgotten what great things the Lord hath done for us, in delivering us out of the hands of Laban, and also that we should obtain the record?" (1 Nephi 7:11).

Laman and Lemuel were in no mood to demonstrate covenantal loyalty. They let their anger burn hot and drive their actions. Seeking to murder Nephi, they tied him up. In so doing, they were no better than generations of Israelites who refused to listen to humble and prophetic voices. Because he knew that he had been devoted to God, Nephi had total faith and trust that God would deliver him. Nephi trusted the God of Abraham who would deliver the faithful.

> But it came to pass that I prayed unto the Lord, saying: O Lord, according to my faith which is in thee, wilt thou deliver me from the hands of my brethren; yea, even give me strength that I may burst these bands with which I am bound. And it came to pass that when I had said these words, behold, the bands were loosed from off my hands and feet, and I stood before my brethren, and I spake unto them again. (1 Nephi 7:17–18)

Each chapter of 1 Nephi we've reviewed so far shows the clear strands and intermingling of the Mosaic and Abrahamic covenants. Without knowing of these fundamental covenants from the Old Testament (and the language, terminology, and structure of these covenants), we would miss much of the covenantal nature and significance of the Book of Mormon. We would miss that Nephi (as well as later prophetic writers and record keepers of the Book of Mormon) was deeply influenced by these two covenants in his thinking, writing, preaching, and living.

## 1 Nephi 9, 13, and 19: Nephi Recorded and Preserved God's Covenants, the Most Plain and Precious Parts

When Nephi paused for yet another editorial insertion explaining why he was writing his record, he expressed themes from the Abrahamic covenantal tradition. Like Abraham, Nephi knew that God would fulfill all His words and promises.

> But the Lord knoweth all things from the beginning; wherefore, he prepareth a way to accomplish all his works among the children of men; for behold, he hath all power unto the fulfilling of all his words. And thus it is. Amen.
> (1 Nephi 9:6)

God's covenants are some of the most plain and precious things He has ever revealed. Luckily for us, key covenants of the covenant path have been preserved in the Bible. Still, the expression of those covenants has not been easily and readily recognizable for many readers of scriptures. And portions of the Biblical record have been removed or lost, compromising our ability to learn more about God's covenants.

Nephi described how God commanded him to keep a record of the plain and precious teachings he shared during his ministry.

> I have received a commandment of the Lord that I should make these plates, for the special purpose that there should be an account engraven of the ministry [covenantal instruction] of my people. (1 Nephi 9:3)

In the quotation below, notice Nephi's use of the word "instruction" and remember that the Torah is the covenantal instruction manual. Without instructing people in the covenant, they cannot keep the covenant. Having lived in Jerusalem, Nephi had seen firsthand what happens to a people who are ignorant of the things of God, especially His covenants. They fall into apostasy and they are removed from the promised land. Given his awareness of covenantal duties, Nephi recognized that his people could not be saved in ignorance. They needed access to the covenantal instruction manual, the Torah and other scriptures that Nephi preserved or produced.

> And after I had made these plates by way of commandment, I, Nephi, received a commandment that the ministry and the prophecies, the more plain and precious parts of them, should be written upon these plates; and that the things which were written should be **kept for the instruction of my people** [Torah, Mosaic covenant], who should possess the land, and also for other wise purposes, which purposes are known unto the Lord. (1 Nephi 19:3; emphasis added)

When we pair 1 Nephi 19:3 with passages from 1 Nephi 13, we see the serious need to preserve the knowledge of and instruction about God's covenants for His people. We can feel thankful that Nephi was so covenantally loyal and devoted to God that He received the promise of being prospered, of having God's Spirit with him, which guided him on what to preserve in the covenantal text we call the Book of Mormon. For example, Nephi had seen in his vision "the Gentiles do stumble exceedingly, because of the most plain and precious parts of the gospel of the Lamb which have been kept back" (1 Nephi 13:34). How can anyone walk the covenant path if they have not been shown the way? Should we be surprised that those who have not had the covenant path revealed to them stumble? Can we be loyally devoted to God, to follow in His footsteps if we don't know how to walk or where to walk? The command to walk before God, or to walk with God (as we've demonstrated before, that is covenantal language) cannot be fulfilled without instructions. The scriptures are the instruction manual for how to walk with God. Because some of the covenantal instructions in the Bible have been removed, people have stumbled in ignorance.

Nephi knew, because of his visionary experience, that the fullness of the gospel message would be had among his descendants. He also knew that they would become like the people of Israel who dwindled in unbelief because they stopped walking on the covenant path. Nephi knew that the records of God's covenant would be preserved for a later time to come forth when God restored all things and revealed anew the path that led back into His presence. The Book of Mormon preserves a fullness of the basic saving truths necessary for any one of us to walk the covenant path with the guidance and presence of God.

> I will manifest myself unto thy seed, that they shall write many things which I shall minister unto them, which shall be plain and precious; and after thy seed shall be destroyed, and dwindle in unbelief, and also the seed of thy brethren, behold, these things shall be hid up, to come forth unto the Gentiles, by the gift and power of the Lamb. (1 Nephi 13:35)

## 1 Nephi 16: The Liahona as Manna and as Guide for the Covenant Path

After the narrative pause to share Lehi's dream and his own visionary experiences, Nephi picked up the story again of his family's travels through the wilderness. When we read Nephi's story, he hoped for us as readers to see that his family was a new Israel being guided by God through the wilderness to the promised land. Just as the ancient Israelites required ongoing nourishment from God as they wandered in the wilderness, the same held true for Nephi's family. In fact, in 1 Nephi 16, God gave to Nephi's family something very much like manna—the Liahona.

> And it came to pass that the voice of the Lord spake unto my father by night, and commanded him that on the morrow he should take his journey into the wilderness. And it came to pass that as my father arose in the morning, and went forth to the tent door, to his great astonishment he beheld upon the ground a round ball of curious workmanship; and it was

of fine brass. And within the ball were two spindles; and the one pointed the way whither we should go into the wilderness. (1 Nephi 16:9–10)

The tribe of Lehi was like the Israelites who woke one morning to discover something unexpected on the ground.

> And when the dew that lay was gone up, behold, upon the face of the wilderness there lay a small round thing, as small as the hoar frost on the ground. And when the children of Israel saw it, they said one to another, It is manna: for they wist not what it was. And Moses said unto them, This is the bread which the LORD hath given you to eat. (Exodus 16:14–15)

The Israelites were curious about the unknown object. They didn't know what it was. They said to one another "what is it?" using the Hebrew words *ma* meaning "what" and *na* meaning "is it." The resulting word is *manna*, which literally means "what is it?" We can almost hear Nephi's family when first seeing the Liahona exclaiming in Hebrew *manna* or "what is it?" Like manna, the Liahona provided substance and sustenance. Like manna, the Liahona provided hope. Like manna, the Liahona demonstrated "Emmanuel" meaning "God is with us." Like manna, the Liahona demonstrated God's covenant path that He would provide a way for His people to fulfill the things that He had commanded them. Like manna that was bread for the Israelites to eat, the Liahona was like the bread of life delivering the word of God whenever they diligently sought through faith to receive.

God had commanded Lehi's party to continue their journey, but He didn't leave them on their own. He provided guidance for them in the form of the Liahona, fulfilling Nephi's testimony expressed in 1 Nephi 3:7, "I will go and do the things which the Lord hath commanded, for I know that the Lord giveth no commandments unto the children of men, save **he shall prepare a way** for them that they may accomplish the thing which he commandeth them" (emphasis added).

Like Abraham, who trusted God, Nephi acted on trusting God that He would do what He had promised to do—to provide a way to walk the covenant path. God will create a way, or a path, a covenant path, that He will reveal to us so that we may cross through life and find ourselves back in His presence. That is God's Abrahamic promise to us, if we are faithful.

If we listen carefully, we'll see how Nephi had been constructing his narrative around the covenant path. Lehi's dream and Nephi's vision revealed the covenant path guided by a rod of iron representing the word of God. How did Nephi and his family access the word of God? By obtaining the brass plates and by seeking new revelation from God via the Liahona, as they exercised faith. As they were loyal to God, God was loyal to them. He delivered them through His power as they were faithful to the covenant path.

> And we did follow the directions of the ball, which led us in the more fertile parts of the wilderness. . . . And it came to pass that I, Nephi, beheld the pointers which were in the ball, that they did work according to the faith and diligence and heed which we did give unto them. (1 Nephi 16:16, 28)

In the human context, faith and diligence are covenantal concepts evoking the imagery of the Mosaic covenant. As we are faithful, we prosper in the land. Our faith is centered on God, who made an eternal promise to grant us prosperity in proportion to how wide we open our faith-door of receiving.

## 1 Nephi 17: The Interplay between the Abrahamic and Mosaic Covenants

As they continued their toilsome journey in the wilderness, Nephi described their experience in the covenantal terms of Mount Sinai:

> And thus we see that the commandments of God must be fulfilled. And **if it so be** that the children of men keep the commandments of God he doth nourish them, and strengthen

them, and provide means whereby they can accomplish the thing which he has commanded them; wherefore, he did provide means for us while we did sojourn in the wilderness. (1 Nephi 17:3; emphasis added)

We see the conditional phrase "if it so be" that Nephi included. He knew that his continued access to God's promises was conditioned on covenantally loyalty. The commandments were the guardrails, or the discipline, or the sign posts, or the instructions for how to show loyalty to God. Those who paid attention would see God's mighty arm providing means for them to endure to the end. Those who wandered in forbidden paths would find themselves lost in dreary wastes and would only fully experience the fruit of the tree of God's love when they returned to firmly and loyally holding onto the iron rod that marks the covenant path.

We might wonder where Nephi acquired his rock-ribbed and uncompromising faith and trust in God. If we see Nephi as an Abraham figure, as one who has learned to trust God fully, implicitly, without question, then we begin to understand the character of Nephi. When God commanded Nephi to build a ship, Nephi was like Abraham willing to go to Mount Moriah, not knowing beforehand what he was going to do or how God would fulfill the covenant path. But like Abraham who had received the Abrahamic covenant, Nephi trusted. He knew that God would be true.

In fact, when God did reveal Himself to Nephi in Bountiful, He first told Nephi to go into the mountain (see 1 Nephi 17:7). Only after Nephi was alone in the mountain praying did God reveal the next assignment (see 1 Nephi 17:8–9). We might wonder, why didn't God simply reveal His will when He first spoke to Nephi in Bountiful? Why make him climb a mountain? One reason is that God wants us to make an effort to be in communion with Him. Another reason is that God wants us to put ourselves in locations of limited or no distractions so that He can have our full attention. If we are so busy in the cares of the day, in conversations with friends and family, in the incessant disruption of technology devices, how will we ever know that God is seeking to communicate with us? How can God fulfill His purposes in the Abraham covenant if we never are in a position to *hear* Him that we might act on covenantally loyalty?

When God commanded Nephi to build a ship, why didn't Nephi sensibly say, "Umm, hey God, I've never built a ship before and I know you want a faithful people in a new promised land. But if they all drown because of my ineptitude, won't that throw a wrench into your whole plans? And remember, God, my apprenticeship in metalworking and my school days training to be a scribe never had any lessons on ship building. Are you sure have the right guy?" Nephi didn't respond in a sensible way to God's request to build a boat. Instead, he responded in a faithful way. Nephi had trust and faith like his ancestor Abraham who had trusted fully and implicitly in the God of Abraham.

God would do His part to inspire and instruct Nephi on how to build a ship. Thus it became Nephi's job to demonstrate covenantal devotion to God by listening to and obeying instructions. "Not faithful" Laman and Lemuel were *unwilling* to be covenantally devoted to God. "They did **not believe** that [Nephi] could build a ship" (1 Nephi 17:18; emphasis added; remember that Laman's name may mean "not believing" from *La* "not" *aman* "faithful/believing"). They did not believe that God could talk to Nephi (as He had spoken to Abraham). They did not believe that God could do great deeds, as He had done for the Israelites. They did not believe that they should have ever left Jerusalem in the first place. In fact, so far gone in their faithlessness and unbelief were Laman and Lemuel that they actually twisted and confused the meaning, responsibility, and purposefulness of the Mosaic covenant. They called evil good and good evil.

> And we know that the people who were in the land of Jerusalem were a **righteous people** [i.e., covenantally loyal to God]; for they **kept the statutes and judgments** of the Lord, and all his commandments, according to the law of

Moses; wherefore, we know that they are a **righteous people** [i.e., covenantally loyal to God]; and our father hath judged them, and hath led us away because we would hearken unto his words; yea, and our brother is like unto him. And after this manner of language did my brethren murmur and complain against us. (1 Nephi 17:22; emphasis added)

Laman and Lemuel *believed* (Hebrew *aman, amen*) that the people of Jerusalem had been righteous. Their expressed belief was contrary to God's chosen prophets saying otherwise, including Jeremiah, Lehi, Zephaniah, Nahum, Habakkuk, Huldah, Urijah, Daniel, Ezekiel, and Obadiah. Laman and Lemuel's false belief led them to false conclusions with spurred them to false actions resulting in covenantal disloyalty. In fact, worse than not keeping the covenant, Laman and Lemuel *worked against* God's commands. They actively acted to make it so others could not be covenantally faithful. It's bad enough to leave the covenantal relationship with God. It is far worse to commit spiritual murder (as Alma the Younger termed it) by disrupting and disallowing another individual's ability to be in a covenantally committed and devoted relationship with God. Orthodoxy (correct beliefs in the covenantal context) leads to orthopraxis (correct faithful actions that demonstrate loyalty to God).

Turning to the paradigmatic example of following God's commands, Nephi recites a litany of examples from the life of Moses (see 1 Nephi 17:23–39). Did Moses know how to lead a host of people out of bondage? No. But he trusted God and acted to fulfill the command. Did Moses know how to part the waters? No. but he listened to God's command and acted. Did Moses know in advance to strike the rock to find water for the people? No. But in following God's commands, he saved the people. Moses had no special academic training or journeyman apprenticeship experience that could have prepared him to participate in such marvelous acts of physical salvation. Moses simply was God's servant, loyally willing to do as God commanded. In acting, God empowered him to become great, and his name has become great, just as God promised to Abraham and his descendants, "and I will make . . . thy name great" (Genesis 12:2). Moses was the model of devoted loyalty Nephi followed. In this regard Nephi was like Moses, leading the people safely through the waters to the promised land!

Nephi expected his brothers to similarly get in line and follow the faithful example of Moses. Nephi knew that whatever the God of Abraham, Isaac, and Jacob commanded, He would prepare a way for people to successfully endure on the covenant path. He would provide a way for those commands to be fulfilled, just as He did for Abraham on Mount Moriah where the ram became the provided substitute for Isaac. As Nephi had so astutely observed earlier in the Book of Mormon, Laman and Lemuel "did murmur because they knew not the dealings of that God [which God? The God of Abraham, Isaac, and Jacob who was entirely trustworthy in the covenant] who had created them" (1 Nephi 2:12). Unlike Abraham, or Moses, or Nephi, Laman and Lemuel did not believe that God would provide a way.

Nephi demonstrated the interplay between the Abrahamic and Mosaic covenants as expressed in the peak of his prophetic interpretation of Israelite history for his brothers. Look at all the covenantal language packed into these verses signaling God's obligations in the Abrahamic covenant and our obligations in the Mosaic covenant:

> And he **loveth** [i.e., is covenantally loyal to] those who will have him to be their God. Behold, he **loved** [i.e., showed His covenantal faithfulness to] our fathers, and he **covenanted** with them, yea, even **Abraham, Isaac, and Jacob** [this is God's covenantal title "the God of Abraham, Isaac, and Jacob"!]; and he **remembered the covenants** [He showed loyalty] which he had made; wherefore, he did bring them out of the land of Egypt [as He was covenantally obligated to do]. And he did straiten them in the wilderness with his rod [as He was covenantally obligated to do to those who did not keep their end of the bargain]; for they **hardened their**

**hearts** [were not covenantally loyal to the Mosaic covenant], even as ye have; and the Lord straitened them because of their iniquity. He sent fiery flying serpents among them; and after they were bitten he prepared a way that they might be healed; and **the labor which they had to perform was to look** [akin to weekly partaking of the sacrament to look to God and proclaim, "I am committed to you and I trust you!"]; and because of the **simpleness of the way** [covenant path], or the easiness of it, there were many who perished. (1 Nephi 17:40–41; emphasis added)

Laman and Lemuel persisted in their unbelief to the point that they wanted to commit murder, one of the major ways to break covenantal loyalty with God, as expressed in the Ten Commandments. Calling upon the power of God, Nephi stopped them with the command,

In the name of the **Almighty God**, I command you that ye touch me not, for I am filled with the power of God, even unto the consuming of my flesh; and whoso shall lay his hands upon me shall wither even as a dried reed; and he shall be as naught before the power of God, for God shall smite him. (1 Nephi 17:48; emphasis added)

Nephi used a title of God that had been revealed by God to Abraham in a covenantal ceremony,

The LORD appeared to Abram, and said unto him, **I am the Almighty God**; walk before me [be on the covenant path], and be thou perfect [covenantally loyal]. And I will make my covenant between me and thee, and will multiply thee exceedingly. (Genesis 17:1–2; emphasis added)

Like Abraham, Nephi trusted that God would fulfill His promises, "I will bless them that bless thee, and curse him that curseth thee" (Genesis 12:3) and "The LORD will fight for you; you need only to be still" (Exodus 14:14, NIV). Therefore, Nephi had complete trust that God would deliver him from his brothers' murderous rage.

Nephi concluded this conflicted experience with his brothers by testifying of something he likely learned from faithful Abraham who learned to trust God: "If God had commanded me to do all things I could do them. If he should command me that I should say unto this water, be thou earth, it should be earth; and if I should say it, it would be done. And now, if **the Lord has such great power**, and has wrought so many miracles among the children of men [such as with Abraham, Moses, and the House of Israel], how is it that he cannot instruct me, that I should build a ship?" (1 Nephi 17:50–51; emphasis added).

The concluding verse of this chapter intertwines the two covenant traditions again. Nephi has experienced the Abrahamic promise of God being with him and his faithful descendants (see Genesis 26:24; 28:15) and Nephi urges his brothers to show loving loyalty to God by keeping the commandments to "love God" (summarizing the first four of the Ten Commandments) and "love thy neighbor" (summarizing the last six of the Ten Commandments), specifically loving father and mother. We can see the covenantal language in Laman and Lemuel's reaction and then Nephi's response:

> We know of a surety that **the Lord is with thee**, for we know that it is the power of the Lord that has shaken us. And they fell down before me, and were about to worship me, but I would not suffer them, saying: I am thy brother, yea, even thy younger brother; wherefore, **worship the Lord thy God** [be loyal, believing, and faithful to God], and **honor thy father and thy mother**, that thy days may be long in the land [the promised land!] which the Lord thy God shall give thee. (1 Nephi 17:55; emphasis added)

Why am I doing such a detailed and deep dive on 1 Nephi and on 1 Nephi 4 and 1 Nephi 17 in particular? I'm hoping to provide convincing evidence that the Book of Mormon is thoroughly saturated in the covenantal ideology, themes, and ideas of the two key covenants originating in the Bible: the Abrahamic and the Mosaic covenants. My book will not do a deep dive on every book or chapter of the Book of Mormon. But the selections I offer the reader should provide a compelling case that the Book of Mormon is best understood as a covenantal text. If we want to understand the purposefulness and testimony of the Book of Mormon writers, we need to enter into their world of covenants. Otherwise, we may miss some of the most profound insights about the gospel of Jesus Christ preserved in this record written and kept for our day.

# CHAPTER 11

## ISAIAH IN THE BOOK OF MORMON: THE INTERWEAVING OF THE ABRAHAMIC AND MOSAIC COVENANTS

### What is Isaiah Doing in the Book of Mormon?

Readers have long puzzled, even fretted, over the inclusion of Isaiah in the Book of Mormon. I invite us to reread all quoted selections of Isaiah in the Book of Mormon through the lens of the Abrahamic and Sinai covenants. My thesis is that since these two covenants are foundational for understanding the character of God (Jehovah) and His work among the children of men to save them, then we'll better understand Isaiah's message when we read his words as expressions of the covenant path. We should look for the covenants of Mount Moriah and Mount Sinai, symbolically and thematically, in the words of Isaiah. I believe that as we do so, Isaiah's testimony of God as the covenant path creator and revealer will shine bright and pure.

I won't provide an exhaustive review of the Isaiah passages in the Book of Mormon. Rather I'll provide a few examples to demonstrate that the covenant path aids our comprehension of Isaiah's writings.

One of the fascinating discoveries I've made about Isaiah in the Book of Mormon is how selective Nephi and other Book of

Mormon writers were in choosing what to include from Isaiah. Earlier we discussed some of Nephi's likely background in the scribal and Deuteronomistic world of Jerusalem near 600 BC that interpreted Israelite history through the lens of how well the people of Israel kept the commanded stipulations of loyalty. We've also discussed God's covenant with King David. Here's what's interesting. During the time of Nephi there was significant religious controversy and disagreement about God. Some people put all their trust in God's covenant with King David, believing that God would never let Jerusalem, the temple, or the throne of David fall. They interpreted God's promise to David that these things could *never fall*: the dynasty of David, the city of Jerusalem where the dynasty resided, and the temple that provided legitimacy to the kingship. If the city couldn't fall, then the people could not be destroyed, or so went the reasoning. These ancient Israelites believed that Jerusalem could never fall. In summary, the people who trusted in their interpretation of God's covenant to David preached "All is well in Zion [Jerusalem]" (2 Nephi 28:21)!

Arrayed opposite the "All is well in Zion" religious movement was that of the Deuteronomists who believed that the only way to achieve and maintain access to God's protecting presence was to stay loyal to Him. Yes, God's presence was in the temple of Jerusalem. But God's presence was *not* the originating cause of the peace and prosperity that the people enjoyed. Their covenantal faithfulness provided an ongoing invitation for God's presence to remain with the temple and the people. If the people failed to live the commands revealed in the Law of Moses, eventually God, as the owner of the temple, city, and land, would remove His presence and His people from the land.

It seems strongly reasonable that Nephi, Lehi, and Jeremiah were squarely in the camp of the Deuteronomists preaching the Mosaic covenant. What religious party do you think Laman and Lemuel adhered to?

**Neither did they believe** [Laman = *La* (not) *aman* (believing)] that Jerusalem, that great city, could be destroyed according to the words of the prophets. And they were like unto the Jews who were at Jerusalem, who sought to take away the life of my father. (1 Nephi 2:13; emphasis added)

Laman and Lemuel seemed to put all their trust in the Davidic covenant, forgetting about their duties and obligations to God spelled out in the Mosaic covenant. This may provide one of the key reasons why there was so much conflict between Lehi and Nephi on one side and Laman and Lemuel on the other. It seems that the family was split right down the middle on religio-political questions. One side (Lehi and Nephi) believed and preached that individuals had to show covenantal loyalty. The other side (Laman and Lemuel) believed and acted as though their citizenship in Jerusalem automatically protected them. I can't pass by this opportunity to say that unfortunately there are members of the Church today who believe that because they lived in a promised land (wherever they may draw those borders) that they are automatically protected. They believe, like the ancient Jews, that the temple on the hill is a sign that God's presence is them and therefore there is nothing to worry about. We have modern-day members living and preaching "All is well in Zion!" Yes, there are many prosperous things happening in the Restoration today, and God's presence is spreading throughout the world. But the rise of God's presence does not create an invitation for us to lower our guard or our faithfulness to God. We should not become complacent or lazy, as Laman and Lemuel were. We should be ever diligent to check ourselves to ensure that we are fully committed to God and His kingdom.

Now this is where things get interesting. One of the greatest prophets to explain God's covenant with David was Isaiah, some one hundred years before the time of Nephi. We've already made the strong case that Nephi really didn't admire David and didn't want to preserve the Davidic covenant as it was preached and interpreted during his day. So if Isaiah so often wrote in positive terms about the Davidic covenant and if Nephi was so skittish about Davidic ideology, why would Nephi claim that Isaiah was one of the greatest prophets and so often quote from him?

Would you be surprised to learn that Nephi selectively quoted from Isaiah? Would you be surprised to see that for the most part Nephi, and other Book of Mormon writers, avoided quoting any Isaiah passages that glorified the kingdom of David? Take a look at this table below. It represents all the major Book of Mormon quotes of Isaiah and labels which of the Isaiah passages are devoted to David. You'll notice that the Book of Mormon authors appear to selectively and strategically only use the covenantal words of Isaiah *that do not involve King David*, although there is one minor exception to this rule within Nephi's lengthy block quote of Isaiah 2–14.

Of the 102 Isaiah passages deemed by scholars to explicitly focus on the Davidic covenant, only six of those passages appear in the Book of Mormon. That is less than 6% of the total. Hardly a meaningful amount. Notice how there is a big section of Isaiah devoted to the ideas of the Davidic covenant in Isaiah 24, 25, 26, 30, and 31. But none of those sections are included in the Book of Mormon. Instead, it appears as though Nephi intentionally selected Isaiah chapters that did not discuss the Davidic covenant. Within Isaiah 24–31 there are only three chapters (Isaiah 27, 28, and 29) that *do not* reference the Davidic covenant. Where does Nephi quote from? Isaiah 28 and 29, effectively finding the open area between Isaiah 24–31 where the Davidic covenant is not expressed. This seems to be further evidence that Nephi wanted to be a prophet like Moses (one who follows the commands of the Law of Moses to demonstrate covenantal faithfulness) and not a king like David (who sits in stupor upon his throne while his brethren languish in ignorance of the Law).

| Isaiah Chapters | Where Are Davidic Covenant Ideas in Isaiah? | Isaiah Quotes in the Book of Mormon | Book of Mormon Reference |
|---|---|---|---|
| 1 | | | |
| 2 | | Isaiah 2 | 2 Nephi 12 |
| 3 | | Isaiah 3 | 2 Nephi 13 |
| 4 | | Isaiah 4 | 2 Nephi 14 |
| 5 | | Isaiah 5<br>Isaiah 5:26 | 2 Nephi 15<br>2 Nephi 29:2–3 |
| 6 | | Isaiah 6 | 2 Nephi 16 |
| 7 | | Isaiah 7 | 2 Nephi 17 |
| **8** | **8:5–10** | **Isaiah 8** | **2 Nephi 18** |
| 9 | | Isaiah 9 | 2 Nephi 19 |
| 10 | | Isaiah 10 | 2 Nephi 20 |
| 11 | | Isaiah 11<br>Isaiah 11:4<br>Isaiah 11:5–9<br>Isaiah 11:11 | 2 Nephi 21<br>2 Nephi 30:9<br>2 Nephi 30:11–15<br>2 Nephi 25:17<br>2 Nephi 29:1 |
| 12 | | Isaiah 12 | 2 Nephi 22 |
| 13 | | Isaiah 13 | 2 Nephi 23 |
| 14 | | Isaiah 14 | 2 Nephi 24 |
| 15 | | | |
| 16 | | | |
| 17 | 17:12–14 | | |
| 18 | | | |
| 19 | | | |
| 20 | | | |
| 21 | | | |
| 22 | | | |
| 23 | | | |
| 24 | 24:21–22 | | |
| 25 | 25:6–12 | | |

## The Covenant Path in the Bible and the Book of Mormon 193

| | | | |
|---|---|---|---|
| 26 | 26:1–7 | | |
| 27 | | | |
| 28 | | Isaiah 28:10 | 2 Nephi 28:30 |
| | | Isaiah 28:13 | 2 Nephi 28:30 |
| 29 | | Isaiah 29:3–4 | 2 Nephi 26:15–16 |
| | | Isaiah 29:4 | 2 Nephi 27:6–9 |
| | | Isaiah 29:5 | 2 Nephi 26:18 |
| | | Isaiah 29:6 | 2 Nephi 6:15 |
| | | Isaiah 29:6–10 | 2 Nephi 27:2–5 |
| | | Isaiah 29:11 | 2 Nephi 26:17 |
| | | Isaiah 29:11–12 | 2 Nephi 27:15–19 |
| | | Isaiah 29:13 | 2 Nephi 28:9 |
| | | Isaiah 29:13 | 2 Nephi 28:14 |
| | | Isaiah 29:13–24 | 2 Nephi 27:25–35 |
| | | Isaiah 29:14 | 1 Nephi 14:7 |
| | | Isaiah 29:14 | 1 Nephi 22:8 |
| | | Isaiah 29:14 | 2 Nephi 25:17 |
| | | Isaiah 29:14 | 2 Nephi 28:9 |
| | | Isaiah 29:21 | 2 Nephi 28:16 |
| 30 | 30:27–33 | | |
| 31 | | | |
| 32 | | | |
| 33 | 33:5–6, 14–24 | | |
| 34 | | | |
| 35 | | | |
| 36 | | | |
| 37 | 37:33–38 | | |
| 38 | | | |
| 39 | | | |
| 40 | | Isaiah 40:3 | 1 Nephi 10:7 |
| | | Isaiah 40:3 | 1 Nephi 10:8 |
| 41 | | | |
| 42 | | | |
| 43 | | | |
| 44 | | Isaiah 44:27 | Helaman 12:16 |
| 45 | | Isaiah 45:18 | 1 Nephi 17:36 |

| 46 | | | |
|---|---|---|---|
| 47 | | Isaiah 47:14 | 1 Nephi 22:15 |
| 48 | | Isaiah 48:1–49:26 | 1 Nephi 20:1–21:26 |
| 49 | | Isaiah 48:1–49:26<br>Isaiah 49:22<br>Isaiah 49:22–23<br>Isaiah 49:22–23<br>Isaiah 49:22–23<br>Isaiah 49:24–52:2 | 1 Nephi 20:1–21:26<br>2 Nephi 29:2<br>1 Nephi 22:6<br>1 Nephi 22:8<br>2 Nephi 6:6–7<br>2 Nephi 6:16–8:25 |
| 50 | | | |
| 51 | | Isaiah 51:10 | Helaman 12:16 |
| 52 | | Isaiah 52:1–2<br>Isaiah 52:1–3<br>Isaiah 52:6–7<br>Isaiah 52:7<br>Isaiah 52:7<br>Isaiah 52:7<br>Isaiah 52:7–10<br>Isaiah 52:8<br>Isaiah 52:8–10<br>Isaiah 52:8–10<br>Isaiah 52:8–10<br>Isaiah 52:10<br>Isaiah 52:10<br>Isaiah 52:11–15<br>Isaiah 52:12<br>Isaiah 52:15 | Moroni 10:31<br>3 Nephi 20:36–38<br>3 Nephi 20:39–40<br>1 Nephi 13:37<br>Mosiah 15:14<br>Mosiah 15:15–18<br>Mosiah 12:21–24<br>3 Nephi 20:32<br>Mosiah 15:29–31<br>3 Nephi 16:18–20<br>3 Nephi 20:34–35<br>1 Nephi 22:10<br>1 Nephi 22:11<br>3 Nephi 20:41–45<br>3 Nephi 21:29<br>3 Nephi 21:8 |
| 53 | | Isaiah 53:1–12<br>Isaiah 53:7<br>Isaiah 53:10 | Mosiah 14:1–12<br>Mosiah 15:6<br>Mosiah 15:10 |
| 54 | | Isaiah 54:1–17<br>Isaiah 54:2 | 3 Nephi 22:1–17<br>Moroni 10:31 |
| 55 | | Isaiah 55:1<br>Isaiah 55:1<br>Isaiah 55:2 | 2 Nephi 9:50<br>2 Nephi 26:25<br>2 Nephi 9:51 |
| 56 | | | |
| 57 | | | |

| 58 | | | |
| --- | --- | --- | --- |
| 59 | | | |
| 60 | 60:1–22 | | |
| 61 | 61:1–11 | | |
| 62 | 62:1–12 | | |
| 63 | | | |
| 64 | | | |
| 65 | 65:17–27 | | |
| 66 | | | |

The main takeaway from this table is to demonstrate that Nephi and other Book of Mormon writers were focused primarily on the two covenantal mountains expressed in the Abraham and Moses stories *and not* on the covenant God gave to David that he would retain kingship. The conclusion we draw from this is that we can reasonably and meaningfully read Isaiah in the Book of Mormon through the lens of the Abrahamic and Mosaic covenants and not distract ourselves with the Davidic covenant.

### Isaiah, Abraham, Moses, and Nephi

Why did Nephi include Isaiah in his writings? Nephi shared Isaiah as a word of warning and for comfort. Nephi essentially wanted his people to reflect on Israelite history and see what happened to those who didn't remain faithful to God. The core of Nephi's message was this: "We have a new promised land. Let us be faithful to God and find prosperity in the land. Let us not be like the other Israelites who forgot the Lord and forgot their covenants. We have seen what happened to them. Isaiah reminds us of what happened to them."

Nephi quoted Isaiah so that his people would see the consequences of covenantal fidelity o r f aithlessness. L et's e xplore 1 Nephi 20, which quotes Isaiah 48 and see how revealing it can be to read Isaiah through the lens of the unconditional covenant to Abraham and the conditional covenant to Moses and his people. You can then repeat this exercise for the remainder of the Isaiah quotes in the Book of Mormon. You should look for the key themes, ideas, phrases, and ideology of the Abrahamic and Mosaic covenants. When you see evidence of the Abrahamic covenant, you'll see that the true nature and character of God is being revealed. When you see the Mosaic covenant, you'll see that God is reminding His people how and why to be faithful, or He is acting for or against them based on their faithfulness to their covenants with Him.

| 1 Nephi 20 (Isaiah 48) Abrahamic covenantal words are underlined *Mosaic covenantal words are italicized* | Notes on Reading through the Lens of Abrahamic and Mosaic Covenant |
|---|---|
| [1] *Hearken and hear this, O house of Jacob, who are called by the name of Israel, and are come forth* out of the waters of Judah, *or out of the waters of baptism, who swear by the name of the Lord, and make mention of the God of Israel, yet they swear not in truth nor in righteousness.* | The house of Israel are God's chosen people whom He chose to save, as an act of covenantal love (Abrahamic covenant), from Egyptian bondage. He gave them the Mosaic law as covenantal instructions for the Israelites to show their love to Him. Baptism is part of the covenantal path for how we show our love to God. But Isaiah calls out the Israelites to repent for not being firm and faithful in their covenantal commitments, "they swear not in truth nor in righteousness." Metaphorically, they have "taken the Lord's name in vain" because that they made covenants without intending to keep the commitment. |
| [2] *Nevertheless, they call themselves* of the holy city, *but they do not stay themselves upon the God of Israel, who is the Lord of Hosts; yea, the Lord of Hosts is his name.* | The people claim they deserve the blessings of the Abrahamic covenant, "they call themselves of the holy city [Jerusalem]," but they do not actually stay committed to the God of the fathers as they were commanded to do in the Mosaic covenant. The God of the fathers is the God of Israel, the Lord of Hosts (Abrahamic covenant). |

| | |
|---|---|
| [3] Behold, I have declared the former things from the beginning; and they went forth out of my mouth, and I showed them. I did show them suddenly. | This speaks of the nature and character of God (Abrahamic covenant). God speaks truth. God reveals His covenants. God has all power. |
| [4] And I did it because I knew that *thou art obstinate, and thy neck is an iron sinew, and thy brow brass;* | But we are fickle humans. We are often too proud to return loving fidelity to God, as He instructed us in the Mosaic covenant to show. |
| [5] And I have even from the beginning declared to thee; before it came to pass I showed them thee; and I showed them for fear lest thou shouldst say—*mine idol hath done them, and my graven image, and my molten image hath commanded them.* | There is no god but God (the God of Abraham, Isaac, and Jacob), but we want to replace the God of the Abrahamic covenant with our own imagined gods. God will give us all the promises of Abraham, but then in our fallen natures, we claim that some other god gave us these promises or that we acquired these Abrahamic promises on our own. |
| [6] *Thou hast seen and heard all this; and will ye not declare them?* And that I have showed thee new things from this time, even hidden things, *and thou didst not know them.* | God has shown His mighty arm to save, most marvelously when He led the Israelites out of Egyptian captivity. He had covenanted with Abraham to do so. The Israelites saw and heard all of the great deeds of the God of Abraham. But then the Israelites seem to fail to remember these great deeds, they fail to remember the loving kindnesses of God's deliverance and salvation. |
| [7] They are created now, and not from the beginning, even before the day when thou heardest them not they were declared unto thee, *lest thou shouldst say—Behold I knew them.* | God has taught all these covenantal truths. God has revealed His plan in fullness and plainness (Abrahamic covenant). But we resist. We claim that He has not taught us, or that we did not know (breaking the Mosaic covenant). |
| [8] *Yea, and thou heardest not; yea, thou knewest not; yea, from that time thine ear was not opened; for* I knew that *thou wouldst deal very treacherously, and wast called a transgressor from the womb.* | We close our ears to the God's covenantal truths. We walk away from our covenantal obligations (Mosaic covenant) and thus lose our access to the Abrahamic promises. |

| | |
|---|---|
| [9] <u>Nevertheless, for my name's sake will I defer mine anger, and for my praise will I refrain from thee, that I cut thee not off.</u> | God made an immutable covenant with Abraham (see Genesis 15) and He promised in His own sacred name that He would not permanently cut the House of Israel out of the promises that He made to their father Abraham. At some future day, God will gather in the House of Israel again and seek to redeem them, insofar as they are willing to live His covenants (as symbolized by the Mosaic covenant). |
| [10] <u>For, behold, I have refined thee, I have chosen thee in the furnace of affliction.</u> | God allows us to suffer the consequences when we break the Mosaic covenant. But God, committed to the Abrahamic covenant, continues to choose us. |
| [11] <u>For mine own sake, yea, for mine own sake will I do this, for I will not suffer my name to be polluted, and I will not give my glory unto another.</u> | When God says "For mine own sake," He is referring to His covenantal obligations to prepare and make ready the covenant path of salvation. |
| [12] *Hearken unto me, O Jacob, and Israel my called,* <u>for I am he; I am the first, and I am also the last.</u> | God, as the God of Abraham, Isaac, and Jacob, declares His trustworthy nature. Those who enter into covenant with Him (as symbolized by the Mosaic covenant) will receive the promises of the Abrahamic covenant. |
| [13] <u>Mine hand hath also laid the foundation of the earth, and my right hand hath spanned the heavens. I call unto them and they stand up together.</u> | God describes more of His nature and characteristics. He is the God of creation. He is the God of the hosts of heaven. |

| | |
|---|---|
| [14] *All ye, assemble yourselves, and hear;* <u>who among them hath declared these things unto them?</u> The Lord hath loved him; yea, and he will fulfill his word which he hath declared by them; and he will do his pleasure on Babylon, and his arm shall come upon the Chaldeans. | As a covenantal God (within the Abrahamic covenant) God declares His intentions and plans. No one else has declared God's will but God. He will fulfill His obligations within the Abrahamic covenant to bring the House of Israel out of Babylonian captivity and give them an opportunity yet again to be faithful to Him by living the covenantal instructions revealed to Moses (and updated by subsequent prophetic revelation). |
| [15] *Also, saith the Lord;* <u>I the Lord, yea, I have spoken; yea, I have called him to declare, I have brought him, and he shall make his way prosperous.</u> | God is God alone. He will fulfill His word. And who does He fulfill His word for? The children of Abraham. "I have brought him [the children of Abraham], and [the Lord] shall make [the children of Abraham's, the children of the promise] way prosperous." |
| [16] *Come ye near unto me;* <u>I have not spoken in secret; from the beginning, from the time that it was declared have I spoken; and the Lord God, and his Spirit, hath sent me.</u> | God wants us to trust Him for He is a covenant-making and covenant-keeping God. He will fulfill His promises to Abraham. He explains to His people how and why He will fulfill the covenant. God does nothing in secret save He sends His prophets to declare it. |
| [17] *And thus saith the Lord, thy Redeemer, the Holy One of Israel;* <u>I have sent him, the Lord thy God who teacheth thee to profit, who leadeth thee by the way thou shouldst go, hath done it.</u> | More expressions of the trustworthy and enduring character of God to lead and to save (this represents the Abrahamic covenant). |
| [18] *O that thou hadst hearkened to my commandments*—<u>then had thy peace been as a river, and thy righteousness as the waves of the sea.</u> | God revealed the Mosaic covenant as covenantal instructions. If we are faithful, we receive the Abrahamic promises. If we are faithless, we lose our access to the Abrahamic promises until we repent and turn to the God of Abraham, Isaac, and Jacob. |

| | |
|---|---|
| [19] <u>Thy seed also had been as the sand; the offspring of thy bowels like the gravel thereof; his name should not have been cut off nor destroyed from before me.</u> | God is referencing His promise to Abraham that his seed would be as many as the sands of the sea. Abraham's seed will always have access to God's promises, they simply have to show covenantal loyalty (Mosaic covenant) to walk through that door to claim what God has to offer. God will never break His covenant with Abraham. |
| [20] *Go ye forth of Babylon, flee ye from the Chaldeans, with a voice of singing declare ye, tell this, utter to the end of the earth; say ye:* <u>The Lord hath redeemed his servant Jacob.</u> | What should we do? Return to God! Stay in the covenant. Keep the commandments as revealed at Mount Sinai (Mosaic covenant) and as updated by God's living prophets. God is the Redeemer (Abrahamic covenant) who saves all those who come to Him (Mosaic covenant). |
| [21] <u>And they thirsted not; he led them through the deserts; he caused the waters to flow out of the rock for them; he clave the rock also and the waters gushed out.</u> | God reminds readers of the mighty and great deeds He had done for their fathers in the wilderness when He saved them from Egyptian bondage and from the wilderness. As the covenantal God of Abraham, God was obligated to do these loyal and faithful deeds. He led the people to Mount Sinai and invited them to covenant with Him, to be loyal to Him and to do deeds of covenantal righteousness, just as He had done deeds of covenantal righteousness for them. |
| [22] <u>And notwithstanding he hath done all this, and greater also,</u> *there is no peace, saith the Lord, unto the wicked.* | But even though God fulfilled His obligations in the Abrahamic covenant, if we do not stay faithful to God as He instructed in the Mosaic covenant, we will have no peace. |

My hope is that, by reading this one chapter of Isaiah quoted in the Book of Mormon through the covenantal lens, Isaiah becomes much more understandable. Furthermore, we see the covenantal purposefulness for why Nephi would have inserted Isaiah. Nephi wanted to teach his people about covenants. Nephi wanted to be like Moses who faithfully instructed the Israelites on their covenantal duties. Isaiah was one of the powerful ways Nephi could get his covenantal message across. Why, you might ask, didn't Nephi simply quote more of the Law of Moses? Because Isaiah had several hundreds of years of Israelite history to work with to share examples of what had and had not worked in Israelite society. Instead of reading the Law of Moses that speaks in general terms about the consequences of living faithfully or not to God, Nephi could quote Isaiah and show with evidence the good, the bad, and the ugly. Unfortunately, much of what Isaiah had to report was that the Israelites had consistently failed to acquire the promises of Abraham because they did not stay on the covenant path revealed in the Law of Moses. Nevertheless, God being God still beckoned to His people to come to Him and partake of all the blessings promises to the patriarchs. Nephi, like Moroni hundreds of years later, wanted his people to know that they were not cast off forever. Though other Israelites had provided clear negative examples to not follow of covenantal faithlessness, Nephi's people could rouse themselves to devoted loyalty to God and claim the prize of His presence in their lives. In that regard, the words of Isaiah provided some of the clearest examples and instructions on what happens as a consequence of living God's law or not.

My invitation to you at this point is to study other Isaiah passages in the Book of Mormon and look for the covenantal themes that are found throughout. As you read, ask yourself, "How am I doing at showing my love and devotion to God? What do I learn from the examples Isaiah records?"

# CHAPTER 12
## THE SMALL PLATES OF NEPHI AS TORAH OR INSTRUCTIONAL MANUAL FOR THE COVENANT PATH

**The Book of Mormon as Torah**

Earlier we discussed that the Hebrew word *Torah* means "law," or more precisely, "instruction." The Five Book of Moses, which are the first five book of the Bible (Genesis, Exodus, Leviticus, Numbers, and Deuteronomy) are the source for the two foundational covenants of the covenant path: The Abrahamic covenant and the Sinai covenant. The Five Books of Moses are called the Torah, or the instruction, because they provide instructions for how to walk the covenant path by preserving stories that show how these covenants function and that explain the duties of each party in the covenant.

The Book of Mormon also preserves stories about how these covenants function and the duties within the covenant. The Book of Mormon also contains and shares significant covenantal instructions. The Book of Mormon is a covenantal instruction manual, like the Five Books of Moses or Torah. Therefore, the Book of Mormon is a Torah. We can and should read the Book of Mormon as Torah, as instruction, as covenantal guidance, just as the Five Books of Moses were preserved to do.

## Lehi's Last Will and Covenantal Speech (2 Nephi 1–4)

One of the defining features of the Mosaic covenant, as found in the Bible, is that when a great leader was about to die and leadership would pass to another, the great leader left his final testament, or testimony with the people. Typically these testimonies review the key expectations that God has for people to live faithful to Him and include warnings of the consequences of faithlessness as well as promises to those who remain true and faithful. Some beautiful final testaments or speeches in the Bible are as follows:

- Moses (the entire book of Deuteronomy with specific focus on Deuteronomy 31–33)
- Joshua (Joshua 23–24, i.e., "Choose ye this day whom ye will serve!")
- Samuel (1 Samuel 12)
- David (1 Chronicles 29)
- Jesus (John 13–17)
- Paul (Acts 20)

2 Nephi 1 is full of Lehi's loving and final admonition to his family, especially to his unbelieving sons, Laman and Lemuel, (and their allies, the sons of Ishmael) to be loyal to God as revealed in the Mosaic covenant. Let's explore the Mosaic themes that mark the substance of Lehi's last speech to his family, with specific focus on 2 Nephi 1. Below I've quoted several salient verses and emphasized key covenant terms.

### *Lehi Preaches Faithfulness to God by Echoing the Sinai Covenant (2 Nephi 1:6–7, 9, 16, 19–20)*

> Wherefore, I, Lehi, prophesy according to the workings of the Spirit which is in me, that there shall none come into this land save they shall be brought by the hand of the Lord. Wherefore, this land is consecrated unto him whom he shall bring. And if it so be that they shall serve him according to the **commandments which he hath given**, it shall be a land

of liberty unto them; wherefore, they shall never be brought down into captivity; if so, it shall be because of iniquity; for if iniquity shall abound cursed shall be the land for their sakes, but unto the **righteous** it shall be blessed forever. . . . Wherefore, **I, Lehi, have obtained a promise**, that inasmuch as those whom the Lord God shall bring out of the land of Jerusalem shall **keep his commandments, they shall prosper** upon the face of this land; and they shall be kept from all other nations, that they may possess this land unto themselves. And if it so be that they shall **keep his commandments they shall be blessed** upon the face of this land, and there shall be none to molest them, nor to take away the land of their inheritance; and **they shall dwell safely forever**. . . . And I desire that ye should **remember to observe the statutes and the judgments of the Lord**; behold, this hath been the anxiety of my soul from the beginning. . . . O my sons, that these things might not come upon you, but that ye might be a choice and a favored people of the Lord. But behold, his will be done; for his ways are **righteousness forever**. And he hath said that: **Inasmuch as ye shall keep my commandments ye shall prosper in the land; but inasmuch as ye will not keep my commandments ye shall be cut off from my presence.**

I won't expand into a lengthy explanation of each significant phrase since we've now seen these repeatedly throughout scripture. What I hope for you to see is how thoroughly embedded into Lehi's preaching are the themes, words, and purposes of the Mount Sinai covenant. Lehi knew with full surety that the only way to claim the promises of Abraham was through disciplined loyalty to God. So he repeated, again and again: Keep the commandments, be righteous, in so doing, you will reap the greatest rewards—peace and prosperity in the land. We see here Lehi summarizing the entire purpose and meaning of the Mount Sinai covenant with this sweeping covenantal phrase "Inasmuch as ye shall keep my commandments ye shall prosper in the land; but inasmuch as ye will not keep my commandments ye shall be cut off from my presence" (vs. 20). That phrase is the paradigmatic example of the conditional covenant theology of Sinai.

## The Book of Mormon Record Keepers Demonstrate Their Covenantal Fidelity

If we remember back to the covenant at Mount Sinai, one of the provisions or expectations of the covenant is that the covenant and attending instructions be recorded and preserved. Why did Nephi write? He was under covenantal obligation to do so. Why did Nephi command his prophetic-scribal followers to follow his example? Because Nephi knew that God would provide explanations and understanding of the covenant for each generation. Those revelations would help guide people on the covenant path. Do we see evidence of Nephite record keepers consciously expressing their covenantal duty to record the truth for their and future generations to see and stay on the covenant path? Yes. The prophetic writers of the small plates were influenced by the Mosaic covenant to write and preserve the words of wisdom that would guide people to covenantal loyalty. They focused primarily on our obligations within the Mosaic covenant, highlighting the blessings or afflictions we should expect depending on our loyalty to God.

Here are some brief examples from the writings found on the small plates of Nephi where I emphasize significant words or phrases related to the covenant path.

### *Jacob 1:1–2, 4, 6–8*

> Nephi gave me, Jacob, a **commandment** [stipulation for loyalty] concerning the small plates, upon which these things are engraven. And he gave me, Jacob, a commandment that I should write upon these plates a few of the things which I considered to be most **precious** [instructions on how to live aligned with God in the covenant]. . . . And if there were preaching which was sacred, or revelation which was great, or prophesying, that I should engraven the heads of them

upon these plates, and touch upon them as much as it were possible, **for Christ's sake** [because He has covenantally loved us, revelation can teach us how to love Him], and for the **sake of our people** [that they might have instruction for how to be loyal to Christ].... And we also had many revelations, and the spirit of much prophecy; wherefore, we knew of Christ and his kingdom, which should come. Wherefore we labored diligently among our people, that **we might persuade them to come unto Christ** [just like at Sinai where God invited His people to come unto Him in covenantal relationship], and partake of the goodness of God, that they might **enter into his rest** [as promised in the Abrahamic covenant], lest by any means he should swear in his wrath **they should not enter in** [if they did not live the stipulations of the Mount Sinai covenant], as in the provocation in the days of temptation while the children of Israel were in the wilderness. Wherefore, we would to God that we could persuade all men **not to rebel against God** [stay within the covenantal relationship that God had revealed at Sinai and updated with revelation to His prophets], to provoke him to anger, but that all men would **believe in Christ** [be faithful to Christ, that is covenantal loyalty!], and view his death, and suffer his cross and bear the shame of the world; wherefore, I, Jacob, take it upon me to fulfil the commandment of my brother Nephi.

## Enos 1:15–18

Wherefore, I knowing that the Lord God was able to preserve our records, I cried unto him continually, for he had said unto me: Whatsoever thing ye shall ask in faith, believing that ye shall receive in the name of Christ, ye shall receive it. And I had faith, and I did cry unto God that he would preserve the records; and **he covenanted with me** [God is renewing and extending the Abrahamic promise. God is a covenant-making and covenant-keeping God!] that he would **bring them forth** [the records, such as the Book of Mormon, that contain the instructions for how to be faithful] unto the Lamanites in his own due time. And I, Enos, **knew it would be according**

**to the covenant which he had made** [just like Abraham believed and trusted God and it was counted to him for righteousness (see Genesis 15:6)]; wherefore my soul did rest. And the Lord said unto me: **Thy fathers** [including Abraham, Isaac, and Jacob] have also required of me this thing; and it shall be done unto them **according to their faith** [according to their loyalty within the covenantal obligations]; for their **faith** [trust] was like unto thine.

## Jarom 1:1–2

Now behold, I, Jarom, write a few words according to the **commandment** [stipulation for living loyally within the covenant] of my father, Enos.... And as these plates are small, and as these things are written for the intent of the **benefit of our brethren the Lamanites** [preserving instructions so that they might be invited into the covenant and live it], wherefore, it must needs be that I write a little; but I shall not write the things of my prophesying, nor of my revelations. **For what could I write more than my fathers have written? For have not they revealed the plan of salvation?** [The preserved covenantal instructions on the small plates of Nephi are sufficient to show you the covenant path.] I say unto you, Yea; and this sufficeth me.

## Omni in Omni 1:3

I had kept these plates according to the **commandments of my fathers** [Omni was faithful]; and I conferred them upon my son Amaron. And I make an end.

Why did Omni and other writers within his small book write so few words? They deemed that the covenants had been revealed and there was nothing significant "to add to or take away" from the instructions and agreements that God had so far revealed. "Carry on in the covenant path as it has been revealed" was their theme.

## Amaron in Omni 1:4–6

> And now I, Amaron, write the things whatsoever I write, which are few, in the book of my father. Behold, it came to pass that three hundred and twenty years had passed away, and the more wicked part of the Nephites were destroyed. For the Lord would not suffer, after he had led them out of the land of Jerusalem and kept and preserved them from falling into the hands of their enemies, yea, he would not suffer that the words should not be verified [God is covenantally bound to do what He promised to do], which he spake unto our fathers, saying that: **Inasmuch as ye will not keep my commandments ye shall not prosper in the land.**

Amaron had no need to repeat the entire Book of Deuteronomy, which contains the covenantal instructions God gave to us for us to show loving devotion to Him, when he could summarize the entire covenant in a single pithy phrase.

## Chemish in Omni 1:9

> Now I, Chemish, write what few things I write, in the same book with my brother; for behold, I saw the last which he wrote, that he wrote it with his own hand; and he wrote it in the day that he delivered them unto me. And after this manner we keep the records, for it is according to **the commandments of our fathers** [maintaining the faith]. And I make an end.

Incidentally, Chemish's name may come from the Hebrew word for five (5). If that is the case, he may have that name because he is the fifth record keeper since the records were given to his forefather Enos: Enos (1), Jarom (2), Omni (3), Amaron (4), Chemish (5). That is five witnesses! When you only need two or three witnesses to establish the truth, what need is there for the fourth or fifth witness to say more?

## Abinadom in Omni 1:11

And behold, the record of this people is engraven upon plates which is had by the kings, according to the generations; **and I know of no revelation save that which has been written, neither prophecy; wherefore, that which is sufficient is written.** And I make an end.

Once again, Abinadom had nothing to add because the covenantal instruction manual that has already been revealed in the small plates was sufficient to teach anyone of the covenant path.

## Amaleki in Omni 1:17, 18, 20–21, 25–26

Amaleki narrated how the covenantally faithful Nephites followed the covenantally faithful King Mosiah into the land of Zarahemla where they discovered the Mulekites.

And at the time that Mosiah discovered them, [the Mulekites] had become exceedingly numerous. Nevertheless, they had had many wars and serious contentions, and had fallen by the sword from time to time; and their language had become corrupted; and **they had brought no records with them** . . . (Omni 1:17)

[Without the covenantal instructions as recorded in scripture they could not know of the commandments of the Lord! They were just like the Jews who lost the Book of Law and therefore fell into apostasy because they didn't know how to keep their covenants with God and they were led into captivity.]

and they **denied the being of their Creator.** . . . (Omni 1:17)

[The first commandment is to love God. How can you be faithful to God and His covenants if you deny who God is? The people of Zarahemla were outside the covenant until Mosiah brought them in via the records his people had preserved.]

But it came to pass that Mosiah caused that they should be taught in his language. . . . And it came to pass in the days of Mosiah, there was a large stone brought unto him with engravings on it; and he did interpret the engravings by the gift and power of God. And they gave an account of one Coriantumr, and **the slain of his people**. (Omni 1:18, 20–21)

The large stone told the story of the Jaredites, who broke their covenants with God and were destroyed from the face of the promised land. That story confirms that this is a covenantal land and when people fail to show covenantal loyalty to God they are removed from the land.

Amaleki, the last writer of the small plates, ends his record focused on the covenant path, urging everyone to walk the covenant path and to not turn aside from it. Amaleki testified that the Lord does live and that He is covenantally bound to save you in His eternal promised land if you walk the covenant path!

> And it came to pass that I began to be old; and, having no seed, and knowing king Benjamin to be a just man before the Lord, wherefore, I shall deliver up these plates unto him, exhorting all men to come unto God, the Holy One of Israel, and believe in prophesying, and in revelations, and in the ministering of angels, and in the gift of speaking with tongues, and in the gift of interpreting languages, and in all things which are good; for there is nothing which is **good** save it **comes from the Lord** [all these things teach us of the covenant path]: and that which is **evil cometh from the devil** [who wants you to be ignorant of God's covenants, who wants you to *not* be on the covenant path]. And now, my beloved brethren, I would that ye should **come unto Christ**, who is **the Holy One of Israel** [the God of Abraham, Isaac, and Jacob, and the God of the Israelites], and **partake of his salvation** [as promised in the Abrahamic covenant], and the power of his redemption. Yea, come unto him, and **offer your whole souls** [be wholly and entirely committed and devoted to God through covenant] as an offering unto him, and continue in fasting and praying, and **endure to the end**; and **as the Lord liveth ye will be saved**. (Omni 1:25–26)

The Book of Mormon now transitions from the small plates to the edited and abridged Nephite records preserved by

Mormon. Mormon explained this transition briefly in his short insertion called The Words of Mormon. If we listen carefully, we can hear the covenantal purposes, and the Spirit of God, driving his writing.

*Words of Mormon 1:8–9*

> And my prayer to God is concerning my brethren, that they may once again **come to the knowledge of God, yea, the redemption of Christ** [to be in covenant with God, we must know who He is and what He has done for us]; that they may once again **be a delightsome people** [covenant keepers become the Lord's treasure]. And now I, Mormon, proceed to finish out my record, which I take from the plates of Nephi; and I make it according to the **knowledge** [covenantal vocabulary, you cannot keep the covenant if you do not know the covenant] and the **understanding** [covenantal vocabulary, you cannot live the covenant if you do not understand the covenant] which God has given me.

# CHAPTER 13

## THE BOOK OF MOSIAH: THE BOOK OF THREE KINGS AND THE STORY OF THEIR COVENANT PATHS

**Overview**

The book of Mosiah is beautifully structured around the stories and deeds of three kings and the consequences of their covenantal faithfulness or faithlessness. We discussed earlier that the True King is God Himself. The Israelites had wanted a human king. That request was grievous to Samuel the prophet and to God. But God allowed it. We saw that all the kings of Israel and many of the kings of Judah modeled covenantal *unfaithfulness*. In each instance, because the kings failed to model covenantal faithfulness, their people were led into captivity.

Nephi knew that history. He knew that kings had enormous power to lead their people along the covenant path or disastrously off the path. Nephi, though acting like a king, would not take the title of kingship, stating, "And it came to pass that they would that I should be their king. But I, Nephi, was desirous that they should have no king; nevertheless, I did for them according to that which was in my power [which was to teach and model the covenant path, especially as revealed in the Law of Moses]" (2 Nephi 5:18). The way that Nephi served as the ruler over the Nephites was to do exactly as God demanded of kings in Deuteronomy 17:14–20 by living, teaching, and preserving the covenant path (i.e., the law of God) for the people at all times.

After Nephi died, the people appointed themselves another king and called him Nephi, a bit like how in the ancient Roman imperial leaders took on the title of Caesar, who had been a great former leader. The title of Caesar has remained for more than two thousand years in names like Czar (i.e., the Czar of Russia) and Kaiser (i.e., the Kaiser of Germany). Though Nephi hadn't wanted to be a king, it seems that his name became the term for "king"!

In each generation, God wants to create or renew the covenant relationship between Him and His people that they might live in peace and prosperity in the promised land. Righteous kings either receive the conditional covenant of the promised land from God and then deliver it to the people (that is what we saw with Moses's story) or they preserve, retain, explain, and teach the existing covenant to their people. That is what we saw Nephi do. The prophetic writers in the small plates following in Nephi's footsteps adhered to this latter model.

Generations after Nephi, King Mosiah came to power and led the people to Zarahemla. We pick up the story near the end of the life of his son, King Benjamin.

## King Benjamin's Speech: Preaching Covenantal Loyalty

Because the people had arrived in a new land (Zarahemla), we should expect, as occurred in the Sinai covenant, a review and renewal of the law of the land and an explanation of the conditions for righteousness in the land. And that was exactly what happened. The people were in a promised land, therefore they were required to understand the covenantal obligations protecting the land. If you want to have prosperity in the land, you must keep the commandments. Those commandments must be revealed so that the people know with clarity the instructions God expects them to live by in order to reap the benefits He has prepared for them in the land. The book of Mosiah opens with the story of King Benjamin giving his farewell speech to his people (like what we saw earlier with Lehi, Moses, Joshua, and others). Significantly, King Benjamin's speech was modeled on the structure of the conditional covenant God entered into with His people at Mount Sinai!

Let's review the covenantal language and structure of King Benjamin's speech. Remember, that the Mosaic/Mount Sinai covenant provides the conditions for how we maintain our access to God's promises unconditionally offered in the Abrahamic covenant. I've included again a table summarizing key scriptural texts that follow the structure of the Mount Sinai covenant.

|  | Exodus | Deut. | Joshua | Mosiah | D&C 58–59 |
|---|---|---|---|---|---|
| **Introduction of Covenant Parties** | Ex. 20:1–2 | Deut. 1:1–5 | Joshua 24:1–2 | Mosiah 1:1–2:9 | D&C 59:24 |
| **Historical Review of Great Deeds** | Ex. 20:2 | Deut. 1:6–3:29 | Joshua 24:2–13, 16–18 | Mosiah 2:9–21, 23–30 | D&C 58 |
| **Stipulations and Instructions for Showing Loyalty in the Covenant** | Ex. 20–23 (especially 20:3–17) | Deut. 1:1–5 | Joshua 24:14, 18, 23 | Mosiah 2:22, 24, 31–41; 4:6–30 | D&C 59:5–15, 21–23 |
| **Witnesses** | Ex. 24:3 | Deut. 31:19–32:45 | Joshua 24:16, 19, 21–23 | Mosiah 5:2–8 | D&C 59:24 |
| **Blessings and Curses** | Ex. 23:20–33 | Deut. 27–28 | Joshua 24:19–20 | Mosiah 5:9–15 (see also 3:24–27) | D&C 59:1–4, 16–20, 23 |
| **Record the Covenant and Store it in a Sacred Location** | Ex. 24:7 | Deut. 31:1–9 | Joshua 24:25–27 | Mosiah 2:8–9; 6:1–3, 6 | D&C 59:24 |

(Modified from "The Treaty / Covenant Pattern in King Benjamin's Address (Mosiah 1–6)" by Stephen D. Ricks, BYU Studies Vol. 24, No. 2 (Spring 1984), pp. 151–162.)

## Part 1 of the Covenant: God or the King Introduces Himself (Mosiah 1, 2:1–9. Compare to Exodus 20:1–2)

The book of Mosiah begins with King Benjamin's preparations to give his last will and testament to his people. As a righteous (covenant-abiding) king, he taught his sons from the scriptures about how to demonstrate loyalty to God so that they might reap the rewards of God's promised blessings. As a ruler who emulated covenant keeping to his people, he ensured that the records were preserved and transmitted for posterity because these records both contained the covenantal instructions and ensured that God's people stayed on the covenant path. In the expected fashion of Mosaic covenant terminology, King Benjamin urged his sons to remember the true instructions of the covenant and to be loyal to God so that they could have God's promised blessings.

> O my sons, I would that ye should **remember** that these sayings are true, and also that **these records are true**. And behold, also the plates of Nephi, which contain the records and the sayings of our fathers from the time they left Jerusalem until now, and they are true; and we can know of their surety because we have them before our eyes. And now, my sons, I would that ye should remember to search them diligently, that ye may profit thereby; and I would that ye should **keep the commandments of God, that ye may prosper in the land according to the promises which the Lord made unto our fathers.** (Mosiah 1:6–7; emphasis added)

King Benjamin gave instructions for the people to gather to hear his final words. Mormon editorialized on the people's love for King Benjamin and their love for God, explaining that King Benjamin had labored ceaselessly to teach the covenant path to his people. The people were reaping the benefits of God's promised prosperity for the covenantally faithful. In thanks they offered sacrifices to God, "that they might give thanks to the Lord their God, who had brought them out of the land of Jerusalem, and who had delivered them out of the hands of their enemies, and had appointed just men to be their teachers, and also a just man to be their king, who had established peace in the land of Zarahemla, and who had **taught them to keep the commandments of God**, that they might rejoice and be filled with **love towards God** [summary of first four of the Ten Commandments] and all men [summary of the final six Ten Commandments]" (Mosiah 2:4).

With that introduction to the leader of the covenant ceremony, we see a king who was totally devoted to God's people, who served the interests of God so that His people would experience the joy and peace God intends. Because we know the structure of this covenant, we should next expect to see King Benjamin review the deeds of covenant loyalty he performed on behalf of the people. This review was intended to humble the people so that they were willing to enter into a covenant to be God's people.

## Part 2 of the Covenant: God or King Reviews His Great Deeds to Encourage Loyalty (Mosiah 2:9–21, 23–30. Compare to Exodus 20:1–2)

In Exodus, God descended upon Mount Sinai in a storm cloud and reviewed the deeds He had done on behalf of the Israelites. He then delivered the commandments to them. Afterward, "all the people saw the thunderings, and the lightnings, and the noise of the trumpet, and the mountain smoking: and when the people saw it, they removed, and stood afar off. And they said unto Moses, Speak thou with us, and we will hear: but let not God speak with us, lest we die" (Exodus 20:19–20).

What did Benjamin do when he reviewed the great deeds he had done to help save the people? Benjamin made clear that *he was not a god!* How many kings in the ancient world took upon themselves divine honors, took the place of God, or had others do so for them? Remember Julius Caesar and Caesar Augustus? Upon their deaths the Roman senate voted them into the Roman heavenly pantheon. King Benjamin would never do such a thing. He knew who the real King was and he was not about to substitute himself for the real King. He did not want people to worship him or think of himself as anything more than a man, explaining, "I have not commanded you to come up hither that ye should fear me, or that ye should think that I of myself am more than a mortal man. But **I am like as yourselves**" (Mosiah 2:10–11; emphasis added).

Benjamin reviewed his great deeds (see Mosiah 2:9–21, 23–30): he served the people, he didn't over tax them, he didn't put people in dungeons, he did not allow slavery, he taught them to keep the commandments. But Benjamin knew his real place in the grand cosmos.

> Behold, I say unto you that because I said unto you that I had spent my days in your service, I do not desire to boast, for I have only been **in the service of God** [that is covenantal loyalty]. And behold, I tell you these things that ye may **learn wisdom** [learn how to show covenantal loyalty, which is true wisdom]; that ye may learn that when ye are in the service of your fellow beings ye are only in the service of your God. Behold, ye have called me your king; and if I, whom ye call your king, do labor to serve you, then ought not ye to **labor to serve one another** [that is fulfilling the last six of the Ten Commandments, which God revealed to us in order to show our covenantal loyalty]? And behold also, if I, whom ye call your king, who has spent his days in your service, and yet has been in the service of God, do merit any thanks from you, O how you ought to thank your heavenly King! (Mosiah 2:16–19)

The real purpose of an earthly ruler is to model Godly service for the people while leading the people back to God. In this regard, Benjamin was the ideal example of leadership!

## Part 3 of the Covenant: God Instructs on How to Show Covenantal Loyalty (Mosiah 2:22, 24, 31–41; 4:6–30. Compare to Exodus 20–23, especially 20:3–17)

Now that the people had been invited into humility by listening to the great deeds of loving service done on their behalf that they might prosper in the land and be saved, they were prepared to learn what God expected of them to show their loving devotion to Him. These were the stipulations. In the Mount Sinai covenant we learned that the Ten Commandments are the major stipulations, or methods, or instructions for showing covenantal loyalty to God. What did King Benjamin reveal to the people that God expected of them?

Benjamin detailed God's expectations throughout Mosiah 2 and Mosiah 4. Benjamin paused on the stipulations to deliver revelation in Mosiah 3 that focused on the means by which we are all saved—the Atonement of Jesus Christ. The covenant path is made possible by that love from Jesus. At the center spot of King Benjamin's speech is the covenant pathway illuminated by Jesus.

King Benjamin did not create an exhaustive list of all the ways that we can show our devoted love to God through covenantal commitment. In fact, Benjamin concluded the covenantal stipulations with this summary statement about faithful loyalty.

> And finally, I cannot tell you all the things whereby ye may commit sin; for there are divers ways and means, even so many that I cannot number them. But this much I can tell you, that if ye do not watch yourselves, and your thoughts, and your words, and your deeds, and observe the commandments of God, and continue in the faith of what ye have heard concerning the coming of our Lord, even unto the end of your lives, ye must perish. And now, O man, remember, and perish not. (Mosiah 4:29–30)

Although all of us will fail from time to time in meeting the stipulations of the conditional covenant, if we remember Jesus Christ and His Atonement for us, our efforts will be accepted.

## Part 4 of the Covenant: Witnesses Certify or Ratify the Covenant (Mosiah 5:2–8. Compare to Exodus 24:3)

Once the terms of the agreement had been delivered, the people were invited to accept the covenant. King Benjamin asked if they "**believed** [covenantal term indicating that someone is in the covenant] the words which he had spoken unto them" (Mosiah 5:1; emphasis added). The people responded in unison that they were willing to join the covenant, "Yea, we believe all the words [instructions about how to be in a covenant with God] which thou hast spoken unto us" (Mosiah 5:2). Further they declared, "We are willing to enter into a covenant with our God to do his will [as it was just revealed in King Benjamin's speech], and to be obedient to his commandments in all things that he shall command us, all the remainder of our days" (Mosiah 5:5).

## Part 5 of the Covenant: God Explains the Conditions of the Covenant (Mosiah 5:9–15; see also Mosiah 3:24–27. Compare to Exodus 23:20–33)

After exhorting his people to "take upon you the name of Christ, all you that have entered into the covenant with God that ye should be obedient unto the end of your lives" (Mosiah 5:8), King Benjamin reveals the next stage of the covenant—blessings and curses conditioned on faithfulness.

> And it shall come to pass that **whosoever doeth this [taking the name of Christ upon themselves] shall be found at the right hand of God** [blessing for faithfulness], for he shall know the name by which he is called; for he shall be called by the name of Christ. And now it shall come to pass, that **whosoever shall not take upon him the name of Christ** must be called by some other name; therefore, he **findeth himself on the left hand of God** [curses for unfaithfulness]. (Mosiah 5:9–10; emphasis added)

## Part 6 of the Covenant: Covenant is Recorded and Preserved in a Sacred Location (Mosiah 2:8–9; 6:1–3, 6. Compare to Exodus 24:7)

Finally, the covenantal ceremony, which was modeled on the Mosaic covenant at Mount Sinai detailed in the Bible, concluded with the king enrolling the names of those who had made the covenant, recording the covenant, and storing those records in a sacred location.

> And now, king Benjamin thought it was expedient, after having finished speaking to the people, that he should take the names of all those who had entered into a covenant with God to keep his commandments. (Mosiah 6:1)

Though we don't have any information about where the covenantal texts were stored, the fact that we have King Benjamin's speech is evidence that, as a sign of covenantal devotion to God, this update to the Mosaic covenant at Sinai was kept, preserved, and taught among the Nephites as long as there were faithful covenant keepers among them.

## Review of King Benjamin's Covenantal Speech

Why did we spend our time reviewing highlights of King Benjamin's speech? Because it provides strong evidence for the covenant path in the Book of Mormon. First, King Benjamin's speech is clearly modeled on the covenantal structure revealed at Mount Sinai. We are meant to read King Benjamin's speech as a covenantal invitation to loyalty to God. Second, the covenant path is marked clearly, especially by the revelatory interlude provided by King Benjamin in Mosiah 3 that focused on declaring the Messianic mission and atoning sacrifice of Jesus Christ. Those revealing words are some of the most direct, clarifying, and inviting words about Jesus Christ anywhere in scripture. It is only fitting that they are embedded within a covenantal framework. Without Jesus Christ, there would be no promised land no matter the faith we exercised. Without Jesus Christ there would be no posterity or property, no matter our heed and diligence at living the stipulations delivered to us through prophetic voices. Jesus is the very substance of the covenant path. Without Him there is nothing. Therefore it is necessary, needful, appropriate, and expected that the source of all covenants be discussed—Jesus Christ.

We began this chapter briefly mentioning that the book of Mosiah is structured on three separate kings. We've reviewed righteous King Benjamin who lived, modeled, and taught the covenant path. The next king did the exact opposite—faithless and covenant-breaking King Noah.

## King Noah: The Paradigmatic Example of Covenantal Unfaithfulness

We discussed earlier God's expectations for a human king. King Noah did everything exactly opposite of what God expected of a covenantally faithful king as detailed in Deuteronomy 17:14–20. We shouldn't be surprised that because of King Noah's disastrous unfaithfulness to the expectations of the Mount Sinai covenant God had to send a new Moses (Abinadi) to remind Noah and his priests about what they should be living and teaching to the people.

> I know if ye keep the commandments of God ye shall be saved; yea if ye keep the commandments which the Lord delivered unto Moses in the mount of Sinai . . . (Mosiah 12:33)

When Abinadi reviewed the covenantal stipulations of the Ten Commandments (see Mosiah 13), which Noah and his priests were not living or teaching, Mormon even described Abinadi as looking like Moses at Mount Sinai.

> Now it came to pass after Abinadi had spoken these words that the people of king Noah durst not lay their hands on him, for the Spirit of the Lord was upon him; and **his face shone with exceeding luster, even as Moses' did while in the mount of Sinai**, while speaking with the Lord. (Mosiah 13:5; emphasis added)

The covenantal relationship between the Book of Mormon and the Bible is as clear as could be in the Abinadi-as-Moses story in the book of Mosiah. The Book of Mormon is a covenantal text, structured and influenced by the key covenantal mountains from the Bible.

After hearing the covenantal stipulations, and the condemnation for not showing loyalty to God, we shouldn't be surprised that King Noah was eventually killed and his people scattered or taken into captivity. This story arc is so common across scriptures, and especially in the Book of Mormon, we may miss the covenantal significance out of sheer familiarity of the well-worn path of the pride cycle. Pride always leads people into unfaithfulness and off the covenant path. King Noah was a spectacular failure of covenantal faithfulness.

Let's remind ourselves of what God expects of a covenantally loyal human king. (If you review King Benjamin's speech, you'll see that he thoroughly aligned himself with God's instructions for kings.)

### *What a Covenantally Faithful King Should Not Do*

- Don't acquire many horses (don't raise a military) (see Deuteronomy 17:16).
- Don't return the people to Egypt (don't return people to the house of bondage/apostasy) (see Deuteronomy 17:16).
- Don't acquire many wives (see Deuteronomy 17:17).
- Don't seek after silver and gold (see Deuteronomy 17:17).

### *What a Covenantally Faithful King Should Do*

- Have a copy of the scriptures (see Deuteronomy 17:18).
- Read the scriptures every day (see Deuteronomy 17:18).
- Teach the scriptures (see Deuteronomy 17:19–20).
- Do not lift yourself up above your brethren (see Deuteronomy 17:20).

How does King Noah do as a covenantal king? The two tables below review his deeds according to his covenantal faithfulness or faithlessness.

*The Covenant Path in the Bible and the Book of Mormon* 223

## King Noah Evaluated Against Deuteronomy 17

| What a Covenantally Faithful King Should *Not* Do | How Did Noah Do? Disastrous King |
|---|---|
| Deuteronomy 17:16<br>Don't acquire many horses (don't raise a military). | Mosiah 11:18–19<br>Noah raised a military; he put his trust in the arm of flesh, not in God, who is the Divine Warrior! |
| Deuteronomy 17:16<br>Don't return the people to Egypt (don't return people to the house of bondage/apostasy). | Mosiah 11:2; 19:28; 21:3–5<br>Noah's actions led the people into apostasy and bondage. |
| Deuteronomy 17:17<br>Don't acquire many wives. | Mosiah 11:2<br>Noah "had many wives and concubines." |
| Deuteronomy 17:17<br>Don't seek after silver and gold. | Mosiah 11:3–4<br>Noah sought the gold and silver of the people for his own purposes. |

The table above summarizes what a faithful king should *not* do and saw that Noah didn't listen at all to God. What do we see when we review what God expects a covenantally faithful king to do?

| What a Covenantally Faithful King Should Do | How Did Noah Do? Disastrous King |
|---|---|
| Deuteronomy 17:18<br>Have a copy of the scriptures. | Mosiah 11:27, 29<br>Noah was apparently ignorant of scriptures. |
| Deuteronomy 17:19<br>Read the scriptures every day. | Mosiah 12:18–29<br>Noah gave that role to the priests. (No scripture indicates that Noah had any awareness of scripture. Instead, the priests were the primary agitators in the trial of Abinadi, misusing scripture to attempt to trap Abinadi.) |

| | |
|---|---|
| Deuteronomy 17:19<br>Live and teach the scriptures. | Mosiah 12:18–29<br>Noah did not live or teach the scriptures. (In fact, the priests, to whom he delegated his role as scriptorian, appeared to be familiar with scripture but they misused scripture in an attempt to destroy Abinadi.) |
| Deuteronomy 17:20<br>Do not lift yourself up above your brethren. | Mosiah 11:9–12; 19:6–11<br>Noah lifted himself up above the people. |

As we see from the table above, King Noah was exactly the type of king that God feared would usurp authority and lead people into apostasy. Because the people of King Noah were led into captivity, only God could deliver them.

## Trust in the God of Abraham, Isaac, and Jacob

### *The People of Limhi Delivered from Bondage as a Fulfillment of the Abrahamic Covenant*

After the death of King Noah, his son, King Limhi, came to power. Though he understood and forsook the wickedness (i.e., covenantal unfaithfulness) of his father, he and the people suffered the consequences of apostasy for some time. They attempted to free themselves from Lamanite bondage by resorting to the arm of strength. Because they had temporarily lost the presence of God, they did not prosper. Remember, to prosper means to have the presence of God. When they went to fight, they did so only with their own limited strength instead of in the strength of God. Had they been covenantally firm, the presence of God would have remained with them and He would have fought their battles so that they would not have remained in captivity. In fact, that is eventually what happened. The people of Limhi humbled themselves. They realized that only God could deliver them. They eventually developed that implicit faith and trust that we see demonstrated in scriptural heroes like Abraham and Nephi who accomplished great things because of the power of God who was with them.

A path of salvation was offered to the people, in the guise of Ammon coming from the land of Zarahemla to find them. Limhi gathered his people together at the temple and preached to them the foundational truths of the Abrahamic covenant. God has promised deliverance to all who trust Him!

> Therefore, lift up your heads, and rejoice, and put your **trust** in God, in that **God who was the God of Abraham, and Isaac, and Jacob** [Abrahamic covenant]; and also, that God who brought the children of Israel out of the land of Egypt, and caused that they should walk through the Red Sea on dry ground, and fed them with manna that they might not perish in the wilderness; and many more things did he do for them. And again, that same God has brought our fathers out of the land of Jerusalem, and has kept and preserved his people even until now; and behold, it is because of our iniquities and abominations that he has brought us into bondage [Mosaic covenant]. (Mosiah 7:19–20; emphasis added)

The phrase "the God of Abraham, and Isaac, and Jacob" (and derivations of that phrase) appear only eight times in all of the Book of Mormon. And each instant is consistently and specifically used to evoke *trust* in God. He is the God who covenanted with and fulfilled *and will fulfill* His promises to Abraham and his children. As children of Abraham, the people of Limhi could trust in those promises, especially when they were willing to accept God in their lives through covenant.

## *The People of Alma Delivered from Bondage as a Fulfillment of the Abrahamic Covenant*

Like the people of Limhi, Alma's people were brought into captivity as well. Like the people of Limhi, they groaned under the oppressive burdens, pleading with God to deliver them. And like in the Limhi story, the people were delivered by God. Mormon provides an editorial comment reminding us of the Abrahamic covenant and instructing us on covenantal trust.

> Nevertheless the Lord seeth fit to chasten his people; yea, he trieth their patience and their faith. Nevertheless—whosoever putteth his **trust** in him the same shall be lifted up at the last day. Yea, and thus it was with this people. For behold, I will show unto you that they were brought into bondage, and none could deliver them but the Lord their God, yea, even **the God of Abraham and Isaac and of Jacob**. And it came to pass that he did deliver them, and he did show forth his mighty power unto them, and great were their rejoicings. (Mosiah 23:21–24; emphasis added)

When we reflect on the Abraham story we see that God created circumstances where Abraham had to exhibit faith, patience, and trust. How can God teach us to trust Him if there are *never* any circumstances where faith, patience, and trust are required? Of course, most of us are not aching to have more trials and difficulties in our lives, but God uses the inequalities and injustices of life to give us testimony-building experiences to see His true character in action—God is a God of covenant making and covenant keeping. He has promised to provide a way for the children of Abraham. As we are children of the promise, we can trust Him. That is what Alma's people did. They trusted God. He delivered them from bondage. They were tested. They passed the test and thereby they built a testimony of what they knew to be true—that God is trustworthy. Now we as readers can have our testimonies fortified by reading about the tests that others successfully endured on the covenant path. If anything, the most difficult concept about the covenant path is enduring to the end, for God will continue to provide opportunities for us to show Him that we are trustingly holding to the rod of iron, which is the word of God, and according to the Gospel of John, that word is Jesus Christ Himself!

We have paused in our conversation of Nephite kingship to look at the causes and consequences of suffering and how the

God of Abraham, Isaac, and Jacob will deliver us, if we are faithful and trust Him. Let's return to the story of the last of the three kings that dominates the narrative of the book of Mosiah. We've seen that Benjamin was covenantally faithful. Noah was decidedly not faithful. What do we see when we read about the last king of the book of Mosiah, King Mosiah II?

## King Mosiah II: Kingship Is a Stumbling Block for Covenantal Loyalty. Expand Covenantal Loyalty by Giving Agency to the People by Removing Kingship

King Mosiah was a covenantally loyal and righteous king. So interested was he that his people stay on the covenant path that he changed the political order to enhance Nephite faithfulness. Thus, the thrust of the King Mosiah II story in the Book of Mormon is the transition from kingship to judgeship. Why would King Mosiah jettison kingship? In Mosiah 29, King Mosiah himself lays out many of the reasons for changing the Nephite political order.

- He wanted to protect his sons from death.
- He wanted to protect the people from oppression, especially kingly oppression.
- He wanted to protect the people from civil war.
- He wanted to protect the people from apostasy, especially that led by failed kings.
- He wanted people to exercise their freedom in Jesus Christ more fully.

These are all powerful and compelling reasons to set kingship aside for a new political order. In my reasoning, I believe that King Mosiah was deeply influenced by the stories of failed kingship and the disastrous consequences for covenantal unfaithfulness unleashed on God's people. Like Nephi, Mosiah was literate. He had all the records before him including the Israelite records of failed kingship that led to apostasy, captivity, and destruction. Mosiah also had access to his recent translation of the records relating some two millennia of destructive apostasy among the Jaredites led by covenantally unfaithful kings. Mosiah had the horrifying recent story of King Noah in front of him. Mosiah also knew of the extreme labor required of a king to serve in God's role to model and teach covenantal faithfulness. He was right that it was unjust to expect a human to play the role of God. More importantly, that put one more impediment between the people and direct access to God.

Kingship, therefore, seemed to be the major reason for apostasy among God's children. Instead of having God as their king and being covenantally loyal to Him, people substituted a human leader and pledged all their loyalty to that human leader. Wherever that leader led them, they followed like sheep, whether to salvation in the rare case of a righteous leader (Nephi, Mosiah I, Benjamin, and Mosiah II) or off the cliff into death and destruction (as seen with King Noah and a variety of Jaredite and Israelite kings). If kingship was the major driver of apostasy, then one of the most successful ways to protect people against apostasy was to remove the stumbling block of human-kingship and reinstall God as the real, true, and only King. That is what Mosiah II attempted to do.

We can see that his actions fit comfortably with the context of the Mosaic covenant. God offered His people property, posterity, and prosperity. Only He can truly and fully deliver. Installing a human king disrupts the covenantal relationship between God and His people because they then turn their loyalty to the human king and they expect the human king to fulfill all their needs. They expect the human king to fulfill God's covenantal promises to provide property, posterity, and prosperity. If the human king does temporarily deliver, then who really needs God anyway, would be the thinking, encouraging people to forget God and His promises and their covenantal duties. By installing a human king, it is as though we deny God His covenantal responsibilities to make the promises of Abraham available to us. The human king should not and cannot be the one with whom we make a covenant in order to receive the Abrahamic promises. Only God can do that. Mosiah II was wise, righteous, and inspired, to reanimate the Abrahamic and the Mosaic covenants by removing human kingship from his society.

# CHAPTER 14

# ALMA 1–4: THE PROMISED LAND IS CHALLENGED BY A FALSE KING

We reviewed some of the reasons that Nephite kingship was eliminated, concluding that from a covenantal context, human kingship created significant obstacles.

But were the Nephite people willing to live in covenantal commitment to God as their King? Were the Nephites willing to abandon their desire to replace the throne of God with a human throne? Unfortunately, no. The major theme of the narratives throughout Alma, Helaman, and 3 Nephi is the destructive consequences that befall individuals, families, communities, and nations when people fail to be covenantally faithful to God because they either would rather have a human king and/or they were led off the covenant path by a faithless king.

## Alma 1: Nehor Teaches False Doctrine about the Abrahamic and Mosaic Covenants

One could misread the doctrines contained in the Abrahamic and Mosaic covenants and invent the false teachings of Nehor. First, he taught (contrary to God's express will delivered in Deuteronomy 17:14–20) that leaders should not humbly live, teach, and preserve the covenantal instructions as revealed at Sinai (or updated by later revelation).

> And [Nehor] had gone about among the people, preaching to them that which he termed to be the word of God, bearing down against the church; declaring unto the people that every priest and teacher ought to become popular; and they ought not to labor with their hands, but that they ought to be supported by the people. (Alma 1:3)

Next, Nehor also deceptively manipulated the meaning and intent of the Abrahamic promises and covenant by teaching that everyone would be saved regardless of whether they demonstrated loyalty to God or not. Yes, only God is under obligation within the Abrahamic covenant. And yes, God promises property, posterity, and prosperity (on earth and in heaven) to Abraham and his children. One might superficially conclude, "I'm a child of Abraham, so I'm saved!" That was the mindset of some of the Jews in the time of Jesus. They believed that they were special and saved because they were children of Abraham while John the Baptist (the covenant forerunner) corrected this false doctrine by teaching that God can and will make His promises to Abraham available to any child of God (thus adopting them as children of Abraham) who is willing to loyally enter into the covenant path. John said, "And think not to say within yourselves, We have Abraham to our father: for I say unto you, that God is able of these stones to raise up children unto Abraham" (Matthew 3:9).

Nehor taught some aspects of the substance of the promises of the Abrahamic covenant but made significantly erroneous and damning conclusions:

> And [Nehor] also testified unto the people that all mankind should be saved at the last day, and that they need not fear nor tremble, but that they might lift up their heads and rejoice; for the Lord had created all men, and had also redeemed all men; and, in the end, all men should have eternal life. (Alma 1:4)

The promises of the Abrahamic covenant do promise us salvation (enduring land, posterity, and prosperity), and as we saw in the writings of Paul, those promises are *freely offered to us* but *not freely given*. God will be loyal to His promise to give us salvation. However, if we are disloyal and leave the covenant path, we lose our access. We do not experience the Abrahamic promises if we are not faithful to God as He has been faithful to us. The calamitous doctrine of Nehor deviated from these truths.

Alma appropriately countered this by reminding everyone of their covenantal obligations, of the stipulations for them to show love to God, as revealed to Moses, King Benjamin, and Mosiah II. Because Nehor broke covenantal loyalty by killing Gideon, he broke one of the Ten Commandments, which are the stipulations for us to receive the Abrahamic promises, and thus Nehor forfeited his life:

> Therefore thou art condemned to die, according to the law which has been given us by Mosiah, our last king; and it has been acknowledged by this people; therefore this people must abide by the law. And it came to pass that they took him; and his name was Nehor; and they carried him upon the top of the hill Manti, and there he was caused, or rather did acknowledge, between the heavens and the earth, that **what he had taught to the people was contrary to the word of God**; and there he suffered an ignominious death. (Alma 1:14–15; emphasis added)

God's expectations for us have been revealed through the Law of Moses, and through the writings of Nephi, King Benjamin, and other righteous teachers. Nehor did the opposite. Nehor created his own rules for loyalty to God and taught that to the people. Nehor taught the people to let go of the rod of iron, the word of God, thus walking away from the covenant path, and to follow some other path of his own making. He led people into spiritual death.

Why is the story of Nehor shared in the Book of Mormon? To provide an example of what happens when teachers claiming to speak for God preach false stipulations and false covenant paths. Their purpose is to destroy God's plan and God's people. Ultimately such false teachers will be destroyed, as was Nehor.

## Alma 2: The Amlicites Reject God as Covenantal King and Seek for a Human King

Just when we think that the people have been thoroughly convinced of their covenantal duties and the significant obstacles that human kings create for covenantal fidelity, we see the rise of Amlici among the Nephites, clamoring to rule in the place of God.

Incidentally, I find it fascinating that like so many names in the Book of Mormon that seem to be word plays on the themes of their stories (i.e., Laman "not believing," Sariah "Jehovah is a faithful commander"), the Hebrew meaning of the name "Amlici" may have something to do with his desire for kingship. In Hebrew, words having to do with kingship contain the root letters of *M L* and *K* or *C*. Notice those letters in the name a**MLiC**i. Later in the Book of Alma, we'll see another apostate pretend for the throne of kingship to replace God and His laws. That man's name likewise has the essence of the Hebrew word for kingship packed into his name—a**MaLiCK**iah.

Much of the warfare in the Book of Mormon, especially in Alma, Helaman, and 3 Nephi, is centered on the fight between those who want to be kings and create alternate instructions for how to live life and, on the other side, those faithful to God as the King of covenants and their desire to live faithfully to Him. Those fighting to preserve their land and their religion look to the God of Abraham, Isaac, and Jacob, who gave the promised land and provided the religion (or instructions) for how to maintain peace and prosperity in the land. The apostates, those unbelievers were unwilling to live within the covenantal system. This conflict drove the many years of destructive wars among the Nephites.

The story of Amlici is representative of all these destructive wars. Amlici was a man who loved himself more than he loved God or his fellow man and charismatically convinced others to support him and to be loyal to him and no one else, even to the point of laying down their lives for this pretender to kingship. Alma, the leader of the covenantally faithful, fought with the sword and with the presence and support of God to overthrow this threat to the covenant. Only because the people on Alma's side were covenantally faithful did they receive the full benefit of God's saving promises and prevailed. But the story here, and throughout the Book of Mormon, makes clear that those wishing to be in league with God must ever be vigilant against the threats that distract us from loving God alone.

What were the consequences of Amlici's drive to wrest kingship away from God and to deny God's people their freedom to live in a covenantal relationship with God? Abinadi spoke words that seem to apply to Amlici, "Yea, and ye shall be smitten on every hand, and shall be driven and scattered to and fro, even as a wild flock is driven by wild and ferocious beasts. And in that day ye shall be hunted, and ye shall be taken by the hand of your enemies. . . . Thus God executeth vengeance upon those that destroy his people" (Mosiah 17:17–19).

What was the end of Amlici and his band?

> Yea, they were met on every hand, and slain and driven, until they were scattered on the west, and on the north, until they had reached the wilderness, which was called Hermounts; and it was that part of the wilderness which was infested by wild and ravenous beasts. And it came to pass that many died in the wilderness of their wounds, and were devoured by those beasts and also the vultures of the air; and their bones have been found, and have been heaped up on the earth. (Alma 2:37–38)

Unfortunately, as we will see as we continue reading in the Book of Mormon, the human lust for power and conquest never fully died out and king-seekers continued to disrupt the peace and harmony of the Nephite nation.

Mormon editorialized on the distinction between those who believed and were faithful to their covenants with God by keeping the commandments, and those who did not believe and were unfaithful. The name of each group, Lamanites and Nephites, functioned as a header for a categorizing whether someone was within the covenant.

> Therefore, whosoever suffered himself to be led away by the **Lamanites** [not believe] was called under that head, and there was a mark set upon him. And it came to pass that whosoever would **not believe** in the tradition of the **Lamanites** [not believe], but **believed** [Nephites were covenantally faithful] those records which were brought out of the land of Jerusalem, and also in the tradition of their fathers, which were correct, who believed in the commandments of God and kept them, were called the Nephites, or the people of Nephi, from that time forth. (Alma 3:10–11; emphasis added)

Soon after the war, the covenant people of God experienced prosperity, but they ascribed it to their own goodness instead of to the goodness of God, who had made the promise to give such prosperity.

> And it came to pass in the eighth year of the reign of the judges, that the people of the church began to wax proud, because of their exceeding riches, and their fine silks, and their fine-twined linen, and because of their many flocks and herds, and their gold and their silver, and all manner of precious things, which they had obtained by their industry; and in all these things were they lifted up in the pride of their eyes, for they began to wear very costly apparel. . . . The people of the church began to be lifted up in the pride of their eyes, and to set their hearts upon riches and upon the vain things of the world, that they began to be scornful, one towards another, and they began to persecute those that did not believe according to their own will and pleasure. (Alma 4:6, 8)

Seeing the pride of the people, Alma could not rest but went forth to call people to humility, gratitude, and covenantal fidelity.

# CHAPTER 15

# ALMA 5–16: GOD'S COVENANTAL REPRESENTATIVES TEACH THE PEOPLE HOW AND WHY TO BE COVENANTALLY FAITHFUL TO GOD

After Alma's experience preaching fidelity to God, Mormon documented the process for people joining or leaving God's covenantal community. We see that, as expected, those who partook of the covenantal commitment became witnesses to the agreement between God and His people (compare to Exodus 24:3 and Mosiah 5:2–8):

> And it came to pass that whosoever did not belong to the church who repented of their sins were baptized unto repentance, and were received into the church. And it also came to pass that whosoever did belong to the church that did not repent of their wickedness and humble themselves before God—I mean those who were lifted up in the pride of their hearts—the same were rejected, and **their names were blotted out**, that their names were not numbered among those of the righteous. (Alma 6:2–3; emphasis added)

Those on the covenant path form a community who have associated their names with Jesus Christ. They take upon themselves the name of Jesus,

> To come into the fold of God, and to be called his people, and are willing to bear one another's burdens, that they may be light; Yea, and are willing to mourn with those that mourn; yea, and comfort those that stand in need of comfort, and to stand as witnesses of God at all times and in all things, and in all places that ye may be in, even until death, that ye may be redeemed of God, and be numbered with those of the first resurrection, that ye may have eternal life. (Mosiah 18:8–9)

When Alma continued his preaching in the city of Gideon, he urged the people to enter into the covenant path.

> But behold, the Spirit hath said this much unto me, saying: Cry unto this people, saying—Repent ye, and prepare the way of the Lord, **and walk in his paths** [be on the covenant path], which are straight; for behold, the kingdom of heaven is at hand, and the Son of God cometh upon the face of the earth. (Alma 7:9; emphasis added)

What can we do to stay on the covenant path? Alma answered, "And now I would that ye should be humble, and be submissive and gentle; easy to be entreated; full of patience and long-suffering; being temperate in all things; being diligent in **keeping the commandments of God at all times** [live the stipulations of God's covenants]; asking for whatsoever things ye stand in need, both spiritual and temporal; always returning thanks unto God for whatsoever things ye do receive. And see that ye have faith, hope, and charity, and then ye will always abound in good works" (Alma 7:23–24; emphasis added).

We see in the Book of Mormon righteous teachers and leaders in the mode of Moses teaching the people about God's covenants, what their covenantal responsibilities were, and how they could demonstrate faith in order to reap the blessings of prosperity.

## Alma 8: Destruction for Those Who Would Teach Destruction of God's Covenants

Alma's life seems to have been one continuous round of drama and challenge. After being thrown out of the city of Ammonihah, the Lord appeared to him with instruction. Listen to the covenantal language employed in these verses.

> **Blessed art thou**, Alma; therefore, lift up thy head and rejoice, for thou hast great cause to rejoice; **for thou hast been faithful in keeping the commandments of God** from the time which thou receivedst thy first message from him. Behold, I am he that delivered it unto you. And behold, I am sent to command thee that thou return to the city of Ammonihah, and preach again unto the people of the city; yea, preach unto them. Yea, say unto them, except they repent **the Lord God will destroy them**. For behold, **they do study at this time that they may destroy the liberty of thy people**, (for thus saith the Lord) which is contrary to the statutes, and judgments, and commandments which he has given unto his people. (Alma 8:15–17; emphasis added)

What is striking about the doctrine in these verses is that liberty is possible through and because of covenants. God wants us to have true liberty. We will find that in covenantal relationship with Him. Those who seek to destroy God's covenants are seeking to compromise the liberty that is at the heart of God's gospel. We cannot be truly free to be our very best selves if we ignore God and His promises.

## Alma 9: Those Who Disbelieve God and His Covenants

Alma endeavored again to preach to the people of Ammonihah. Their reception of Alma provided unmistakable evidence that they were not covenant makers or keepers. Notice that they appeared to have no knowledge of God the Wonder Worker who, as He promised to Abraham, can and will save His people, bringing destruction against those who stand in the way of His work, such as the Egyptians who were overthrown in one day. If the people of Ammonihah had known the story of God's overthrow of the Egyptians, would they have so cavalierly queried who was this God who claimed to overthrow cities? "Now they knew not that God could do such marvelous works, for they were a hard-hearted and a stiffnecked people" (Alma 9:5).

Our purpose in reviewing these select passages throughout Alma is to show that by tugging on the thread of covenantal ideology, we see it woven throughout the whole of the Book of Mormon. Our reading of the Book of Mormon is enhanced as we listen to the words of prophets, and of God, through the covenantal framework.

What is the character of the covenant-making and covenant-keeping God? He makes mighty unto the power of deliverance (as promised in the Abrahamic covenant) all those who have faith in Him (by living the revealed stipulations for fidelity):

> Do ye not remember that our father, Lehi, was brought out of Jerusalem by the hand of God? Do ye not remember that they were all led by him through the wilderness? And have ye forgotten so soon how many times **he delivered our fathers out of the hands of their enemies**, and preserved them from being destroyed, even by the hands of their own brethren? Yea, and if it had not been for **his matchless power, and his mercy**, and his long-suffering towards us, we should unavoidably have been cut off from the face of the earth long before this period of time, and perhaps been consigned to a state of endless misery and woe. . . . And not many days hence **the Son of God shall come in his glory**; and his glory shall be the glory of the Only Begotten of the Father, full of grace, equity, and truth, full of patience, mercy, and long-suffering, **quick to hear the cries of his people and to answer their prayers**. And behold, **he cometh to redeem those who will be baptized unto repentance, through faith on his name**. Therefore, **prepare ye the way of the Lord**, for the time is at hand that all men shall reap a reward of their works, according to that which they have been—if they have been righteous

they shall reap the salvation of their souls, according to the power and deliverance of Jesus Christ; and if they have been evil they shall reap the damnation of their souls, according to the power and captivation of the devil. (Alma 9:9–11, 26–28; emphasis added)

The crux of Alma's message to the people of Ammonihah was that they should trust God who had consistently demonstrated His ability to save and bless His faithful people. That trust should be demonstrated by faithful adherences to God's revelations. The covenant path is that straightforward. Of course, humans like complexity. We find a way to make God's straight and narrow path much more complex. But He has a plan for even the monkey wrenches that we insert into the system. If and whenever we are willing to be in a covenant relationship with God, He stands ready to receive us.

God seeks to prepare and preserve a land for a covenant people. If people are unwilling to be in a covenant with God in the land that He has delivered to them, then He will remove them. That is the outcome of breaking the covenant represented by Mount Sinai. This was the message from Alma and Amulek to the people of Ammonihah:

> Yea, and I say unto you that if it were not for the prayers of the righteous, who are now in the land, that ye would even now be visited with utter destruction; yet it would not be by flood, as were the people in the days of Noah, but it would be by famine, and by pestilence, and the sword. But it is **by the prayers of the righteous that ye are spared** [the petitions of those who are faithful in the covenant have convinced God to stay His hand, similar to how in Genesis 19 God was willing to change His plans concerning Sodom and Gomorrah because of Abraham's righteous petition]; now therefore, if ye will cast out the righteous from among you then will not the Lord stay his hand; but in his fierce anger he will come out against you; then ye shall be smitten by famine, and by pestilence, and

by the sword; and the time is soon at hand except ye repent. (Alma 10:22–23; emphasis added)

Later, Amulek preached some beautiful doctrines about the covenant path, describing how the work and role of Jesus is at the center of the covenantal relationship between God and His people.

> And Amulek said unto him: Yea, he is the very Eternal Father of heaven and of earth, and all things which in them are; he is the beginning and the end, the first and the last; And he shall come into the world to redeem his people; and he shall take upon him the transgressions of those who believe on his name; and these are they that shall have eternal life, and salvation cometh to none else. (Alma 11:39–40)

The covenant path, which intertwines God's covenantal responsibilities via the Mount Moriah covenant and our responsibilities represented by the Mount Sinai covenant, can be summarized in this beautiful statement from Alma, "Therefore, **whosoever repenteth, and hardeneth not his heart** [our obligation via the Mount Sinai covenant], **he shall have claim on mercy through mine Only Begotten Son** [God's obligation via the Mount Moriah covenant], unto a remission of his sins; and these shall enter into my rest" (Alma 12:34; emphasis added).

When we show our faith and covenantal loyalty, we repent, we accept Jesus Christ as our atoning Savior, and we receive the power of God (priesthood) in our lives. Who are those that received the priesthood anciently? Those who showed the greatest loyalty and devotion to God and His covenants.

> And those priests were ordained after the order of his Son, in a manner that thereby the people might know in what manner to look forward to his Son for redemption. And this is the manner after which they were ordained—being called and prepared from the foundation of the world according to the foreknowledge of God, **on account of their exceeding faith and good works** [living the requirements of the covenant]; in the first place being left to choose good or evil; therefore they having chosen good, and exercising exceedingly great

faith, are called with a holy calling, yea, with that holy calling which was prepared with, and according to, a preparatory redemption for such. (Alma 13:2–3; emphasis added)

Why did the Lord reveal ordinances to guide us along the covenant path? We read that

Now **these ordinances were given** after this manner, that thereby the people might look forward on the Son of God, it being a type of his order, or it being his order, and this that they might look forward to him for a remission of their sins, **that they might enter into the rest of the Lord** [the ultimate purpose of our covenantal relationship with God]. (Alma 13:16)

What happened after Alma and Amulek preached to the people of Ammonihah the covenant path and the covenantal instructions centered on Jesus Christ? Most people rejected the message. Worse, they destroyed those who believed (who had joined the covenant path) and they destroyed the records or scriptures, which was the instruction manual for how to live faithfully to God.

And they spit upon [Zeezrom, a believer], and cast him out from among them, and also all those who believed in the words which had been spoken by Alma and Amulek; and they cast them out, and sent men to cast stones at them. And they brought their wives and children together, and whosoever believed or had been taught to **believe in the word of God** [which reveals the covenant path] they caused that they should be cast into the fire; and they also brought forth their records which contained the holy scriptures, and cast them into the fire also, that they might be burned and destroyed by fire. (Alma 14:7–8; emphasis added)

We know that God has no patience for those who destroy covenant keepers or who destroy the knowledge and instruction of the covenant. We are saddened, but not surprised, when the city of Ammonihah was later thoroughly destroyed.

*The Covenant Path in the Bible and the Book of Mormon* 243

> On the fifth day of the second month [in the eleventh year], . . . there was a cry of war heard throughout the land. For behold, the armies of the Lamanites had come in upon the wilderness side, into the borders of the land, even into the city of Ammonihah, and began to slay the people and destroy the city. . . . And the people of Ammonihah were destroyed; yea, every living soul of the Ammonihahites was destroyed, and also their great city, which they said God could not destroy, because of its greatness. But behold, in one day it was left desolate; and the carcasses were mangled by dogs and wild beasts of the wilderness. Nevertheless, after many days their dead bodies were heaped up upon the face of the earth, and they were covered with a shallow covering. And now so great was the scent thereof that the people did not go in to possess the land of Ammonihah for many years. And it was called Desolation of Nehors; for they were of the profession of Nehor, who were slain; and their lands remained desolate. (Alma 16:1–2, 9–11)

Alma 16 provides examples in one single chapter of the consequences of living or not living the covenant path. We saw above what happened to Nehor because of their refusal to join and live the covenants of God. But those who were humble experienced all the happiness that God had to provide.

> And thus did Alma and Amulek go forth, and also many more who had been chosen for the work, to **preach the word** [the covenantal instructions] throughout all the land. And the **establishment of the church** [the covenantal community] became general throughout the land, in all the region round about, among all the people of the Nephites. And there was no inequality among them; the Lord did pour out his Spirit [because people kept the commandments, they did prosper by having God's Spirit] on all the face of the land to prepare the minds of the children of men, or to prepare their hearts to receive the word which should be taught among them at the time of his coming. (Alma 16:15–16)

As we see so clearly in these verses, the purpose of covenanting with God is to prepare us to receive more of God's word, truth, teaching, and covenantal instruction.

We've also seen that the covenantal context of Alma 5–16 shows how God's faithful and covenantal representatives (prophets, missionaries, etc.) teach others how and why to be covenantally faithful to God. We've seen examples of those who rejected covenants and those who embraced God's covenants. In the following chapter, we'll learn that those who have discovered the covenant path feel the call and obligation to share those covenantal truths with others.

# CHAPTER 16

## ALMA 17–27: THOSE WHO HAVE DISCOVERED THE COVENANT PATH LABOR TO INVITE OTHERS TO THE PATH

### Alma 17: The Covenants of God Go Forth to the Lamanites

The sons of Mosiah walked away from a life of power, prestige, and wealth when they rejected the crown of Nephite kingship. Instead, they went among their brethren the Lamanites who for so many hundreds of years had been cut off from the saving graces of God's covenants. Mormon describes the Lamanites in these terms, highlighting that one of the major ways that the Lamanites were cut off from the presence of God was because they had no knowledge of God. They worshiped fake gods instead. They did not have God's presence because they were loyal to other gods. Having God's presence is the essence of true prosperity. Those who reject God's covenants are cursed. That is, they experience the curse of not having God's presence. That curse followed the Lamanites wherever they went:

> Thus they were a very indolent people, many of whom did worship idols, and the curse of God had fallen upon them because of the traditions of their fathers; **notwithstanding the promises of the Lord were extended unto them** [Mount

Moriah covenant, plus covenants God made with Enos and other Nephite prophets] on the conditions of repentance [Mount Sinai covenant]. (Alma 17:15; emphasis added)

## Alma 18: The Scriptures Teach Us of the Covenant Path

Ammon taught the Lamanite king Lamoni about God's covenant path beginning with the creation of the world and Adam and Eve and following the path through the scriptures (see Alma 18:36–39). Ammon clarified how Laman and Lemuel had left the covenant and had taught their children to stay off the covenant path. Ammon explained that the path centers on Jesus Christ. A significant editorial phrase Mormon includes is this, "and **all the works of the Lord** did [Ammon] make known unto [Lamoni and his servants]" (Alma 18:39; emphasis added). What are the works of the Lord? God's deeds of covenantal loyalty, continuously leading His people to promised lands and creating the conditions so that they might experience peace and prosperity in the land.

This instruction on the covenant path was necessary so that Lamoni could see the path and understand the great deeds that God has done throughout the generations to bless His people. Lamoni needed to see and feel God's love and loyalty so that he would have the desire to loyally enter into a covenant of love with God. As soon as Lamoni experienced his awakening knowledge of God's good deeds, he believed and wanted to join the covenant. Like the people of King Benjamin, Lamoni cried out for the mercy of God.

> O Lord, have mercy [open your covenant to me]; according to thy abundant mercy which thou has had upon the people of Nephi [God had been in covenant with Nephi's people], have upon me, and my people [God, be in covenant with the Lamanites]." (Alma 18:41)

And like the people of King Benjamin who fell down in humility as they expressed their desire to be in covenant with God, Lamoni fell to the earth.

## Alma 19: The Light of the Covenant Path Enlightens Lamoni's Life

Ammon knew that the covenant path was unfolding to Lamoni.

> Now, this was what Ammon desired, for he knew that king Lamoni was under the power of God; he knew that the dark veil of unbelief [being outside of God's covenant] was being cast away from his mind, and the light which did light up his mind, which was the light of the glory of God, which was a marvelous light of his goodness—yea, this light had infused such joy into his soul, the cloud of darkness having been dispelled, and that the light of everlasting life was lit up in his soul, yea, he knew that this had overcome his natural frame, and he was carried away in God [Lamoni had found the covenant path to the tree of life]. (Alma 19:6)

Because of this experience, the queen was willing to enter into a covenant to join with God. Ammon rejoiced at the willingness that she demonstrated in wanting to be faithful to God, a willingness that was not so readily found among his people the Nephites who had the privilege of knowing the covenant. When Lamoni revived from his transformative experience, he exclaimed in testimony what he learned about the covenant path.

> Blessed be the name of God, and blessed art thou [those who are in covenant with God and who receive the blessings of the Abrahamic promises]. For as sure as thou livest, behold, I have seen my Redeemer; and he shall come forth, and be born of a woman, and he shall redeem all mankind who believe on his name [all those who believe, or choose to be in covenant with God, will have access to redemption]. (Alma 19:12–13)

The joy of Lamoni, the queen, and Ammon was so great that they all fell down as if they were dead. Soon thereafter, all the servants likewise fell down for joy, except for Abish, who had already been converted unto the Lord many years prior "on account of a remarkable vision of her father" (Alma 19:16). When she noised the news about, people throughout the kingdom came to the king's home and wondered at the events. Some thought it was an act of God. Others thought that only evil could account for the scene. One Lamanite was angry with Ammon and sought to slay him. But God protected Ammon. Just as Abraham trusted God to fulfill His promises, so too did King Mosiah trust in God to protect his sons who had been true in the covenant.

> Now, one of them, whose brother had been slain with the sword of Ammon, being exceedingly angry with Ammon, drew his sword and went forth that he might let it fall upon Ammon, to slay him; and as he lifted the sword to smite him, behold, he fell dead. Now we see that Ammon could not be slain, for the Lord had said unto Mosiah, his father: I will spare him, and it shall be unto him according to thy faith—therefore, Mosiah trusted him unto the Lord. (Alma 19:22–23)

Our trust of God is crucial for covenantal faithfulness. We show our love of God by trusting that He will do what He promised to do. And when we keep our end of the bargain, to be loyal to God, we have total surety that the God of promise making and promise keeping will come through. That is what we see here in this story of Ammon.

The conclusion of this chapter uses covenantal terminology, explaining that when people choose to enter into a covenant relationship with God (i.e., to believe in Him), they receive His presence in return, which is the prosperity we all seek:

> And thus the work of the Lord did commence among the Lamanites; thus the Lord did begin to pour out his Spirit upon them; and we see that his arm is extended to all people who will repent and believe on his name. (Alma 19:36)

*The Covenant Path in the Bible and the Book of Mormon* 249

## Alma 22–23: The King of the Lamanites Enters into the Covenant Path

After Ammon's success with Lamoni, the story then moves to the conversion experience of the king of the Lamanites, the father of Lamoni, who was willing to enter into the covenant path with God. "And he said: Yea, I **believe** that the Great Spirit created all things, and I desire that ye should tell me concerning all these things, and I will **believe** thy words [I am willing to enter the covenant path]" (Alma 22:11; emphasis added).

Like Ammon, Aaron taught the king from the covenantal instruction book (the scriptures), elucidating the covenant path by explaining the purpose of creation, commandments, and the needs for a savior:

> And it came to pass that when Aaron saw that the king would **believe** his words, he began from the creation of Adam, reading the scriptures unto the king—how God created man after his own image, and that God gave him commandments [the expectations for covenantal loyalty], and that because of transgression [we failing to be loyal], man had fallen. And Aaron did expound unto him the scriptures from the creation of Adam, laying the fall of man before him, and their carnal state and also the plan of redemption, which was prepared from the foundation of the world, through Christ, for all whosoever would **believe** on his name [or willingly enter into the covenant path]. And since man had fallen he could not merit anything of himself; but the sufferings and death of Christ atone for their sins, through **faith** and repentance [actions to show our loyalty to God], and so forth; and that he breaketh the bands of death, that the grave shall have no victory, and that the sting of death should be swallowed up in the hopes of glory; and Aaron did expound all these things unto the king. (Alma 22:12–14; emphasis added)

The king of the Lamanites felt the stirring power of the Spirit come upon him and wash away his sins. He willingly entered into the covenant with God. As a righteous king who models living and teaching the covenant path, the king of the Lamanites soon thereafter issued a proclamation of religious freedom throughout his land (see Alma 23:1–5).

This proclamation allowed the sons of Mosiah to teach the covenant path (a duty reserved for the king unless he has delegated it to authorized servants) without molestation.

The remaining portion of the missionary journeys of the sons of Mosiah (Alma 24–27) contains additional stories that teach and reveal the covenant path and demonstrate what happens when individuals, families, and nations choose to enter or leave God's covenant path. We see many thousands of the Lamanites join themselves to God in covenant and reap the promised rewards.

# CHAPTER 17

## ALMA 28–35: THE MISSION TO RECLAIM THOSE WHO HAVE FALLEN OFF THE COVENANT PATH

This section of the Book of Alma focuses on the mission to the wayward Zoramites. Alma's deep-seated desire that people everywhere feel the love of God was founded on his visionary and transformative experience with the power of Jesus found in Mosiah 26–28. Alma wishes he had the capacity to do for others what the angel of God did to him—wake him up to the fact that he was off the covenant path but could enter in.

> O that I were an angel, and could have the wish of mine heart, that I might go forth and speak with the trump of God, with a voice to shake the earth, and cry repentance unto every people! Yea, I would declare unto every soul, as with the voice of thunder, repentance and the plan of redemption [the covenant path], that they should repent and come unto our God [the God of Abraham, Isaac, and Jacob, who will save us if we let Him], that there might not be more sorrow upon all the face of the earth. (Alma 29:1–2)

Before Alma embarked with his sons on a mission to reclaim the Zoramites who had strayed off the covenant path into strange paths of their own making, Alma had to address a serious threat against the covenants of God. The false teacher Korihor arose and taught many things contrary to God's revealed covenantal expectations.

## Alma 30: Korihor Leads People Away from the Covenant Path

Alma 30 begins by explaining the covenantal faithfulness of the people, and the positive consequences they experienced, according to the revealed Mosaic law.

> Yea, and the people did **observe to keep the commandments of the Lord**; and they were strict in **observing the ordinances of God**, according to the law of Moses; **for they were taught to keep the law of Moses** [the expectations of the covenant] until it should be fulfilled [in Jesus Christ who would reveal updated expectations for covenantal living]. And thus the people did have no disturbance in all the sixteenth year of the reign of the judges over the people of Nephi. And it came to pass that in the commencement of the seventeenth year of the reign of the judges, **there was continual peace** [which is the promise of keeping the covenant]. (Alma 30:3–5; emphasis added)

But then Korihor taught a series of doctrines that called everything into question. He caused the people to question whether there really was a God (if there wasn't, who would provide the promises given to Abraham?) and whether there really was a Christ (if there wasn't, who would vivify the covenant path?). Korihor taught the people not to believe. Not to trust. Not to read or believe the scriptures (the covenantal instruction manual). He berated believers, saying,

> O ye that are bound down under a foolish and a vain hope, why do ye yoke yourselves with such foolish things? Why do ye look for a Christ? For no man can know of anything which is to come. Behold, these things which ye call prophecies, which ye say are handed down by holy prophets, behold, they are foolish traditions of your fathers [Korihor erroneously claims that the covenantal instructions are foolish]. How do ye know

of their surety? Behold, ye cannot know of things which ye do not see [but we can trust, as Abraham did, and have it counted to us for righteousness; we can also know by the witness of the Holy Ghost]; therefore ye cannot know that there shall be a Christ. Ye look forward and say that ye see a remission of your sins. But behold, it is the effect of a frenzied mind; and this derangement of your minds comes because of the traditions of your fathers, which lead you away into a belief of things which are not so. (Alma 30:13–16)

Korihor's doctrines are all explicitly contrary to the covenant path, which is what made his preaching so dangerous that it required prophetic correction. At its core, Korihor's doctrine was infused with atheism—the belief that there is no God. Consider how destructive this doctrine is. If there is no God, then God has never done any great deeds for the salvation of mankind. If there is no God, there are no covenantal blessings associated with showing loving loyalty to God. If there is no God, then the gods that we create in our own minds are all that we have to provide us any meaningless and transitory comfort. Without God, there is no covenant path. Without God there is no tree of life. Without God there is no delicious fruit of the Atonement. Without God there is, ultimately, nothing. Only death and oblivion await us. This life is purposeless and meaningless. This is what Korihor offered.

By the power of God Korihor was eventually struck dumb so that he could no longer speak such vain, lying, erroneous words that led people away from God's covenants. Mormon provided a covenantal editorial conclusion to the story of Korihor, showing that those who cause others to stray from the covenant path will, in the end, experience their end:

> And thus we see the end of him who perverteth [turns away from or tries to turn others away from] the ways of the Lord; and thus we see that the devil will not support his children at the last day, but doth speedily drag them down to hell. (Alma 30:60)

## Alma 31–35: The Mission to the Self-Exalters (Zoramites)

The key of God's promise to Abraham is that God will exalt the faithful. He will make them great. Abraham's original name was Abram, which in Hebrew means "exalted father" (from *ab* "father" and *ram* "exalted"). Those who are faithful to God become like Abraham and Sarah, exalted fathers and mothers. The Exalted Father makes us to become as He is.

The Zoramites tried to exalt themselves, which is contrary to the covenant path! God's covenantal role is to exalt us (the Abrahamic covenant). Our covenantal role is to show loyalty to God (the Mosaic covenant). The Zoramites tried to create their own path back to God. And in so doing they misled many from the true covenant path, which was why Alma sought to reclaim them by teaching them the true nature of God and His covenants.

The name Zoram likely means "he who is exalted" or "this one is exalted" (Hebrew *zo* "he" or "this one" and *ram* "exalted"). What better name for a group of self-exalters than Zoramites? Unfortunately, the Zoramites seemed to not understand the purpose of the Tower of Babel and Abraham stories in the Bible. They failed to see that when they built a Rameumptom (note: *ram* "exalted" eumptom!), it was as though they were repeating the failed mission of those in the Bible attempting to exalt (Hebrew *ram*) themselves by building the tower of Babel. That story takes place in Genesis 11. In Genesis 12, Abraham and the promises from God to Abraham are introduced (we reviewed those stories earlier in this book). The story of Babel and Abraham are placed side by side for covenantal instruction. And the Zoramites seemed to have missed the lesson.

Following the pattern of comparing people of Babel against Abraham, you may find it valuable to compare the haughty Zoramites (who rejected Alma) against their humble brethren (who accepted Alma).

Only God exalts us. We cannot build our own towers or paths to God and exalt ourselves. We already saw in Genesis 11 what happens to those who try to create alternative covenant paths back to the presence of God. They are scattered. Only those who are faithful to God will be exalted and have their names be made great, which is the purpose of the promises God made to Abraham in Genesis 12:1–3. The Zoramites were on the same deadly path and Alma desired to save them by inviting them back to the covenant path. That is the purpose of Alma 31–35.

## Alma 32: Test the Covenant Path by Planting the Seed of Faith

Alma taught people to show faithfulness to God by experimenting on His word. Trust God. Try Him. Just like Abraham did, and it was counted to Him for righteousness. What if Abraham had *not* trusted God to fulfill His covenant to him? What if Abraham walked off the covenant path? Would his faith like a mustard seed ever sprout into a glorious tree? No. Similarly, Alma taught that we must be like Abraham, trusting in God and experimenting on His word. God has promised to be loyal to us. How will we ever know God will be true to His word to us if we don't let Him show us? How can we expect to receive the blessings of God if we remove the very conditions that are required for the blessings to be received—faith? How can we expect a seed to grow if we don't first put it into the ground? Those who want to eat the fruit of the tree of life but refuse to show trust in God by first putting their seed of faith in the ground will reap nothingness.

## Alma 35: Those Joining God's Covenant Must Renounce Covenants with Other Groups

Those Zoramites who chose to join God's covenant were kicked out of the false "covenantal" community of the Zoramites. What else would we expect? An individual is either covenantally committed in the kingdom of God or is not. We cannot covenant with God and then expect to make covenants with other gods (such as those offered by Korihor or the Zoramites). The very first stipulation of covenantal loyalty is to have no other gods besides God.

# CHAPTER 18

# ALMA 36–42: ALMA MODELS AND TEACHES THE COVENANT PATH

This section demonstrates that Alma was the covenant-keeping father-leader who taught his sons to be faithful, and as a faithful teacher and father, he commissioned his sons to teach others to do likewise. After spending a lifetime teaching and leading others on the covenant path, Alma knew that he would soon die. Like other great and righteous covenant-keeping and covenant-teaching leaders who left their last will and testament before dying (such as Lehi, Samuel, King Benjamin, Mosiah II, etc.), Alma delivered a final round of covenantal instruction to his three sons.

## Alma 36: Jesus is the Source and the Center of the Covenant Path

As discovered by Book of Mormon scholar Jack Welch, Alma 36 is one of the most beautiful, sophisticated, and literarily brilliant chiastic structures anywhere in scripture. The center spot of the chiasm is Jesus Himself: "Behold, I remembered also to have heard my father prophesy unto the people concerning the coming of one Jesus Christ, a Son of God, to atone for the sins of the world" (Alma 36:17). A chiasm is an "x" structure in literature;

The Covenant Path in the Bible and the Book of Mormon  257

here is Alma 36 formatted to highlight that structure and with comments on the covenantal language:

  A My son give ear to my words (v. 1)
    B Keep the commandments and ye shall prosper in the land [summary of Mosaic covenant] (v. 1)
      C Do as I have done (v. 2)
        D Remember the captivity of our fathers (v. 2)
          E They were in bondage (v. 2)
            F He surely did deliver them [summary of Abrahamic covenant] (v. 2)
              G Trust in God [like Abraham did] (v. 3)
                H Supported in trials, troubles, and afflictions (v. 3)
                  I Lifted up at the last day (v. 3)
                    J I know this not of myself but of God (v. 4)
                      K Born of God (v. 5)
                        L I sought to destroy the church (vv. 6–9)
                          M My limbs were paralyzed (v. 10)
                            N Fear of being in the presence of God (vv. 14–15)
                              O Pains of a damned soul (v. 16)
                                P Harrowed up by the memory of sins (v. 17)
                                  **Q I remembered Jesus Christ, a Son of God (v. 17)**
                                  **Q' I cried, Jesus Christ, thou Son of God (v. 18)**
                                P' Harrowed by the memory of sins no more (v. 19)
                              O' Joy as exceeding as was the pain (v. 20)
                            N' Long to be in the presence of God (v. 22)
                          M' My limbs received strength again (v. 23)
                        L' I labored to bring souls to repentance (v. 24)
                      K' Born of God (v. 26)
                    J' Therefore my knowledge is of God (v. 26)
                I' Supported under trials, troubles, and afflictions (v. 27)
              H' Trust in Him (v. 27)
            G' He will deliver me (v. 27)
          F' And raise me up at the last day (v. 28)
        E' As God brought our fathers out of bondage [summary of Abrahamic covenant] (vv. 28–29)
      D' Retain a remembrance of their captivity (v. 29)
    C' Know as I do know (v. 30)

B' Keep the commandments and ye shall prosper in the land [summary of Mosaic covenant] (v. 30)

A' This according to His word (v. 30)

(Modified from *Charting the Book of Mormon*, Welch and Welch [1999], Foundation for Ancient Research and Mormon Studies, Chart 132.)

Jesus is the source of the covenant path. He is the path. He is the word of God. He is the iron rod. He is the tree of life. He is the center.

## Alma 37: The Scriptures Preserve the Covenants of God

As we have seen elsewhere when we read the scriptures through the lens of covenants, we should expect to find covenant-keeping record keepers who preserve the scriptures as God's covenants with His people. Sure enough, Alma fulfills that role and delivers that sacred commission to his son Helaman. Without the covenantal instructions, people fall into disbelief and disloyalty. They lose access to the blessings promised to Abraham and his descendants.

> And now, my son Helaman, I command you that ye take the records which have been entrusted with me; And I also command you that ye keep a record of this people, according as I have done, upon the plates of Nephi, and keep all these things sacred which I have kept, even as I have kept them; for it is for a wise purpose that they are kept. (Alma 37:1–2)

What is the purpose of the records Alma entrusted to his son (and we have them now in summary form as the Book of Mormon!)?

> And now, it has hitherto been wisdom in God that these things should be preserved; for behold, they have **enlarged the memory of this people** [so that they might know of the covenant path and their duties within the covenant], yea, and convinced many of the error of their ways, and brought them to the knowledge of their God unto the salvation of their souls. Yea, I say unto you, were it not for these things that these

records do contain, which are on these plates, Ammon and his brethren could not have convinced so many thousands of the Lamanites of the incorrect tradition of their fathers; yea, **these records and their words brought them unto repentance** [the word of God is the iron rod on the covenant path]; that is, they brought them to the knowledge of the Lord their God, and to rejoice in Jesus Christ their Redeemer. And who knoweth but what they will be the means of bringing many thousands of them, yea, and also many thousands of our stiffnecked brethren, the Nephites, who are now hardening their hearts in sin and iniquities, to the knowledge of their Redeemer? (Alma 37:8–10; emphasis added)

The records that Alma received and preserved led people to understand and embrace God's saving covenants. Those records were abridged by Mormon and preserved for our day so that we might have a bright and clear understanding of God's covenantal nature and our obligations to Him.

## Alma 38: Alma Summarizes the Interlocking Nature of the Abrahamic and Mosaic Covenants

Alma offered fewer recorded words of wisdom and counsel to his son Shiblon than he did to his other two sons. Nevertheless, what we learn from these few words is precious indeed. Perhaps the most important covenantal words in this chapter are these:

> And now my son, Shiblon, I would that ye should remember [covenantal terminology], that as much as ye shall put your trust in God [just as Abraham did, and as the Mosaic covenant instructs] even so much ye shall be delivered out of your trials, and your troubles, and your afflictions, and ye shall be lifted up at the last day [the promise of the Abrahamic covenant for those who show loyalty as instructed in the Mosaic covenant]. (Alma 38:5)

## Alma 39–42: Alma Instructs Corianton on Covenantal Faithfulness

Remember that according to the covenant path a righteous father or mother and leader is duty bound to teach those within their sphere of responsibility the covenant path and the expectations for loyalty that God has revealed. Alma spent time with Corianton, teaching him specifically and clearly about the covenant path, about the role of Jesus Christ in saving us, and about our need to show loyalty by not breaking the commandments.

Alma was indeed troubled by the immorality Corianton had fallen into, thus showing covenantal disloyalty to God. What also really disturbed Alma was that Corianton's covenantal disloyalty made it more difficult for others to choose to be loyal to God, to believe the words that Alma had taught. In this sense, the Zoramites were no better than the nonbelieving Lamanites who were outside of God's covenantal protection. And Corianton was responsible for keeping people out of covenantal relationship with God. That truly is a spiritual crime.

> Behold, O my son, how great iniquity ye brought upon the Zoramites; for when they saw your conduct they would **not believe** [*la* "not" *aman* "believe"] in my words. (Alma 39:11; emphasis added)

Alma continued to teach his son the doctrine of resurrection and restoration. The covenant path is meant to be a path of happiness and prosperity. Those who humbly follow that path find themselves surrounded by joy and purpose. Those who seek that covenantal joy in this life will experience it now and for the eternities. That is justice and mercy. God gives us what we want. For those who live outside of God's covenant, they will receive whatever is available outside of God's relationship. But for those who enfold themselves into God's merciful covenantal promises will receive everything He has.

> And now behold, is the meaning of the word restoration to take a thing of a natural state and place it in an unnatural

state, or to place it in a state opposite to its nature? O, my son, this is not the case; but the meaning of the word restoration is to bring back again evil for evil, or carnal for carnal, or devilish for devilish—good for that which is good; righteous for that which is righteous; just for that which is just; merciful for that which is merciful. (Alma 41:12–13)

God will not force us to accept the promises He made to Abraham. God will not compel us to make covenants. God will not require us to live in His promised lands. God loves and invites. He makes the covenants available. He has prophetic writers preserve the stories of faithful individuals who trusted God and reaped the covenantal rewards so that we as readers will be encouraged to also trust the God of covenants. The purpose of this life is for us to choose to be on the covenant path. If we demonstrate through our words, deeds, and actions that we have no desire to be part of God's promises, God honors that desire. But we shouldn't be surprised that in the final scenes God restores to us what we have desired in this life.

Using the analogy of a bank again, no bank forces us on where to live. No bank requires us to live in this house or that house, or to live on that land versus other land. It is our choice where to live and which house to inhabit. But if we are to receive the "blessings" of the bank to have the resources to live in the land, we are required to live the obligations that the bank has established. There is *no* injustice when the bank exercises the covenantal agreement and throws out of the house and off the land anyone who does not adhere to the agreement. There is *no* injustice when the bank does not, at the very last day, make available the homes or lands to the buyer, which the buyer *never* showed interest in.

Alma summarized the mercy and justice of God, as a covenant-making and covenant-keeping God, with these resounding words.

> For behold, justice exerciseth all his demands, and also mercy claimeth all which is her own; and thus, none but the truly penitent are saved [those who devoted themselves to covenantal

loyalty]. What, do ye suppose that mercy can rob justice? I say unto you, Nay; not one whit. **If so, God would cease to be God.** [Since God will *not* cease to be God, like Abraham, we can perfectly trust Him within the covenantal relationship.] And thus God bringeth about his great and eternal purposes, which were prepared from the foundation of the world. And thus cometh about the salvation and the redemption of men, and also their destruction and misery. Therefore, O my son, whosoever will come may come and partake of the waters of life freely [promised by God to Abraham and those who are loyal to Him]; and whosoever will not come the same is not compelled to come; but in the last day it shall be restored unto him according to his deeds. (Alma 42:24–27; emphasis added)

We've reviewed a number of chapters in Alma that center on teaching others of the covenant path. We'll turn to the final chapters of the Book of Alma and ask, "Why did Mormon include so much warfare in his sacred record? What does a covenantal perspective suggest as a reason?"

# CHAPTER 19

## ALMA 43–63: THREATS TO THE PROMISED LAND

We need a land where we can live the covenant path. False leaders and kings who teach different paths will cause us to leave the covenant path and lose the promised land. False leaders and kings who seek their own glory will condemn us and compromise the promised land. False leaders and kings who require our loyalty and obedience to them seek to replace God and we will lose the promised land where only God is King. When we give our loyalty to false leaders and kings, we cannot give our loyalty to God and we cannot have the promised land. The promises of the promised land become frayed when we are not loyal to God. And the covenantal promises are lost until we return to God's revealed covenant path.

The war chapters in the Book of Mormon, especially in Alma 43–63, provide evidence for what happens to the promised land when people are—or are not—faithful to God's covenants. The key players in these chapters were, on one side, the covenant-breakers and apostate kingmakers Amalickiah and his brother Ammoron and, on the other side, the leaders of cove-nant-makers, covenant-teachers, and covenant-keepers Captain Moroni and Nephihah.

Amalickiah wanted to be a king. He wanted to rule in place of Jehovah. Amalickiah wanted the people to be loyal to him and his vision for the world. The covenant-keeping Nephites knew that the apostasy of Amalickiah and his followers would lead to the promises of the promised land being forfeited. Posterity and property would be destroyed (through war) and the prosperity of God's presence would flee the land. Captain Moroni resisted Amalickiah with faith and trust in God. But Captain Moroni did not simply sit back and wait for God to save the Nephites from the clear and present danger of Amalickiah's apostasy.

As you read the war chapters in Alma 43–63, look for covenantal terminology and phraseology. Look for the consequences of breaking covenants. Look for the blessings of keeping covenants. Look for how God blesses covenant keepers with strength and inspiration to fight and win defensive battles. And look for instances of when those who are outside the covenant fail to achieve their objectives.

## Alma 43: Moroni Inspires His Men with Covenants

We saw earlier in Alma's writings that the Zoramites would not believe (*la aman*) in the covenantal instruction (see Alma 39:11). They had become, in essence, Lamanites, outside of the covenant. In fact, these were the very words Mormon used to describe the choice the Zoramites made after rejecting Alma's invitation to return to the covenant path: "it came to pass that the Zoramites became Lamanites [*la aman* "unbelievers" or "those outside the covenant"]" (Alma 43:4).

The noncovenanters (Zoramites/Lamanites) decided to fight against the covenanters (Nephites). Mormon editorialized to explain the covenantal obligation for righteous people to defend their lands:

> And now the design of the Nephites was to support their lands [the promised land], and their houses, and their wives, and their children, that they might preserve them from the hands

of their enemies; and also that they might preserve their rights and their privileges, yea, and also their liberty [to keep the covenant], that they might worship God according to their desires [show loyalty to God in the covenant]. For they knew that if they should fall into the hands of the Lamanites, that whosoever should worship God in spirit and in truth, the true and the living God, the Lamanites would destroy. (Alma 43:9–10)

Mormon also recorded how Captain Moroni used the context of covenants to inspire the Nephites to defend their God-given lands. He inspired them to fight "for their homes and their liberties, their wives and their children, and their all, yea, for their rites of worship and their church. And they were doing that which they felt was the duty which they owed to their God" (Alma 43:45–46). In the heat of a battle when the Nephites were about to yield to the Lamanites, Captain Moroni roused his men to faithfulness, "they turned upon the Lamanites, and they cried with one voice unto the Lord their God, for their liberty and their freedom from bondage" (Alma 43:49). God empowered the faithful Nephites to win the battle.

The lesson here is that if we are faithful to God, who is the King of the promised land, He will empower us and deliver us so that we are not ensnared by our enemies. Will the path be a bed of roses? Absolutely not. We have to labor and fight and defend. We may be wounded along the way. Loved ones may die. Since this is the cause of God, we ultimately triumph through Him. That is the covenantal surety of the promised land.

Soon after this great victory that God had given the faithful people, Amalickiah arose with flattering words, convincing many, including many within the church, that if they would be loyal to him and empower him, he would make them rulers over the people.

> And Amalickiah was desirous to be a king; and those people who were wroth were also desirous that he should be their king; and they were the greater part of them the lower judges

> of the land, and they were seeking for power. And they had been led by the flatteries of Amalickiah, that if they would support him and establish him to be their king that he would make them rulers over the people.... And there were many in the church who believed in the flattering words of Amalickiah, therefore they dissented even from the church; and thus were the affairs of the people of Nephi exceedingly precarious and dangerous, notwithstanding their great victory which they had had over the Lamanites, and their great rejoicings which they had had because of their deliverance by the hand of the Lord. (Alma 46:4–5, 7)

These very church members who had the blessings of the eternities in their grasp where they could rule as kings and queens of righteousness forever and ever, decided to sell their covenantal birthright for a mess of pottage. Mormon used this moment to instruct on how easy it is to fall off the covenant path.

> Thus we see how quick the children of men do forget the Lord their God, yea, how quick to do iniquity, and to be led away by the evil one. Yea, and we also see the great wickedness one very wicked man can cause to take place among the children of men. Yea, we see that Amalickiah, because he was a man of cunning device and a man of many flattering words, that he led away the hearts of many people to do wickedly; yea, and to seek to destroy the church of God, and to destroy the foundation of liberty which God had granted unto them, or which blessing God had sent upon the face of the land for the righteous' sake. (Alma 46:8–10)

How do righteous, covenant-making and covenant-keeping people respond to false gods and false kings, like Amalickiah, who would usurp authority and threaten the peace of the people? Captain Moroni is an indefatigable example. He invoked the Nephites' best values and then required them to demonstrate their devotion to God and these pure values through covenant making.

And it came to pass that [Captain Moroni] rent his coat; and he took a piece thereof, and wrote upon it—In **memory** of our God, our religion, and freedom, and our peace, our wives, and our children—and he fastened it upon the end of a pole. And he fastened on his head-plate, and his breastplate, and his shields, and girded on his armor about his loins; and he took the pole, which had on the end thereof his rent coat, (and he called it the title of liberty) and he bowed himself to the earth, and he prayed mightily unto his God for the **blessings of liberty** to rest upon his brethren, so long as there should a band of Christians remain to **possess the land**—For thus were all the **true believers** of Christ, who belonged to the church of God, called by those who did not belong to the church. And those who did belong to the church were **faithful** [they remained true to their covenants with God]; yea, all those who were **true believers** in Christ took upon them, gladly, the name of Christ, or Christians as they were called, because of their **belief** in Christ who should come. And therefore, at this time, Moroni prayed that the cause of the Christians, and the **freedom of the land** might be favored. And it came to pass that when he had poured out his soul to God, he named all the land which was south of the land Desolation, yea, and in fine, all the land, both on the north and on the south—**A chosen land**, and the land of liberty. And he said: Surely God shall not suffer that we, who are despised because we take upon us the name of Christ, shall be trodden down and destroyed, until we bring it upon us by our own transgressions. [In other words, if we show loyalty to God as revealed to the prophets, God will be loyal to us and deliver us from our enemies.] And when Moroni had said these words, he went forth among the people, waving the rent part of his garment in the air, that all might see the writing which he had written upon the rent part, and crying with a loud voice, saying [note the covenantal terms Captain Moroni offers: if you do x you will receive y]: Behold, whosoever will maintain this title upon the land, let them come forth in the strength of the Lord, and **enter into a covenant** that they will maintain their rights, and their religion, that the Lord God may bless them. And it came to pass that when Moroni had proclaimed these words, behold, the people came running together with their armor girded about their loins, rending their garments in token, or as **a covenant**, that they would not forsake the Lord their God; or, in other words, if they should transgress the **commandments** of God, or fall into transgression, and be ashamed to take upon them the name of Christ, the Lord should rend them even as they had rent their garments. Now this was the **covenant** which they made, and they cast their garments at the feet of Moroni, saying: We **covenant** with our God, that we shall be destroyed, even as our brethren in the land northward, if we shall fall into transgression; yea, he may cast us at the feet of our enemies, even as we have cast our garments at thy feet to be trodden under foot, if we shall fall into transgression. (Alma 46:12–22; emphasis added)

The Nephites then went up to battle against the followers of Amalickiah and routed them, though Amalickiah escaped. Those dissenting Nephites who were unwilling to covenant to preserve the promised land were put to death. Those who entered into covenant to preserve the land were incorporated back into the Nephite society.

> And it came to pass that whomsoever of the Amalickiahites that would not enter into a covenant to support the cause of freedom, that they might maintain a free government, he caused to be put to death; and there were but few who denied the covenant of freedom. (Alma 46:35)

God promises peace and posterity to those who covenant to live the commandments of the land. Mormon demonstrated the consequences, or rather the blessings, of covenantal living with these statements.

> And they began to have peace again in the land; and thus they did maintain peace in the land until nearly the end of the nineteenth year of the reign of the judges. And Helaman and the high priests did also maintain order in the church; yea,

even for the space of four years did they have much peace and rejoicing in the church. (Alma 46:37–38)

Mormon described what a covenant-keeping righteous leader looks like, one who teaches and lives God's covenants and defends His people so that they can also live the covenant. When we look around the world today at "leaders," we can look to the covenantal leadership on display in the Book of Mormon as a guide for the type of leader that God really loves and that we should be willing to support. Captain Moroni was such a leader.

> And this was their faith, that by so doing God would prosper them in the land, or in other words, if they were **faithful in keeping the commandments of God** [Mosaic covenant] that he would **prosper them in the land** [Abrahamic covenant]; yea, warn them to flee, or to prepare for war, according to their danger; And Moroni was a strong and a mighty man; he was a man of a **perfect** understanding [covenantal loyalty]; yea, a man that did not delight in bloodshed; a man whose soul did joy in the liberty and the **freedom** of his country, and his brethren from bondage and slavery; Yea, a man whose heart did swell with **thanksgiving to his God**, for the many **privileges** and **blessings** which he bestowed upon his people; a man who did labor exceedingly for the welfare and safety of his people. Yea, and he was a man who was **firm in the faith** of Christ, and he had **sworn with an oath** to defend his people, his rights, and his country, and his religion, even to the loss of his blood. . . . This was the **faith of Moroni**, and his heart did glory in it; not in the shedding of blood but in doing good, in **preserving** his people, yea, in **keeping the commandments of God** [covenantal loyalty], yea, and resisting iniquity. Yea, verily, verily I say unto you, if all men had been, and were, and ever would be, like unto Moroni, behold, the very powers of hell would have been shaken forever; yea, the devil would never have power over the hearts of the children of men. (Alma 48:11–13, 15–17; emphasis added)

We won't delve further into the war chapters here. The covenantal theme is clear and consistent. Those who covenant with the God of the promised land will be blessed with peace and security in the promised land. Those who try to usurp God's authority, by establishing men as kings who refuse to live or teach God's covenant, will eventually fall. As you read the rest of the war chapters, look for the covenantal themes at play. How did God bless the people with His presence to empower them to defend themselves against their enemies? How was God true to His covenantal promises? How were the people faithful, or not, to God and what were the consequences?

A concluding thought from Mormon on the Lamanite/Nephite wars in the Book of Alma orients our understanding. This thought is saturated in covenantal thinking.

> And thus ended the thirty and first year of the reign of the judges over the people of Nephi; and thus they had had wars, and bloodsheds, and famine, and affliction, for the space of many years. And there had been murders, and contentions, and dissensions, and all manner of iniquity among the people of Nephi; nevertheless for the **righteous'** [covenant keepers'] sake, yea, because of the prayers of the **righteous** [covenant keepers], they were spared [God fulfills His covenantal obligations]. But behold, because of the exceedingly great length of the war between the Nephites and the Lamanites many had become hardened, because of the exceedingly great length of the war; and many were softened because of their afflictions, insomuch that they did **humble themselves before God**, even in the depth of humility. . . . And it came to pass that they did **establish again the church of God**, throughout all the land. . . . And the people of Nephi began to **prosper** again in the land, and began to multiply and to wax exceedingly strong again in the land. And they began to grow exceedingly rich. But notwithstanding their riches, or their strength, or their **prosperity**, they were not lifted up in the pride of their eyes; neither were they slow to **remember the Lord their God**; but they did **humble** themselves exceedingly before him. Yea, they did **remember how great things the Lord had done for them**, that he had **delivered**

them from death, and from bonds, and from prisons, and from all manner of afflictions, and he had **delivered** them out of the hands of their enemies. And they did pray unto the Lord their God continually, insomuch that the Lord did bless them, according to his word, so that they did wax strong and **prosper in the land**. (62:39–41, 46, 48–51; emphasis added)

# CHAPTER 20
# THE BOOK OF HELAMAN: COVENANT KEEPERS AND COVENANT COUNTERFEITERS

## Helaman 1–6: The Rise of Covenant Counterfeiters

Nephite society took a turn for the worse in the pages of the Book of Helaman. The people's covenantal unfaithfulness led to more warfare internally as well as with their enemies the Lamanites. And because of a lack of covenantal vigilance, a new threat arose. Instead of Nephites grouping together in covenantal solidity to be faithful to God, a group of Nephites hijacked the purposes of covenant making and covenant keeping to practice evil deeds. Kishkumen and then Gadianton administered oaths and covenants to their followers to do unspeakable deeds. Instead of covenanting to serve and love God and neighbor, the followers of Kishkumen and Gadianton created covenants to reject God and to destroy their neighbors. Instead of entering into sacred covenants of love and service, they entered into secret combinations of self-serving interest. These counterfeit covenants eventually led to the destruction of the Nephite nation, as Mormon states: "And behold, in the end of this book [of Mormon] ye shall see that this Gadianton did prove the overthrow, yea, almost the entire destruction of the people of Nephi" (Helaman 2:13). This same false covenant making was also the downfall of the Jaredite nation. The lesson? Stay on the covenant path! Do not create alternative covenants. Do not try to create your own self-serving ends. Do not mimic the sacred nature of covenants God has revealed for evil, self-interested purposes. To do so will lead to the destruction of individuals, families, communities, and nations.

After Kishkumen murdered the chief judge (because he and his friends wanted a different ruler),

> He went unto those that sent him, and they all entered into a **covenant**, yea, **swearing** by their everlasting Maker, that they would tell no man that Kishkumen had murdered Pahoran. Therefore, Kishkumen was not known among the people of Nephi, for he was in disguise at the time that he murdered Pahoran. And Kishkumen and his band, who had **covenanted** with him, did mingle themselves among the people, in a manner that they all could not be found; but as many as were found were condemned unto death. (Helaman 1:11–12; emphasis added)

Soon thereafter, Gadianton took over leadership of this band of covenantal evil-doers. The promised land cannot long endure as a promised land when such dastardly acts of evil are committed in the name of malevolent covenants. The essence of their terrible and misguided covenants was this.

> But behold, Kishkumen, who had murdered Pahoran, did lay wait to **destroy** Helaman also; and he was upheld by his band, who had **entered into a covenant that no one should know his wickedness**. For there was one Gadianton, who was exceedingly expert in many words, and also in his craft, to carry on the **secret** work of **murder** and of **robbery**; therefore he became the leader of the band of Kishkumen. Therefore he did **flatter** them, and also Kishkumen, that if they would place him in the judgment-seat he would grant unto those who belonged to his band that they should be placed in **power** and **authority** among the people; therefore Kishkumen sought to **destroy** Helaman. (Helaman 2:3–5; emphasis added)

Look at what they were trying to achieve. Power and authority through secret means so that they might destroy others. This is the opposite of the covenant path of Abrahamic and Mosaic covenants, where God promises to make our names great and to give us peace, property, posterity, and prosperity. We are not supposed to grab these for ourselves, or rob them from others. God freely gives us these things when we show Him covenantal faithfulness. The Gadianton robbers acted on the exact opposite of God's intended covenantal purposes for the promised land.

As we have seen elsewhere in the Book of Mormon, the constant question is this, "Who is to be king?" The Book of Mormon narrative is dominated by this question. How this question was answered determined the peace and happiness among the Nephites. This question "Who is to be king?" is a covenantal question. Jacob was right when he said that only God is king, though He is willing to have human kings *if* they keep and teach the covenants.

> And this land shall be a land of liberty unto the Gentiles, and there shall be no kings upon the land, who shall raise up unto the Gentiles. . . . For **he that raiseth up a king against me shall perish**, for **I, the Lord, the king of heaven, will be their king**, and I will be a light unto them forever, that hear my words. (2 Nephi 10:11, 14; emphasis added)

God covenanted that this promised land would be free as long as no kings were raised up against God. Kishkumen and the Gadianton robbers sought to overthrow God as king. That can only end in disaster. What did Kishkumen, Gadianton, and their evil covenant makers want? Human kingship for their own power and prestige. They had no interest in serving and loving the people. They only wanted to be worshiped and served by those under their control.

At this same time with the rise of so much wickedness, righteous leaders stepped forward to preserve and share the covenant path. Nephi and Lehi were the sons of Helaman (the son of Helaman, the son of Alma the Younger). Helaman instructed his sons to remember the righteous, covenant-keeping deeds of their ancestors Nephi and Lehi, for whom they were named (see Helaman 5:6).

Nephi and Lehi, like the sons of Mosiah, ached for others to know the joy of walking the covenant path. Like Enos, they desired that the Lamanites would be brought back into the covenant fold. With such loving devotion to God and their neighbor, they sallied forth into Lamanite lands to teach the people of God's covenants. After exercising tremendous faith, patience, and perseverance, Nephi and Lehi helped the majority of Lamanites be converted and become more righteous (i.e., faithful to God's covenants) than were the Nephites.

Remember that at the founding of the Lehite nation, Laman and Lemuel were unfaithful. They did not teach their children about the covenant path, about God's great deeds in saving them, or of their obligations to show faith and love to God if they expected to see blessings of peace and prosperity inherent in the promised land. Because of this lack of knowledge about the covenant path, for many generations the Lamanites dwindled in unbelief, being outside the covenantal protection offered by God. Multiple generations of faithful Nephites sought to reclaim them with varying levels of success, though usually their efforts were met with failure.

Now, after so many hundreds of years, a major breakthrough had been achieved by Nephi and Lehi. A significant portion, perhaps a majority, of the Lamanites had agreed to the covenantal conditions. They were now righteous; they were part of the covenant. They began to reap the rewards God had always desired to deliver to them.

But while the Lamanites were covenanting to be God's people, the Nephites were replacing God's covenants with catastrophic and evil covenants delivered to them from Satan by Kishkumen and Gadianton. The Nephites abandoned God and embraced depravity, wrapped in the secret combinations of perverted covenants. They walked in their own paths. They no longer trusted God. They no longer put their faith in God. They no longer would have God to be their God. They walked after the interests of their own eyes and their own lusts. They were becoming rotten and corrupt. And God was under covenantal obligation to bring upon them the disasters promised against covenant breakers. If you cannot be loyal to the Landlord and faithful to the agreement, then the Landlord has no other options than to exercise the full force of the agreement to throw you off the promised land.

This is exactly what the enemy of God desires for us, to *not* covenant with God but to covenant with the master of all evil instead!

> But behold, Satan did stir up the hearts of the more part of the Nephites, insomuch that they did unite with those bands of robbers, and did enter into their **covenants** and their **oaths**, that they would protect and preserve one another in whatsoever difficult circumstances they should be placed, that they should not suffer for their **murders**, and their **plunderings**, and their **stealings**. And it came to pass that they did have their signs, yea, their **secret signs**, and their **secret words**; and this that they might distinguish a brother who had entered into the **covenant**, that whatsoever wickedness his brother should do he should not be injured by his brother, nor by those who did belong to his band, who had taken this **covenant**. . . . Now behold, it is these **secret oaths and covenants** which Alma commanded his son should not go forth unto the world, lest they should be a means of bringing down the people unto destruction. Now behold, those **secret oaths and covenants** did not come forth unto Gadianton from the records which were delivered unto Helaman; but behold, they were put into the heart of Gadianton by that same being who did entice our first parents to partake of the forbidden fruit— . . . And behold, it is he who is the **author of all sin**. And behold, he doth carry on his **works of darkness** and **secret murder**, and doth hand down their plots, and their **oaths**, and their

**covenants**, and their plans of **awful wickedness**, from generation to generation according as he can get hold upon the hearts of the children of men. (Helaman 6:21–22, 25–26, 30; emphasis added)

The covenant path is bounded by two symbolic mountains. Mount Moriah represents God's promises to Abraham and His covenantal obligations to offer us property, posterity, and prosperity *if* we are faithful to Him, represented by the commandments and covenantal instructions delivered at Mount Sinai and updated from time to time by new revelation delivered by prophets from God.

Those who are in the covenant relationship with God receive His presence. They prosper. Those who refuse or leave the covenant lose God's presence. They do not prosper.

> And now behold, he had got great hold upon the hearts of the Nephites; yea, insomuch that they had become exceedingly wicked; yea, the more part of them had turned out of the away of righteousness, and did trample under their feet the commandments of God [they deliberately showed covenantal disobedience and disloyalty], and did turn unto their own ways [you cannot create your own path of salvation and expect to succeed, as the Tower of Babel and the Zoramite stories teach us. Only God can save you], and did build up unto themselves idols of their gold and their silver. . . . And thus we see that the Nephites did begin to dwindle in unbelief [their covenantal loyalty diminished and disappeared], and grow in wickedness and abominations, while the Lamanites began to grow exceedingly in the knowledge of their God [learning about the covenantal instructions God had revealed]; yea, they did begin to keep his statutes and commandments, and to walk in truth and uprightness before him [just like their ancestor Abraham did, who had been commanded by God "walk before me, and be perfect" (Genesis 17:1)]. And thus we see that the Spirit of the Lord began to withdraw from the Nephites [not prospering], because of the wickedness and the hardness of their hearts. And thus we see that the Lord

began to pour out his Spirit upon the Lamanites [this is what it means to prosper], because of their easiness and willingness to believe [to be in covenantal relationship] in his words. (Helaman 6:31, 34–36)

This turning point in Nephite and Lamanite history is clearly marked by their different responses to the rise of the debauched, degenerate, and falsifying covenant makers—the Gadianton robbers. The Lamanites did as the Nephites had once done for Lamanites. They sought to reclaim them by teaching them of God's covenants.

And it came to pass that the Lamanites did hunt the band of robbers of Gadianton; and they did preach the word of God among the more wicked part of them, insomuch that this band of robbers was utterly destroyed from among the Lamanites. (Helaman 6:37)

Conversely, as a mark of their utter corruption and destitution, the Nephites embraced and supported the Gadianton robbers, who demanded Nephite loyalty first and foremost *before* loyalty to God, breaking the very first covenantal obligation revealed from God "thou shalt have no other gods before me."

And it came to pass on the other hand, that the Nephites did build them up and support them, beginning at the more wicked part of them, until they had overspread all the land of the Nephites, and had **seduced the more part of the righteous** [God's covenant keepers] until they had come down to **believe in their works** [joining the covenant of the Gadianton robbers] and partake of their spoils, and to join with them in their secret murders and combinations. (Helaman 6:38; emphasis added)

What is the mark of a degenerate society? Of a society who has walked away from God's covenants to follow after the false imaginations of their own hearts? They fail to obey God's law to care for the poor, the destitute, the marginalized, the stranger (foreigner or immigrant) in their midst. They forget that they too were once strangers in a strange land, marginalized and oppressed and saved by God's mighty hand. As God revealed in the original instruction delivered through Moses at Mount Sinai,

> Do not mistreat or oppress a foreigner, for you were foreigners in Egypt. Do not take advantage of the widow or the fatherless. If you do and they cry out to me, I will certainly hear their cry. My [covenantal] anger will be aroused, and I will kill you with the sword; your wives will become widows and your children fatherless. (Exodus 22:21–24, NIV translation)

What did the Nephites do? They turned away from God's covenants in order to install leaders who flattered them with lying words of power, prestige, and promises. They supported leaders who did not love God, who did not teach the people to live in covenantal communion with God. They followed leaders who did not live the commandments of God. They supported, loved, and were fiercely loyal to leaders who set themselves up as messiahs and saviors to the people.

> And thus they [the covenant breakers who would rather worship humans than God] did obtain the sole management of the government, insomuch that they did trample under their feet and smite and rend and turn their backs upon the poor and the meek, and the humble followers of God. (Helaman 6:39)

These flattering and charismatic leaders who offer such fair promises, as though they can deliver on God's plan, only truly care about themselves and their own power. They break God's covenants and do not teach others to keep the covenants. Their actions flow from corrupt hearts:

> Condemning the righteous because of their righteousness; letting the guilty and the wicked go unpunished because of their money; and moreover to be held in office at the head of government, to rule and do according to their wills, that they might get gain and glory of the world, and, moreover, that

> they might the more easily commit adultery, and steal, and kill, and do according to their own wills. (Helaman 7:5)

What is the consequence of such wickedness of turning from the covenants of God?

> And thus we see that they were in an awful state, and ripening for an everlasting destruction. (Helaman 6:40)

As a warning to all of us today, we are no different than the Nephites. Do we have eyes to see and ears to hear?

## Helaman 7–12: Nephi Preaches Covenantal Loyalty

Returning from his disappointing mission to the north where the people entirely rejected the word (i.e., the covenantal law) of God, Nephi found seething wickedness at home. In despair, he prayed to God. A gathered crowd marveled at his distraught words. Rising from prayer, Nephi taught the crowd of the covenant path, encouraging and warning them to return to God. Listen to his words and hear the covenantal context of what he preached: Those who forsake God will inherit the disasters promised in the law. Those who break covenants will lose the promised land, they will be thrown out of the land.

> Yea, how could you have given way to the enticing of him who is seeking to hurl away your souls down to everlasting misery and endless wo? O repent ye, repent ye! Why will ye die? Turn ye, turn ye unto the Lord your God [return to the covenant path]. Why has he forsaken you? It is because you have **hardened your hearts**; yea, ye will **not hearken** unto the voice of the good shepherd; yea, ye have **provoked him to anger** against you. [In other words, God is under covenantal obligation to allow destruction to befall those who reject the covenants of the land.] And behold, instead of gathering you, except ye will repent, behold, he shall **scatter you** forth that ye shall become meat for dogs and wild beasts. O, how could **you have forgotten your God** in the very day that he has delivered you? But behold, it is to get gain, to be praised

of men, yea, and that ye might get gold and silver. And ye have **set your hearts upon the riches and the vain things of this world**, for the which ye do murder, and plunder, and steal, and bear false witness against your neighbor, and do all manner of iniquity [all actions in violation of the Sinai covenantal instructions]. (Helaman 7:1–21; emphasis added)

The ultimate promise experienced by those who show faith and loyalty to God by living His revealed covenantal stipulations is His enduring presence. That is true prosperity. As we listen to the words of Nephi, we hear him focus on this very theme. God will not give His strength or presence to the wicked. God cannot. God is covenantally bound to remove His presence from the faithless and disloyal.

> And for this cause **wo shall come unto you** except ye shall repent. For if ye will not repent, behold, this great city, and also all those great cities which are round about, which are in the land of our possession, shall be taken away that **ye shall have no place in them** [in the promised land]; for behold, **the Lord will not grant unto you strength**, as he has hitherto done, to withstand against your enemies. For behold, thus saith the Lord: **I will not show unto the wicked of my strength**, to one more than the other, save it be unto those who repent of their sins, and hearken unto my words. Now therefore, I would that ye should behold, my brethren, that it shall be better for the Lamanites than for you except ye shall repent. (Helaman 7:22–23; emphasis added)

The Nephite fall was precipitated because of their pride. They experienced God's promised prosperity, but then they claimed that they deserved the blessings and prosperity, that they had earned it, that they were favored of God more than anyone, as if their righteousness was the cause of God's goodness, instead of God's goodness leading them to righteousness. For this covenantal treason, God's people the Nephites would lose the promised land, His presence, and ultimately prosperity.

> Yea, wo be unto you because of that great abomination which has come among you; and ye have united yourselves unto it, yea, to that secret band which was established by Gadianton [covenanted to leave God's tribe and join the tribe of Gadianton]! Yea, wo shall come unto you because of that **pride which ye have suffered to enter your hearts**, which has lifted you up beyond that which is good because of your exceedingly great riches! Yea, wo be unto you because of your wickedness and abominations! And except ye repent **ye shall perish**; yea, even **your lands shall be taken from you**, and **ye shall be destroyed from off the face of the earth**. (Helaman 7:25–28; emphasis added)

The covenant path is strict and strait. If we do not join league with the God of the land, we cannot long endure in the land. God takes no pleasure in executing the full force of the law. But as a God of covenants, He is bound by the obligations made to Abraham and his children to give and preserve the promised land. Those who break the covenant of Sinai are removed like so much corruption that threatens the peace and prosperity of the land.

Nephi continued delivering instruction to the Nephites, as was his covenantal duty, encouraging them to remember the great deeds God had done for them. When we reflect back on the covenant delivered at Sinai, God reminded the people of Israel what great deeds He had done as a sign of loyalty (as part of His covenantal duties to the posterity of Abraham) with the intention that the people would be loyal to Him. Nephi continued that covenantal tradition by having them remember God's goodness. A covenant-making and covenant-keeping faithful leader is under obligation to teach people the covenant path and to teach people of the great deeds God has done for His people.

> Behold, my brethren, have ye not read that God gave power unto one man, even Moses, to smite upon the waters of the Red Sea, and they parted hither and thither, insomuch that the Israelites, who were our fathers, came through upon dry ground, and the waters closed upon the armies of the

Egyptians and swallowed them up? And now behold, if God gave unto this man such power, then why should ye dispute among yourselves, and say that he hath given unto me no power whereby I may know concerning the judgments that shall come upon you except ye repent? (Helaman 8:11–12)

Nephi then emphasized the very purpose and meaning of the covenant path—Jesus Christ. He is the way, the path, the gate, the law, the word of God. Jesus models total covenantal fidelity for us. Jesus teaches us the fullness of covenantal loyalty. And Jesus lays down His life so that we might all live again. Jesus is the one who prepared the covenant path, revealed the covenant path, and then vivified all the covenantal promises through His salvific death. All the prophets have testified of Jesus (see Helaman 8:13–22).

> And behold, **he is God, and he is with them, and he did manifest himself unto them, that they were redeemed by him** [this is the purpose of the covenant path!]; and they gave unto him glory, because of that which is to come. And now, seeing ye know these things and cannot deny them except ye shall lie [rejecting the covenant path], therefore in this ye have sinned, for ye have rejected all these things, notwithstanding so many evidences which ye have received; yea, even ye have received all things, both things in heaven, and **all things** which are in the earth, **as a witness that they are true**. (Helaman 8:23–24; emphasis added)

Because of Nephi's extraordinary perseverance in the faith to be a leader who lived and taught the covenant path to others, he received Abrahamic-like promises from God. As you read the words below, think about the promises God made to Abraham and compare their similarities. God made an unconditional promise to Nephi. God identified the covenantal parties (Nephi and God). And God made the covenantal promises to Nephi in the presence of angels who stood as eternal witnesses to God's willingness to fulfill His promises. We may be in awe of Nephi, but we all have the same opportunity to demonstrate covenantal loyalty to God and receive the same promises!

> Blessed art thou, Nephi, for those things which thou hast done; for I have beheld how thou hast with unwearyingness declared the word, which I have given unto thee, unto this people. And thou hast not feared them, **and hast not sought thine own life, but hast sought my will, and to keep my commandments** [Nephi lived the covenantal obligations revealed at Sinai]. And now, because thou hast done this with such unwearyingness [with total loyalty to God], behold, **I will bless thee forever**; and **I will make thee mighty** in word and in deed, in faith and in works; yea, even that all things shall be done unto thee according to thy word, for thou shalt not ask that which is contrary to my will. **Behold, thou art Nephi, and I am God. Behold, I declare it unto thee in the presence of mine angels**, that ye shall have power over this people, and shall smite the earth with famine, and with pestilence, and destruction, according to the wickedness of this people. Behold, I give unto you power, that whatsoever ye shall seal on earth shall be sealed in heaven; and whatsoever ye shall loose on earth shall be loosed in heaven; and thus shall **ye have power among this people**. (Helaman 10:4–7; emphasis added)

Stunningly, the very thing that the false leaders like Amlici, Amalickiah, Ammoron, Kishkumen, and Gadianton wanted was power among the people (and this is the curse of many leaders anciently and today). They sought to usurp God's authority by imposing perverse covenants of secrecy to murder and get gain. Yet what God expects of His people and His leaders is covenantal fidelity. Walk the path. Walk before God in faith and humility. Teach others to do the same. And by such faithfulness, the covenant keepers will gain power among the people. But they won't gain this power with the intent to get glory and gain but rather to encourage people to come unto God and be saved!

Mormon inserts his covenantal editorial voice into the story to explain yet again why humans struggle to remain loyal to God, even after He has been totally loyal to them. We are blessed when we put our trust in God. But too often we put our trust in the arm of flesh, in the vain things of this world. It is then that God allows afflictions to befall us so that we can experience the reality of being without His preserving presence.

> And thus we can behold how false, and also the unsteadiness of the hearts of the children of men; yea, we can see that the **Lord** in his great infinite goodness doth bless and **prosper those who put their trust in him** [like Abraham did]. Yea, and we may see at the very time when he doth prosper his people, yea, in the increase of their fields, their flocks and their herds, and in gold, and in silver, and in all manner of precious things of every kind and art; sparing their lives, and **delivering them out of the hands of their enemies**; softening the hearts of their enemies that they should not declare wars against them; yea, and in fine, **doing all things for the welfare and happiness of his people** [as He covenanted to do at Mount Moriah for Abraham and his posterity]; yea, then is the time that they do harden their hearts, and do forget the Lord their God, and do trample under their feet the Holy One [forgetting their covenantal obligations revealed at Sinai and through ongoing revelation from God's prophets]—yea, and this because of their ease, and their exceedingly great prosperity. (Helaman 12:1–2; emphasis added)

Mormon's tender love for each of God's children rings out from His words of truth, recorded ages ago and preserved for our day that we might not only know of the covenant path but also choose God and His promises. Mormon aches for us to be faithful to God as He has been faithful to us.

> Therefore, **blessed are they who will repent and hearken unto the voice of the Lord their God; for these are they that shall be saved.** And may God grant, in his great fulness, that men might be brought unto repentance and good works, that they might be **restored unto grace** for grace [God's love as promised at Mount Moriah to Abraham and his children], according to their works [loyalty to the obligations revealed

at Mount Sinai]. And I would that all men might be saved. But we read that in the great and last day there are some who shall be cast out, yea, who shall be cast off from the presence of the Lord; Yea, who shall be consigned to a state of endless misery, fulfilling the words which say: They that have done good [those who have striven to live loyal to God] shall have everlasting life; and they that have done evil [those who have had no desire to be among God's people] shall have everlasting damnation. And thus it is. Amen. (Helaman 12:23–26; emphasis added)

## Helaman 13–15: Role Reversal for Lamanites and Nephites. Samuel the Lamanite Preaches Covenantal Fidelity to the Nephites

From among the righteous, covenant-keeping Lamanites, God sent Samuel to preach to the Nephites. Once when the Nephites were pure and delightsome, when they were covenant keepers, they labored diligently to return the Lamanites to the covenant path. Now that the roles had reversed, the Lamanites desired to help the Nephites return to God's way.

Mormon uses covenantal terminology to explain that the Lamanites were now firmly holding to the rod of iron and walking in the covenant path:

> And now it came to pass in the eighty and sixth year, the Nephites did still remain in wickedness, yea, in great wickedness, while the **Lamanites did observe strictly to keep the commandments of God**, according to the law of Moses [which was the covenantal instructions for how to show fidelity to God, as He had shown fidelity to us as He promised to Abraham]. (Helaman 13:1)

There are two significant themes in Samuel the Lamanite's preaching. First, he highlighted the destruction awaiting those who persistently turn away from God, rejecting the covenant of the land of promise. Samuel wanted the Nephites to understand that they would suffer the consequences for breaking covenant with God. Second, Samuel preached of Jesus Christ, who is the source and power and center and life of the covenant path. Without Jesus there is no covenant path. Samuel wanted them to know that God Himself would visit them to confirm the covenant.

> Yea, heavy destruction awaiteth this people, and it surely cometh unto this people, and nothing can save this people save it be repentance and faith on the Lord Jesus Christ [return to the covenant path and be loyal to God], who surely shall come into the world, and shall suffer many things and shall be slain for his people. (Helaman 13:6)

Samuel the Lamanite went on to teach many things about what would befall the Nephites, prophesying of great destruction—as a consequence of being covenantally disobedient and disloyal—and the subsequent appearance of Jesus Christ to the people to confirm and update the covenantal instructions.

Samuel the Lamanite called with urgency and love. With the voice of God he invited the people to remember God's great deeds, that He is true and faithful and stands ready to deliver the promises to them. But fallen nature takes over and we seek to save ourselves. We grasp at trying on our own to make God's promises be realized. We think to do these things on our own terms and in our own way. We reject God's plan, thinking that we have a better plan for bringing peace and prosperity to our lives.

> But behold, your days of probation are past; ye have procrastinated the day of your salvation until it is everlastingly too late, and your destruction is made sure; yea, for **ye have sought all the days of your lives for that which ye could not obtain**; and ye have sought for happiness in doing iniquity, **which thing is contrary to the nature of that righteousness which is in our great and Eternal Head.** [In other words, the covenant path cannot and does not allow for prosperity and happiness except by being loyal to God.] O ye people of the land, that ye would hear my words! And I pray that the

anger of the Lord be turned away from you, and that ye would repent and be saved. (Helaman 13:38–39; emphasis added)

Samuel continued his words of covenantal warning with a description of the mighty transformation that had occurred among the Lamanites because of their choice to trust the promises God made to Abraham and to show that trust by entering the covenant path of loyalty to keep the commandments as revealed to Moses.

But behold my brethren, the Lamanites hath he hated because their deeds have been evil continually [hate is a covenantal word meaning "off the covenant path, not in covenantal relationship with God"], and this because of the iniquity of the tradition of their fathers. But behold, salvation hath come unto them through the preaching of the Nephites; and for this intent hath the Lord prolonged their days. And I would that ye should behold that the more part of them are in the path of their duty, and **they do walk circumspectly before God**, and they do **observe to keep his commandments** and his statutes and his judgments **according to the law of Moses**. Yea, I say unto you, that the more part of them are doing this, and they are striving with unwearied diligence that they may bring the remainder of their brethren to the knowledge of the truth; therefore there are many who do add to their numbers daily. And behold, ye do know of yourselves, for ye have witnessed it, that as many of them as are brought to the knowledge of the truth, and to know of the wicked and abominable traditions of their fathers, and are led to **believe the holy scriptures** [containing the covenantal instructions], yea, the prophecies of the holy prophets, which are written, which leadeth them to faith on the Lord, and unto repentance, which faith and repentance bringeth a change of heart unto them—Therefore, as many as have come to this, ye know of yourselves are firm and steadfast in the faith, and in the thing wherewith they have been **made free**. [Being made free in Christ is the purpose of the covenant path, as we trust God's covenant to

Abraham we show loyalty by keeping the commandments and receive the promised blessings.] (Helaman 15:4–8)

The final words of Samuel are these, saturated in the doctrines of the Mount Moriah and Mount Sinai covenants.

> Therefore, saith the Lord: **I will not utterly destroy them** [the Lamanites], but I will cause that in the day of my wisdom they shall return again unto me, saith the Lord [as He covenanted to Father Abraham to do]. And now behold, saith the Lord, concerning the people of the **Nephites: If they will not repent, and observe to do my will, I will utterly destroy them**, saith the Lord, because of their unbelief [their covenantal disloyalty] notwithstanding the many mighty works which I have done among them [God's covenantal loyalty]; and as surely as the Lord liveth shall these things be, saith the Lord. (Helaman 15:16–17)

The word of God is simple and pure. God is loyal to His covenants. He offers us salvation. He does great deeds and wonders to convince us to believe and trust Him. He then teaches us His expectations for our loyalty—the commandments. But whoever persistently and consistently rejects the word of God, resists the word of God, and refuses to show loyalty to God, will ultimately experience the consequences of such covenantal disloyalty—to be eternally shut out of the presence of God.

# CHAPTER 21

## 3 NEPHI: THE COVENANT IS FULFILLED IN JESUS CHRIST

The rotten and corrupting wickedness of the Nephites increased in the years after Samuel the Lamanite. Despite a momentary mass conversion as people remembered God's goodness when the star of Jesus's birth was revealed, soon thereafter the people returned to the perverting covenants of the Gadianton robbers.

Massive destruction hung over the Nephites and Lamanites because of the Gadianton robbers. Those who were faithful to God's covenants joined together as a single people while everyone else covenanted to be followers of the leaders of the Gadianton robbers. The people of God were threatened with extermination by the mighty power of the robbers. But there were yet righteous leaders in the land who lived and taught people their covenantal duties: "Now behold, this Lachoneus, the governor, was a just man [he walked and taught the covenant path]" (3 Nephi 3:12). Lachoneus had total trust in God, like Abraham did. He knew that if he and his people were true and faithful to God, they would be preserved in the land. In addition to giving commands to prepare for their physical salvation (see 3 Nephi 3:12–14),

Lachoneus went forth among the people preaching repentance and covenantal fidelity:

> [Lachoneus] did cause that his people should cry unto the Lord for strength against the time that the robbers should come down against them. . . . Yea, he said unto them: As the Lord liveth, except ye repent of all your iniquities, and cry unto the Lord, ye will in nowise be delivered out of the hands of those Gadianton robbers. And so great and marvelous were the words and prophecies of Lachoneus that they did cause fear to come upon all the people; and they did exert themselves in their might to do according to the words of Lachoneus. . . . And they did fortify themselves against their enemies; and they did dwell in one land, and in one body, and they did fear the words which had been spoken by Lachoneus, insomuch that they did repent of all their sins; and they did put up their prayers unto the Lord their God, that he would deliver them in the time that their enemies should come down against them to battle. (3 Nephi 3:12, 15–16, 25)

Because of their faithfulness, God preserved the righteous, covenant-keeping Lamanites and Nephites from the Gadianton robbers. When their war was over, they cried out to God in gratitude and recognition that only He could save them. Notice the title they use for God in these praises of joy. The people specifically refer to "the God of Abraham, and the God of Isaac, and the God of Jacob." We learned earlier that this phrase specifically evokes the covenantal obligations of God to save His faithful people, so that His people can have total faith and trust in Him just as their patriarchal ancestors did.

> May the Lord preserve his people in righteousness and in holiness of heart, that they may cause to be felled to the earth all who shall seek to slay them because of power and secret combinations, even as this man hath been felled to the earth. And they did rejoice and cry again with one voice, saying: **May the God of Abraham, and the God of Isaac, and the God of Jacob, protect this people in righteousness** [God's

covenantal duties], **so long as they shall call on the name of their God for protection** [our covenantal duties]. And it came to pass that they did break forth, all as one, in singing, and praising their God for the great thing which he had done for them, in preserving them from falling into the hands of their enemies. (3 Nephi 4:29–31; emphasis added)

God's people also praised Him using the words and titles also used by Abraham. By this we can see that the covenant people recognized and accepted that the God of Abraham is the one who is mighty to save. He can be trusted to fulfill His covenantal promises.

> Yea, they did cry: Hosanna to the **Most High God**. And they did cry: Blessed be the name of the **Lord God Almighty, the Most High God**. And their hearts were swollen with joy, unto the gushing out of many tears, because of the great goodness of God in delivering them out of the hands of their enemies; and they knew it was because of their repentance and their humility [keeping the covenantal instructions revealed to Moses] that they had been delivered from an everlasting destruction. (3 Nephi 4:32–33; emphasis added)

Had the people not been faithful to God, they could not have had access to His mighty saving power. That is the deal. That is the agreement. God freely and fully offers His mighty power. But we can lose access to that free gift when we turn off the covenant path. Only by turning (repenting) back to loyalty through covenant making and covenant keeping can we again experience the saving presence of God in our lives.

## 3 Nephi 5: Mormon's Personal Disclosure and Introduction

What is remarkable about Mormon as an author, historian, editor, and abridger is how little he has us focus on him. He knew that his real purpose was to reveal Jesus to his readers and to reveal the covenant path. The purpose of the Book of Mormon is *not* for us to know Mormon, but for us to know the source of our covenantal salvation—Jesus Christ. 3 Nephi 5 contains one of the rare autobiographical moments that Mormon disclosed. When he did, his language was thoroughly covenantal language.

> Behold, I am a disciple of Jesus Christ, the Son of God. [Mormon is a loyal covenant-maker and -keeper.] I have been called of him to declare his word among his people, that they might have everlasting life. [Faithful leaders are under covenantal obligation to teach the covenant path.] (3 Nephi 5:13)

Further, Mormon explained his covenantal obligations to preserve and record the covenants for future generations, "And it hath become expedient that I, according to the will of God, that the prayers of those who have gone hence, who were the holy ones, should be fulfilled according to their faith, should make a record of these things which have been done" (3 Nephi 5:14).

Mormon went on to highlight God's good deeds (from the perspective of the Abrahamic covenant) while reinforcing that we owe our loyalty to God.

> I have reason to bless my God and my Savior Jesus Christ, that he brought our fathers out of the land of Jerusalem [Abrahamic covenant], (and no one knew it save it were himself and those whom he brought out of that land) and that he hath given me and my people so much knowledge unto the salvation of our souls [Abrahamic covenant, God's covenantal duties]. Surely he hath blessed the house of Jacob, and hath been merciful unto the seed of Joseph [Abrahamic covenant, God's covenantal duties]. And insomuch as the children of Lehi have kept his commandments he hath blessed them and prospered them according to his word [Mosaic covenant, our covenantal duties]. Yea, and surely shall he again bring a remnant of the seed of Joseph to the knowledge of the Lord their God [Abrahamic covenant, God's covenantal duties]. And as surely as the Lord liveth, will he gather in from the four quarters of the earth all the remnant of the seed of

Jacob, who are scattered abroad upon all the face of the earth [Abrahamic covenant, God's covenantal duties]. And as he hath covenanted with all the house of Jacob, even so shall the covenant wherewith he hath covenanted with the house of Jacob be fulfilled in his own due time, unto the restoring all the house of Jacob unto the knowledge of the covenant that he hath covenanted with them [Abrahamic covenant, God's covenantal duties]. And then shall they know their Redeemer, who is Jesus Christ, the Son of God; and then shall they be gathered in from the four quarters of the earth unto their own lands, from whence they have been dispersed; yea, as the Lord liveth so shall it be [Abrahamic covenant, God's covenantal duties]. Amen. (3 Nephi 5:20–26)

## 3 Nephi 6–10: The Rise of Pride Leads to Destruction

Unfortunately, soon after the mighty deeds of great salvation God did for the combined faithful of Nephites and Lamanites, they turned away from God and resurrected the awful and damning false covenants taught by Gadianton. Just like the Israelites who saw with their own eyes and experienced God's salvation in their own lives and yet then wandered for years murmuring faithlessly in the wilderness, the Nephites turned to the utmost wickedness, "like a dog to his vomit" (3 Nephi 7:8).

We know this story arc. Those who are covenantally unfaithful must suffer the consequences of broken covenants. God will destroy them.

That terrible destruction is detailed in 3 Nephi 8. Mormon then recorded in 3 Nephi 9–10 God's covenantal explanation for the destruction that befell the people using phrases that sound reminiscent of why God wiped out humanity with a flood in the days of Noah.

> To hide their iniquities and their abominations from before my face, that the blood of the prophets and the saints shall not come any more unto me against them. (3 Nephi 9:5)

To hide their wickedness and abominations from before my face, that the blood of the prophets and the saints shall not come up any more unto me against them. (3 Nephi 9:7)

To hide their wickedness and abominations from before my face, that the blood of the prophets and the saints should not come up any more unto me against them. (3 Nephi 9:8)

To destroy them from before my face, that the blood of the prophets and the saints should not come up unto me any more against them. (3 Nephi 9:9)

That their wickedness and abominations might be hid from before my face, that the blood of the prophets and the saints whom I sent among them might not cry unto me from the ground against them. (3 Nephi 9:11)

Sadly, had the people turned to God for atonement, they would have been covered and protected. Remember the Israelites who were told to take blood from a slain lamb and cover the lintels of their doorposts? The destroying angel passed those households by because they have been covered, hidden, or protected by the atoning blood of the lamb. The word "atonement" in Hebrew means to cover or hide. Because the people would not accept the covering of the Atonement, to hide (or blot out) their sins, God was covenantally obligated to hide their sins using other means.

As the destruction ceased and darkness covered the land, God introduced Himself and explained the covenantal purposes of the plan of salvation.

> Behold, I am Jesus Christ the Son of God. I created the heavens and the earth, and all things that in them are. I was with the Father from the beginning. I am in the Father, and the Father in me; and in me hath the Father glorified his name. I came unto my own, and my own received me not. And the scriptures concerning my coming are fulfilled. And as many as have received me, to them have I given to become the sons of God [Abrahamic covenant, God's obligations]; and even so will I to as many as shall believe on my name [Mosaic covenant, our

obligations], for behold, by me redemption cometh, and in me is the law of Moses fulfilled. (3 Nephi 9:15–17)

Instead of demonstrating faithful loyalty by sacrificing animals, the new covenantal stipulation is to sacrifice our own hearts and be baptized.

And ye shall offer up unto me no more the shedding of blood; yea, your sacrifices and your burnt offerings shall be done away, for I will accept none of your sacrifices and your burnt offerings. And ye shall offer for a sacrifice unto me a broken heart and a contrite spirit. And whoso cometh unto me with a broken heart and a contrite spirit, him will I baptize with fire and with the Holy Ghost. (3 Nephi 9:19–20)

How has God been faithful to His promises to Abraham?

Behold, I have come unto the world to bring redemption unto the world, to save the world from sin. (3 Nephi 9:21)

God expects us to be loyal, too, as He has been loyal. The final verse of this chapter chiastically lays out the covenant path.

> A Therefore, whoso repenteth and cometh unto me as a little child [Mosaic covenant, our obligations],
> > B him will I receive [Abrahamic covenant, God's obligations],
> > B' for of such is the kingdom of God. Behold, for such I have laid down my life, and have taken it up again [Abrahamic covenant, God's obligations];
> A' therefore repent, and come unto me ye ends of the earth, and be saved [Mosaic covenant, our obligations]. (3 Nephi 9:22)

Who were those that were spared destruction? Given what we know of the covenant path we should expect to see that those who had endeavored to be loyal to God were preserved. That is indeed what Mormon reported in 3 Nephi 10, in chiastic structure.

> A And it was the more righteous part [more loyal to God] of the people who were saved,
> > B and it was they who received the prophets and stoned them not;

B' and it was they who had not shed the blood of the saints,
A' who were spared. (3 Nephi 10:12)

## 3 Nephi 11–26: Jesus Teaches the Ordinances and Doctrines of the Covenant Path

When Jesus visited His people in the Americas, He reinstituted the covenant path. The first thing He did was let the people see, feel, and know that He was the Lamb that God had promised to provide at Mount Moriah (see Genesis 22:14).

> Behold, I am Jesus Christ, whom the prophets testified shall come into the world. And behold, I am the light and the life of the world; and I have drunk out of that bitter cup which the Father hath given me, and have glorified the Father in taking upon me the sins of the world, in the which I have suffered the will of the Father in all things from the beginning. . . . Arise and come forth unto me, that ye may thrust your hands into my side, and also that ye may feel the prints of the nails in my hands and in my feet, that ye may **know that I am the God of Israel** [Abrahamic covenant], and the God of the whole earth, and have been **slain for the sins of the world** [Abrahamic covenant. At Mount Moriah God promised to provide a lamb]. (3 Nephi 11:10–11, 14; emphasis added)

After receiving everyone into His presence, Jesus called forth Nephi (the son of Nephi, son of Helaman) and gave him power to baptize (see 3 Nephi 11:21). Why would this be so crucial? To enter into the covenant path we must proceed through the gate of baptism. We cannot enter into the covenant path without baptism and taking upon ourselves the name of Jesus Christ. God cannot save those who only know His name. These same people must also be willing to follow Him and to be in covenant relationship with Him. Baptism is that invitation to covenantal faithfulness.

Jesus also reiterated several times that there should be no disputation about baptism. Think of it. If we spend our time fighting, wrangling, and haranguing each other about how to baptize, we may mislead ourselves and others away from the very gateway onto the covenant path God has established. God keeps things simple; humans make them more complex. God wants to be our God and He wants us to be His people. We show love by having faith in the God of Abraham, Isaac, and Jacob, who is mighty to save and who will deliver us. We demonstrate that faith by repenting. Repentance is demonstrated through baptism and the reception of the Holy Ghost, who prospers and helps us to endure to the end. Enduring the end includes renewing these covenants and making other priesthood covenants such as those experienced in the temple. We renew our love and loyalty to God on a weekly basis at the Passover renewal ceremony where our sins are covered by the Atonement and the destroying angel passes by us. That ordinance is called the sacrament.

If you ever wondered about your standing before God and your loyalty to Him, ask yourself these simple questions:

- Do I regularly and willingly partake of the sacrament?
- Do I recognize that when I do so, I am showing my love and loyalty to God?
- Do I recognize that when I pledge my love and loyalty to God, I am not claiming to be without sin or blemish because only God can make me whole?
- Do I realize that I am showing my desire to be in a covenantal relationship with God?
- Do I willingly assent to seek to be faithful to God?

Too often we think we have to be perfect (that is, without sin) *before* we partake of the sacrament. But only God can make us whole and without sin and blemish. The only perfection we can attain in this life is the covenantal perfection of being lovingly loyal to God. Sincere, purposeful, and meaningful participation in the weekly sacrament is a powerful way to show loyalty to God.

Jesus further reinforced the fundamental doctrine of the covenantal relationship.

And this is my doctrine, and it is the doctrine which the Father hath given unto me; and I bear record of the Father, and the Father beareth record of me, and the Holy Ghost beareth record of the Father and me; and I bear record that the Father commandeth all men, everywhere, to **repent and believe in me** [Mosaic covenant, our obligations]. And whoso believeth in me, and is baptized, the same shall be saved; and they are they who shall **inherit the kingdom of God** [Abrahamic covenant, God's obligations]. . . . Verily, verily, I say unto you, that this is my doctrine, and I bear record of it from the Father; and whoso **believeth in me** [covenant with the Son] **believeth in the Father** also [covenant with the Father]; and unto him will the Father bear record of me, for he will visit him with fire and with the Holy Ghost. (3 Nephi 11:32–33, 35; emphasis added)

And He taught how the Mosaic and Abrahamic covenants mutually reinforce each other. When we live loyal to God, His blessings are fully available to us. And God's chosen leaders are those who preserve and teach the instructions revealed by God of the covenant path.

Verily, verily, I say unto you, that this is my doctrine, and whoso buildeth upon this buildeth upon my rock [Mosaic covenant, our obligations], and the gates of hell shall not prevail against them [Abrahamic covenant, God's obligations]. And whoso shall declare more or less than this, and establish it for my doctrine, the same cometh of evil [don't teach false covenants, and do not change the stipulations of the covenantal agreement], and is not built upon my rock; but he buildeth upon a sandy foundation, and the gates of hell stand open to receive such when the floods come and the winds beat upon them. Therefore, go forth unto this people, and declare the words which I have spoken, unto the ends of the earth. [In other words, covenantally faithful leaders live and teach the instructions of the covenant path.] (3 Nephi 11:39–41)

Some wonder why Jesus would declare the Sermon on the Mount to the Nephites. When we read the Book of Mormon through the lens of the covenant path, the answer is obvious. In fact, as covenant readers, we should expect to hear Jesus, as the new Moses, update and clarify the obligations, stipulations, and instructions for covenantal loyalty. That is exactly what happens in the Book of Mormon. After the people had been taught over so many centuries to live the Law of Moses, Jesus fulfilled the law and then appeared to the people to show them a higher way of love and loyalty. And just as Jesus had told the Jews in the old world to be loyal to these new expectations, He invited the same loyalty from the Nephites and Lamanites.

Notice the difference in His statement to the Nephites and Lamanites compared to what He said to the Jews. To the Jews, He only highlighted that God had been perfect. But to the Nephites, Jesus included Himself. Because Jesus had fully completed the mission that God had sent Him on, Jesus was fully and totally loyal to God. He had been perfect to the covenantal expectations.

> Therefore I would that ye should be perfect even as I, or your Father who is in heaven is perfect. (3 Nephi 12:48)

After a full day of transforming experiences and instructions (see 3 Nephi 11–16), Jesus asked the people to spend time pondering His words (see 3 Nephi 17). Remember that righteous leaders and people are expected to preserve and ponder the covenantal instructions of God's love. He then instituted the sacrament among them (see 3 Nephi 18). We discussed above the covenantal significance of sacrament. We see here how beautiful and simple is the covenant path. Jesus does not give us confusing instructions, or hard-to-understand commandments. The order of His church—the ordinances—are beautiful in their simplicity and salvific in their intent.

Jesus's second day was fully packed with covenantal instruction. Consider this: The highest concentration of the word "covenant" across any two back-to-back chapters anywhere in the Book of Mormon occurs in 3 Nephi 20–21! If we include the section 3 Nephi 20–22, we see a beautiful literary structure that centers on God's covenants with the House of Israel.

>A The Father and Son work together (3 Nephi 20:10)
>>B Isaiah's words are written, therefore search them (v. 11)
>>>C Isaiah's words and the Father's covenant with Israel will be fulfilled (v. 12)
>>>>D Scattered Israel to be gathered (v. 13)
>>>>>E America an inheritance for the Nephites/Lamanites (v. 14)
>>>>>>F Gentiles to repent & receive blessings or be destroyed (v. 15–20)
>>>>>>>G A New Jerusalem and the Lord's covenant with Moses, the Gentiles, etc. (v. 21–29)
>>>>>>>>H Gospel preached and Zion established; the marred servant (v. 30–44)
>>>>>>>>>I Kings shall be speechless (v. 45)
>>>>>>>>>>J Covenant fulfillment and the work of the Father (v. 46)
>>>>>>>>>>>K A key sign to be given when things are "about to take place" (3 Nephi 21:1)
>>>>>>>>>>>>L Gentiles learn of scattered Israel (v. 2)
>>>>>>>>>>>>>M These things in the Book of Mormon to come from Gentiles to you (v. 3)
>>>>>>>>>>>>>>N Sign of the Father's covenant with the house of Israel (v. 4)
>>>>>>>>>>>>>M' These works in the Book of Mormon to come from Gentiles to you (v.5)
>>>>>>>>>>>>L' Some Gentiles to be with Israel (v. 6)
>>>>>>>>>>>K' Sign as Lamanites begin to know that the work "hath commenced" (v. 7)
>>>>>>>>>>J' Work and covenant of the Father (v. 7)
>>>>>>>>>I' Kings shall be speechless (v. 8)
>>>>>>>>H' A great and marvelous work; the marred servant (v. 9–10; cf. Isaiah 52:14)
>>>>>>>G' Moses, the Gentiles and covenant Israel (v. 11)
>>>>>>F' Unrepentant Gentiles will be cut down (v. 12–21; cf. Micah 5:8–15)
>>>>>E' America an inheritance for the righteous (v. 22–23)

D' Gentiles to help in the gathering of Israel and a New Jerusalem (v. 24–25)

C' Father's work with His people (v. 26–27)

A' The Father and Son work together (v. 28–29)

B' Isaiah's portrayal of Zion (Isaiah 54); search his words. (3 Nephi 22; 23:1–3)

(Modified from "Why Did Jesus Mix Together Micah and Isaiah?" Book of Mormon Central *KnoWhy #214*.)

We should spend a moment on the center spot of this literary unit in the Book of Mormon since Mormon was seeking to concentrate our attention on the covenants of the Father:

> For it is wisdom in the Father that they should be established in this land, and be set up as a free people by the power of the Father, that these things might come forth from them unto a remnant of your seed, that **the covenant of the Father** [the Abrahamic promises] may be fulfilled which he hath covenanted with his people, O house of Israel. (3 Nephi 21:4; emphasis added)

God's promises cannot be fulfilled without a promised land. It's God's covenantal role to provide the promised land. It is our covenantal role to show loyalty to the God of the land. If we do, we remain free and prosperous. To show disloyalty is to reject God, to reject His covenant, and to reject His promised land. The consequence will be our utter removal from off the land.

This very point is forcefully made a few verses later:

> Therefore it shall come to pass that **whosoever will not believe in my words** [those who will not accept and stay loyal to our covenantal obligations], who am Jesus Christ, which the Father shall cause him to bring forth unto the Gentiles, and shall give unto him power that he shall bring them forth unto the Gentiles, (it shall be done even as Moses said) they shall be cut off from among my people who are of the covenant. . . . For it shall come to pass, saith the Father, that at that day **whosoever will not repent and come unto my Beloved Son** [Mosaic covenant, our obligations], them will

I cut off from among my people, O house of Israel. (3 Nephi 21:11, 20; emphasis added)

But if we are true and faithful to God, if we join in covenantal relationship and strive to be loyal, even though we battle our fallen natures, even though we don't always do everything as perfectly as we wish, if we remain true to God, we have His promise to be in His presence, to prosper eternally:

> But if they will repent and hearken unto my words, and harden not their hearts, I will establish **my church** among them, and they shall come in unto **the covenant** and be numbered among this **the remnant of Jacob**, unto whom I have given this land for their inheritance. . . . And then shall the power of heaven come down among them; and **I also will be in the midst**. (3 Nephi 21:22, 25; emphasis added)

To reinforce covenantal thinking, promises, and possibilities, Jesus then quoted Isaiah 54 (see 3 Nephi 22), explained the words of Isaiah and of Samuel the Lamanite (see 3 Nephi 23), and quoted Malachi 3–4 (see 3 Nephi 24–25).

Jesus declared, "Great are the words of Isaiah" (3 Nephi 23:1). When we listen to Jesus's declaration from a covenantal context, we see Isaiah through fresh eyes. We aren't simply to read Isaiah because he was a powerful prophetic and poetic writer who used vivid word imagery to bring his message home with force. We now see that we should read Isaiah covenantally. When we read Isaiah, especially the Isaiah sections quoted in the Book of Mormon (as well as the quotes from other Bible prophets), we should diligently search for how his words reinforce God's covenantal obligations to Abraham and his descendants while instructing us on our covenantal obligations to God under the Mosaic covenant.

I wonder if the covenant path (marked by the two covenantal mountains) is what Jesus taught the Nephites when Mormon recorded the following: "And now it came to pass that when Jesus **had expounded all the scriptures in** one which they had written, he commanded them that **they should teach** the things which he had expounded unto them" (3 Nephi 23:14; emphasis added). I would not be surprised if this explaining and teaching of scriptures highlighted the covenant path.

Mormon then concluded the section on Jesus's visit to the Nephites by explaining what our duties are. Listen to our covenantal obligations. If we are true and faithful to what has been revealed, we will receive more light and truth. If we fail to stay true to the covenant, we lose what could have been and we lose what we have been given.

> And when they shall have received this [covenantal instruction], which is expedient that they should have first, **to try their faith** [test our loyalty to God in following these covenantal instructions], and if it shall so be that they shall **believe these things** [show covenantal loyalty] then shall the greater things be made manifest unto them. And if it so be that they will **not believe these things** [show covenantal disloyalty], then shall the greater things be withheld from them, unto their condemnation. (3 Nephi 26:9–10; emphasis added)

All those who were there at Jesus's visitation

> taught, and did minister one to another; and they had all things common among them, every man dealing justly, one with another. And it came to pass that **they did do all things even as Jesus had commanded them** [they were within the covenant, they were loyal and faithful]. And they who were baptized in the name of Jesus were called the church of Christ. (3 Nephi 26:19–21; emphasis added)

The original meaning of "church" is "those who are called to gather together." When we join the covenant with God, we are gathered together and that creates a church. To be members of the Church means to be members of God's covenant. Wherever there is the Church, there is the covenant. Covenant making inevitably leads to an organized community of covenant makers and covenant keepers. That is church.

## 3 Nephi 27–30: The Covenantal Purpose of the Book of Mormon Revealed

Before Mormon concluded 3 Nephi, he spends two chapters documenting additional instructions and empowerment from God to His Nephite disciples. These instructions and power enabled the disciples to succeed in their mission to convert people to Jesus and the covenant path in 4 Nephi.

Mormon then used the last two chapters of 3 Nephi to reveal the covenantal purpose of the Book of Mormon. Mormon spoke to us. God is a covenant-making and a covenant-keeping God. God will remember His covenant to Abraham, Isaac, and Jacob. God will do all that He promised. No one can stop Him from His work. And we would be wise to join Him in this loyal labor of love instead of standing in the way as an obstacle on the cov-enant path. 3 Nephi 29 focuses on God's obligations within the Abrahamic covenant:

> And now behold, I say unto you that when the Lord shall see fit, in his wisdom, that these sayings [the Book of Mormon] shall come unto the Gentiles according to his word, then ye may know that the covenant which the Father hath made with the children of Israel [the Abrahamic covenant, God's obligations], concerning their restoration to the lands of their inheritance, is already beginning to be fulfilled. And ye may know that the **words of the Lord**, which have been spoken by the holy prophets, **shall all be fulfilled** [Abrahamic covenant]; and ye need not say that the Lord delays his coming unto the children of Israel. And ye need not imagine in your hearts that the words which have been spoken are vain, for behold, **the Lord will remember his covenant** [Abrahamic covenant] which he hath made unto his people of the house of Israel. And when ye shall see these sayings coming forth among you, then ye need not any longer spurn at the doings of the Lord, for the sword of his justice is in his right hand; and behold, at that day, if ye shall spurn at his doings he will cause that it shall soon overtake you. Wo unto him that spurneth at

the doings of the Lord; yea, wo unto him that shall deny the Christ and his works [in breaking the Mosaic covenant we will suffer the consequences]! Yea, **wo unto him that shall deny the revelations of the Lord** [who deny the covenantal instructions], and that shall say the Lord no longer worketh by revelation, or by prophecy, or by gifts, or by tongues, or by healings, or by the power of the Holy Ghost [these are all signals of a living and vibrant covenantal community]! Yea, and wo unto him that shall say at that day, to get gain, that there can be no miracle wrought by Jesus Christ; for he that doeth this shall become like unto the son of perdition, for whom there was no mercy, according to the word of Christ! Yea, and ye need not any longer hiss, nor spurn, nor make game of the Jews, nor any of the remnant of the house of Israel; for behold, **the Lord remembereth his covenant** [Abrahamic covenant] unto them, and he will do unto them according to that which he hath sworn. Therefore ye need not suppose that ye can turn the right hand of the Lord unto the left [we *cannot* stop Him from fulfilling His covenantal obligations], that he may not execute judgment unto the **fulfilling of the covenant which he hath made unto the house of Israel**. (3 Nephi 29)

3 Nephi 30 focuses on our obligation as revealed through the Mosaic covenant and in subsequent revealed updates through Jesus and other prophets:

> Hearken, O ye Gentiles, and hear the words of Jesus Christ, the Son of the living God, which he hath commanded me that I should speak concerning you, for, behold he commandeth me that I should write, saying: Turn, all ye Gentiles, from your wicked ways; and repent of your evil doings, of your lyings and deceivings, and of your whoredoms, and of your secret abominations, and your idolatries, and of your murders, and your priestcrafts, and your envyings, and your strifes, and from all your wickedness and abominations, and come unto me, and be baptized in my name, that ye may receive a remission of your sins, and be filled with the Holy Ghost, that

ye may be numbered with my people who are of the house of Israel. (3 Nephi 30)

How much clearer could the Book of Mormon be to reveal the covenant path? Mormon was undoubtedly inspired to record and teach us the covenant path in the plainest manner possible.

# CHAPTER 22

# 4 NEPHI: THE RISE AND FALL OF GOD'S COVENANT PEOPLE

After Jesus returned to the Father and His ongoing covenantal work, the disciples of Jesus Christ did as Jesus commanded. They went forth among all the people, teaching with mighty faith and power the covenant path of instructions that Jesus had revealed. Though they suffered and endured many difficulties, over the course of some years a majority of people throughout the land, both Nephites and Lamanites, accepted God's covenants and joined themselves with the church. Thus was initiated the longest period of peace and prosperity ever known in recorded history. When people choose to live God's revealed commands, we receive all the greatest blessings we could ever desire, even the presence of God. Alternatively, when we fear, when we believe that we have to do everything on our own to bring to pass God's promises, that is when we fight, and kill, and steal, and lie, and rage, and drag ourselves and others into the pit of destruction and despair. If only we could all be as believing and faithful as these covenant-making and covenant-keeping Nephites and Lamanites who for generations showed loving loyalty to God and lived in peace and happiness that few people in world's history have truly known.

*The Covenant Path in the Bible and the Book of Mormon* 309

Sadly, as the generations progressed, people allowed their fallen and carnal natures to drive them to reject God as the King and covenantal promise provider. The people sought to bring to pass their own success and happiness following forbidden paths. They wanted human kings to replace God. They wanted the material comforts of the world delivered to them on their terms, not on the covenantal terms God had revealed. They reveled in their pride, creating stories that their own righteousness was the cause of their blessings instead of seeing that only God was the cause behind all that they were and had.

> And now, in this two hundred and first year there began to be among them those who were lifted up in pride, such as the wearing of costly apparel, and all manner of fine pearls, and of the fine things of the world. And from that time forth they did have their goods and their substance no more common among them. And they began to be divided into classes; and they began to build up churches unto themselves to get gain, and began to **deny the true church of Christ.** [In other words, they rejected the covenantal community and the covenant that Jesus revealed as an update to the Mosaic covenant.] (4 Nephi 1:24–26; emphasis added)

Such was the wickedness and pride that people started creating their own churches. They created their own "covenantal" communities. They changed the nature of God's covenants. (Remember in Deuteronomy 12:32, God had explicitly commanded humans to *not* change the covenantal agreement or they would suffer the consequences.) These gospel perverters wanted to dictate to God the terms of His agreements. And they hijacked the powerfully simple ordinance of loyalty, the sacrament, to bind people to their own false covenantal communities.

> And it came to pass that when two hundred and ten years had passed away there were many churches in the land; yea, there were many churches which professed to know the Christ, and yet **they did deny the more parts of his gospel** [rejected the updated Sinai covenant], insomuch that they did receive all

manner of wickedness, and did administer that which was sacred [the sacrament is only meant for those who are sincerely willing to be covenantally loyal to God] unto him to whom it had been forbidden because of unworthiness. (4 Nephi 1:27; emphasis added)

Eventually a clear split occurred in the covenantal community. Those who were true believers, those who were loyal to God, were called Nephites, while those who rejected the covenant and no longer believed were called Lamanites (Laman = *La* "not" *aman* "believing/faithful"):

And it came to pass that in this year there arose a people who were called the Nephites, and they were true believers in Christ. . . . And it came to pass that they who rejected the gospel [the covenant path] were called Lamanites . . . ; and they did not dwindle in unbelief, but they did wilfully rebel against the gospel of Christ; and they did teach their children that they should not believe, even as their fathers, from the beginning, did dwindle. (4 Nephi 1:36, 38)

This is the covenantal summary of 4 Nephi. We can clearly see the doctrine of the two ways: the covenant path or the path of destruction away from God's covenants.

# CHAPTER 23

## MORMON: OUR COVENANTAL INSTRUCTOR AND GUIDE

God's people were ripe for destruction because of infidelity to the covenants. Nevertheless, Mormon continued to labor, as a good leader should do, to physically protect the promised land, and to teach the people their covenantal responsibilities.

Mormon lived during the final years of the Nephite civilization. He witnessed the total and final destruction of his people. Having all the records before him and having a perfect knowledge of the covenant path, Mormon could see clearly the causes and consequences of the fall of the Nephites. They had been covenantally unfaithful. God had waited, persisted, and called to them in loving kindness, asking them to return to the covenant path. As the Landlord of the promised land, God was and is under covenantal obligation to remove from the land those who are disloyal. Mormon reluctantly came to the same conclusion that God had reached.

> And it came to pass that my sorrow did return unto me again, and I saw that **the day of grace was passed with them** [their access to God's freely given promises was blocked because of their unfaithfulness to the covenant], both temporally and spiritually; for I saw thousands of them hewn down in open

rebellion against their God, and heaped up as dung upon the face of the land. (Mormon 2:15; emphasis added)

Mormon was filled with love for his fellow brothers and sisters. In fact, Mormon's name likely comes from the Egyptian phrase "[God's] love endures forever" or "charity never faileth." Mormon wanted his people to feel of God's love. He wanted them to know and taste of the joy of salvation, to find peace and prosperity in the land, as God had promised. But he was heartbroken by the reality of their covenantal disloyalty:

> And I, being fifteen years of age and being somewhat of a sober mind, therefore I was visited of the Lord, and tasted and knew of the goodness of Jesus. And I did endeavor to preach unto this people, but my mouth was shut, and I was forbidden that I should preach unto them; for behold **they had wilfully rebelled against their God**; and the beloved disciples were taken away out of the land, because of their iniquity. But I did remain among them, but I was forbidden to preach unto them, because of the hardness of their hearts; and **because of the hardness of their hearts the land was cursed for their sake.** [As we know, the covenant land is only blessed for those who keep their covenants.] (Mormon 1:15–17; emphasis added)

Despite his searing discouragement at the wickedness he witnessed, Mormon roused himself to fight and defend his land. He encouraged his men to do the same. Like Captain Moroni who convinced the Nephites to fight because of their covenant to defend their religion, their freedom, and the promised land (see Alma 46:12–22, see especially v. 20), Mormon also tried to rouse his men. But he could only encourage the Nephites to fight for their families and homes, not for the covenant of the promised land:

> And it came to pass that I did speak unto my people, and did urge them with great energy, that they would stand boldly before the Lamanites and fight for their wives, and their children, and their houses, and their homes. (Mormon 2:23)

*The Covenant Path in the Bible and the Book of Mormon* 313

Notice how Mormon is different than Captain Moroni. Mormon did not speak to the Nephites in the covenantal terms of religion, freedom, and the promised land. Why? Because the people had left God's covenant, so they no longer had access to His prospering influence. Without the prosperity of God (the presence of His Spirit), they were on their own. God would not fight their battles, and this endangered their property, posterity, and very lives.

> And it came to pass that when they had fled we did pursue them with our armies, and did meet them again, and did beat them; nevertheless **the strength of the Lord was not with us**; yea, we were left to ourselves, that **the Spirit of the Lord did not abide in us** [if we leave the Mount Sinai covenant we have no access to the enduring presence of the Lord]; therefore we had become weak like unto our brethren. (Mormon 2:26; emphasis added)

God gave the Nephites one more opportunity to return to the covenant path. He commanded Mormon to preach these words to the people:

> Cry unto this people—Repent ye, and come unto me, and be ye baptized, and build up again my church, and ye shall be spared. And I did cry unto this people, but it was in vain; and they did not realize that it was the Lord that had spared them, and granted unto them a chance for repentance. And behold **they did harden their hearts against the Lord their God** [they rejected the covenantal invitation to join the covenant path]. (Mormon 3:2–3; emphasis added)

Soon after rejecting Mormon's invitation to return to God through covenant making, the Nephites won a major victory. But who did they glorify? Themselves. Instead of honoring the Divine Warrior who protected them and their promised land, they thought they were the gods and kings who had delivered themselves from the hand of their enemies. They were led away into terrible boasting that sealed the pronouncement of their destruction:

> And now, because of this great thing which my people, the Nephites, had done, they began to **boast in their own strength**, and began to **swear before the heavens** [made a covenant, but not a divine one] that they would avenge themselves of the blood of their brethren who had been slain by their enemies. And they did swear by the heavens, and also by the throne of God, that they would go up to battle against their enemies, and would cut them off from the face of the land. (Mormon 3:9–10; emphasis added)

The people brought damnation upon themselves through false swearing and blood searching. But the only blood that should ever fall has already fallen. That of Jesus Christ so that we might all live.

As the owner of the promised land, only God has the right and responsibility to remove people from the land! God says this by stating, "Vengeance is mine, and I will repay; and because this people repented not after I had delivered them, behold, **they shall be cut off from the face of the earth**" (Mormon 3:15). God is covenantally bound and obligated to remove covenant breakers from the land, and those who take over God's responsibility will find themselves damned and destroyed. Mormon again interjected his purpose for writing and sharing such heartbreaking stories of human corruption. Mormon cries out to us to accept and stay on the covenant path, to not block others from God's covenants, and to trust that God will remember His covenants to do all things He has ever promised.

> And these things doth the Spirit manifest unto me; therefore I write unto you all. And for this cause I write unto you, that ye may know that ye must all stand before the judgment-seat of Christ, yea, every soul who belongs to the whole human family of Adam; and ye must stand to be judged of your works, **whether they be good or evil** [faithful and devoted to God or not]; And also that ye may believe the gospel of Jesus Christ, which ye shall have among you; and also that the Jews, the covenant people of the Lord, shall have other witness

besides him whom they saw and heard, that Jesus, whom they slew, was the very Christ and the very God. And I would that I could persuade all ye ends of the earth to repent and prepare to stand before the judgment-seat of Christ. (Mormon 3:20–22; emphasis added)

As the fall of the Nephite civilization was imminent, Mormon, as a covenantal record keeper and preserver, returned to the hill Shim to retrieve all the covenantal records that had been entrusted to him. From these records he composed the covenantal instruction book we now miraculously have in our hands—the Book of Mormon, a witness of God's covenants.

And this is the commandment which I have received; and behold, they [the words of the Book of Mormon] shall come forth according to the commandment of the Lord, when he shall see fit, in his wisdom. And behold, they shall go unto the unbelieving of the Jews; and for this intent shall they go— that they may be persuaded that Jesus is the Christ, the Son of the living God; that the Father may bring about, through his most Beloved, his great and eternal purpose, in restoring the Jews, or all the house of Israel, to the land of their inheritance, which the Lord their God hath given them, **unto the fulfilling of his covenant** [sealed to Abraham at Mount Moriah]. . . . And behold, the Lord hath reserved their **blessings, which they might have received in the land** [if they had been loyal to God as revealed at the covenant at Mount Sinai], for the Gentiles who shall possess the land. But behold, it shall come to pass that they shall be driven and scattered by the Gentiles; and after they have been driven and scattered by the Gentiles, behold, then will **the Lord remember the covenant which he made unto Abraham** and unto all the house of Israel. (Mormon 5:13–14, 19–20; emphasis added)

Mormon recorded again his role to preserve the records that contain the instructions we should live to show our loyalty to God:

And it came to pass that when we had gathered in all our people in one to the land of Cumorah, behold I, Mormon, began to be old; and knowing it to be the last struggle of my people, and **having been commanded of the Lord that I should not suffer the records** which had been handed down by our fathers, **which were sacred, to fall into the hands of the Lamanites**, (for the Lamanites would destroy them) **therefore I made this record out of the plates of Nephi** [the Book of Mormon], and hid up in the hill Cumorah all the records which had been entrusted to me by the hand of the Lord, save it were these few plates which I gave unto my son Moroni [eventually containing the Book of Ether and the Book of Moroni as well]. (Mormon 6:6; emphasis added)

After the fall of the Nephites, Mormon's heart broke open in unstoppable anguish. We hear him cry out in amazement and wonder that anyone would reject the covenant path that so clearly leads to happiness and salvation. Why are we so foolish as to create our own paths instead of humbly joining the path that God has revealed to us? Why won't we trust God as a covenant maker and covenant keeper? And why won't we show that trust by entering into covenant with God to be loyal to Him?

O ye fair ones, how could ye have departed from the ways of the Lord! O ye fair ones, how could ye have rejected that Jesus, who stood with open arms to receive you! Behold, if ye had not done this, ye would not have fallen. But behold, ye are fallen, and I mourn your loss. . . . O that ye had repented before this great destruction had come upon you. But behold, ye are gone, and the Father, yea, the Eternal Father of heaven, knoweth your [covenantal] state; and he doeth with you according to his justice and mercy. (Mormon 6:17–18, 22)

Mormon's last words call people to follow the covenant path.

And now, behold, I would speak somewhat unto the remnant of this people who are spared, if it so be that God may give unto them my words, that they may know of the things of their fathers; yea, I speak unto you, ye **remnant of the house of Israel**; and these are the words which I speak: Know ye that **ye are of the house of Israel** [therefore you have access to the Abrahamic promises]. Know ye that ye must come unto repentance, or ye cannot be saved [but access to the Abrahamic promises is conditioned on your obedience to the covenantal agreement revealed at Mount Sinai]. . . . Know ye that ye must come to the **knowledge of your fathers** [that they know of the covenant path and the covenantal mountains of Moriah and Sinai], and repent of all your sins and iniquities, and believe in Jesus Christ, that he is the Son of God, and that he was slain by the Jews, and by the power of the Father he hath risen again, whereby he hath gained the victory over the grave; and also in him is the sting of death swallowed up. And he bringeth to pass the resurrection of the dead, whereby man must be raised to stand before his judgment-seat. . . . Therefore repent, and be baptized in the name of Jesus, and lay hold upon the gospel of Christ, which shall be set before you, not only in this record but also in the record which shall come unto the Gentiles from the Jews, which record shall come from the Gentiles unto you. For behold, this is written for the intent that ye may believe that [the covenantal instruction contained in the Bible]; and if ye believe that ye will believe this also [the covenantal instructions contained in the Book of Mormon]; and if ye believe this ye will **know concerning your fathers**, and also the marvelous works which were wrought by the power of God among them [as He promised to Abraham to do, especially to those who live the Mosaic covenant]. And ye will also know that ye are a **remnant of the seed of Jacob**; therefore ye are numbered among the **people of the first covenant** [the Abrahamic covenant]; and if it so be that ye believe in Christ, and are baptized, first with water, then with fire and with the Holy Ghost, following the example of our Savior, according to that which he hath commanded us, it shall be well with you in the day of judgment [the second covenant, which are the conditions for salvation we must live to show faithfulness and loyalty to God]. Amen. (Mormon 7:1–3, 5–6, 8–10; emphasis added)

Moroni picked up the record where his father left off. Like his father, and the righteous record keepers before him, Moroni was a covenant-centered preserver of God's covenants. He returned to the covenant:

> And he that shall breathe out wrath and strifes against the work of the Lord, and against the covenant people of the Lord who are the house of Israel, and shall say: We will destroy the work of the Lord, and the Lord will not remember his covenant which he hath made unto the house of Israel—the same is in danger to be hewn down and cast into the fire; **For the eternal purposes of the Lord shall roll on, until all his promises shall be fulfilled** [that He made to Abraham and His posterity]. Search the prophecies of Isaiah. Behold, I cannot write them. Yea, behold I say unto you, that those saints who have gone before me, who have possessed this land, shall cry, yea, even from the dust will they cry unto the Lord; and as **the Lord liveth he will remember the covenant** [the Abrahamic covenant] which he hath made with them. (Mormon 8:21–23; emphasis added)

Moroni addressed us as if we were present to him. He called out to us with all the energy of his soul that we should accept the covenant path instructions preserved in the Book of Mormon, to not deny or act against the work and covenants of God, who will remember and fulfill His covenantal promises. Moroni even invoked God's covenantal title of trustworthiness, "The God of Abraham, Isaac, and Jacob," to convince us to be faithful to God by turning to and accepting Jesus Christ:

> O then ye unbelieving [not currently on the covenant path], **turn ye unto the Lord** [join the covenant path]; cry mightily unto the Father in the name of Jesus, that perhaps ye may be found spotless, pure, fair, and white, having been cleansed by the blood of the Lamb, at that great and last day. And again I speak unto you who deny the **revelations of God** [the covenantal instructions], and say that they are done away, that there are no revelations, nor prophecies, nor gifts, nor healing, nor speaking with tongues, and the interpretation of tongues [all signs and symbols of God's covenantal reality]; Behold I say unto you, he that denieth these things knoweth

not the gospel of Christ; yea, he has not **read the scriptures**; if so, he does not understand them [for they speak thoroughly of the covenant path]. For do we not read that God is the same yesterday, today, and forever, and in him there is no variableness neither shadow of changing? And now, if ye have imagined up unto yourselves a god who doth vary, and in whom there is shadow of changing, then have ye imagined up unto yourselves a god who is not a God of miracles. But behold, I will show unto you **a God of miracles, even the God of Abraham, and the God of Isaac, and the God of Jacob** [we can trust God for He is loyal, therefore we should be covenantally loyal to Him]; and it is that same God who created the heavens and the earth, and all things that in them are. (Mormon 9:6–11; emphasis added)

Like his father, Moroni primarily focused his writings on calling us to remember God's covenantal trustworthiness so that we too would be faithful to God by entering in and staying on the covenant path.

> And he that believeth and is baptized shall be saved [joining the covenantal community to be on the covenant path], but he that believeth not shall be damned [rejecting the covenant path]. . . . And now, behold, who can stand against the works of the Lord [that He promised to Abraham to do]? Who can deny his sayings? Who will rise up against the almighty power of the Lord? Who will despise the works of the Lord? Who will despise the children of Christ? Behold, all ye who are despisers of the works of the Lord, for ye shall wonder and perish [because you rejected God and His covenants and His covenantal work]. . . . See that ye are not baptized unworthily [be sincere and purposeful when covenanting with God]; see that ye partake not of the sacrament of Christ unworthily [meaningfully and purposefully covenant to be loyal to God]; but see that ye do all things in worthiness, and do it in the name of Jesus Christ, the Son of the living God; and if ye do this, and endure to the end, ye will in nowise be cast out. . . . And may the Lord Jesus Christ grant that their prayers may

be answered according to their faith; and may God the Father remember the covenant which he hath made with the house of Israel; and may he bless them forever, through faith on the name of Jesus Christ. Amen. [This last line is the essence of the covenant God made to Abraham, to bless him and his posterity forever, through Jesus.] (Mormon 9:23, 26, 29, 37)

The Book of Mormon is structured according to the two covenantal mountains revealed in the Bible. Mount Moriah is God's covenantal obligations to bless us, if we are faithful. Our faithfulness does not change God's covenantal obligations, only our access to what He freely offers. God will not force us to accept the promises. We have to accept His blessings by showing love and trust. And Mount Sinai represents our obligations to show faithfulness; *if* we do, we receive all that God has to offer. Moroni, Mormon, and the other Book of Mormon authors understood the boundaries of the covenant path marked by these mountains. They labored diligently to preserve evidence of these covenants and to convince us to be true to God.

# CHAPTER 24

## ETHER: SECOND WITNESS OF THE COVENANT PATH

The Book of Ether is included in the Book of Mormon for our benefit as a second witness of law of covenants. Like the Nephites, the Jaredites had all things given unto them but they fell and lost everything because they consistently and persistently rejected the king of the land—Jesus Christ. They were covenantally disloyal.

Though the people in the Book of Ether left the Old World before the time of Abraham, because God is the same yesterday, today, and forever, the same covenantal promises and expectations that are in force in the promised land now, and during Book of Mormon times, were also in force during the Jaredite time period.

What may be significant for our covenantal discussion is that according to Genesis, the Abraham stories occurred directly following the Tower of Babel episode. In fact, as we discussed earlier in this book, the Tower of Babel and the Abraham stories are placed back-to-back in the Bible so that we can see the difference between those who try to build their own pathways to God (Tower of Babel) versus those who trust God will lead them on the path of salvation (Abraham story). Similarly, the story of the Jaredites immediately follows and emerges from the Tower of Babel. Like the Abraham stories, the Jaredite story reveals God's covenantal promises and purposes and demonstrates all that God is willing to do to bring us to promised lands and preserve us in designated promised lands *if* we are faithful!

The Book of Ether contains a compressed story of a people who failed to stay on the covenant path and lost the promises of the promised land. Their name was not made great. They did not experience enduring peace and prosperity in the land. Just as the fall of the Nephites should be warning to us, the Jaredite covenantal unfaithfulness should serve as a double witness to us to take seriously God's desire to be our God, for us to be His people, and our need to be faithful to Him. Otherwise we suffer the consequences of a broken covenant.

Listen to the similar promises God made to the brother of Jared and his people that He made to Abraham.

> Go to and gather together [your property and family and]. . . . Go . . . down into the valley which is northward [like Abraham leaving with his family from Ur in the south and heading north]. . . . I will go before thee into a land which is choice above all the lands of the earth. And there will I bless thee and thy seed, and raise up unto me of they seed, and of the seed of thy brother, and they who shall go with thee, a great nation. And there shall be none greater than the nation which I will raise up unto me of thy seed upon all the face of the earth. (Ether 1:41–43)

During their travels to the promised land, God revealed the covenantal purposes of the land to the brother of Jared. And Moroni includes an editorial insertion to us as readers to take seriously that God will have us live faithful and devoted to Him as the God of the land or we will be swept off the land:

> And the Lord would not suffer that they should stop beyond the sea in the wilderness, but he would that they should come forth even unto the land of promise, which was choice above all other lands, which the **Lord God had preserved for a**

**righteous people** [those who showed covenantal devotion to God]. And he had sworn in his wrath unto the brother of Jared, that whoso should possess this land of promise, from that time henceforth and forever, should **serve him, the true and only God**, or they should be swept off when the fulness of his wrath should come upon them. . . . And this cometh unto you, O ye Gentiles, **that ye may know the decrees of God** [know the covenantal expectations God has revealed]—that ye may repent, and not continue in your iniquities until the fulness come, that ye may not bring down the fulness of the wrath of God upon you as the inhabitants of the land have hitherto done. Behold, this is a choice land, and whatsoever nation shall possess it shall be free from bondage, and from captivity, and from all other nations under heaven, if they will but **serve the God of the land, who is Jesus Christ**, who hath been manifested by the things which we have written. (Ether 2:7–8, 11–12; emphasis added)

But even the brother of Jared who had received such great promises from the Lord had to be reminded from time to time to be faithful to God:

And it came to pass at the end of four years that the Lord came again unto the brother of Jared, and stood in a cloud and talked with him. And for the space of three hours did the Lord talk with the brother of Jared, and **chastened him because he remembered not to call upon the name of the Lord** [prayer is a way to demonstrate covenantal devotion to God]. And the brother of Jared repented of the evil which he had done, and did call upon the name of the Lord for his brethren who were with him. And the Lord said unto him: I will forgive thee and thy brethren of their sins; but thou shalt not sin any more, for ye shall remember that my Spirit will not always strive with man; wherefore, **if ye will sin until ye are fully ripe ye shall be cut off from the presence of the Lord.** [In other words, God is full of grace and mercy, giving us multiple opportunities to enter and stay on the covenant path. But if we persistently walk away we lose the prospering promise of His presence.] And these are my thoughts upon the land which I shall give you for your inheritance; for it shall be a land choice above all other lands. (Ether 2:14–15; emphasis added)

After the brother of Jared had completed the barges, he approached the Lord asking for a solution to the darkness they would experience crossing the ocean deep. The Lord engaged in an interview of sorts with the brother of Jared where we hear the brother of Jared's testimony about the nature of God. Like Abraham, the brother of Jared had full trust, faith, and belief in God as a God of covenant making and covenant keeping. Because of his full trust in God, the brother of Jared received the ultimate blessing of being brought back into the presence of God.

> And the Lord said unto him: **Believest** thou the words which I shall speak? And he answered: Yea, Lord, **I know** that **thou speakest the truth**, for **thou art a God of truth**, and canst not lie. And when he had said these words, behold, the Lord showed himself unto him, and said: **Because thou knowest these things ye are redeemed from the fall**; therefore ye are brought back into my presence; therefore I show myself unto you. (Ether 3:11–13; emphasis added)

The Book of Mormon has persistently sought to teach us about this element of God's nature. And we have the same promise to receive the same knowledge that the brother of Jared received, if we are faithful to God:

> And in that day that they shall exercise faith in me, saith the Lord, even as the brother of Jared did, that they may become sanctified in me, then will I manifest unto them the things which the brother of Jared saw, even to the unfolding unto them all my revelations, saith Jesus Christ, the Son of God, the Father of the heavens and of the earth, and all things that in them are. And **he that will contend against the word of the Lord** [those who reject the covenantal instructions of God or who teach others to do so]**, let him be accursed**; and he that shall deny these things, let him be accursed; for unto

them will I show no greater things, saith Jesus Christ; for I am he who speaketh. . . . Come unto me, O ye Gentiles, and I will show unto you the greater things, the knowledge which is hid up because of unbelief [because of a failure to enter in and stay committed to the covenant path]. Come unto me, O ye house of Israel, and it shall be made manifest unto you how great things the Father hath laid up for you, from the foundation of the world; and it hath not come unto you, because of unbelief [because of a failure to enter in and stay committed to the covenant path]. (Ether 4:7–8, 13–14; emphasis added)

Moroni again reinforces the covenantal purpose of the Book of Mormon. The miraculous coming forth of the Book of Mormon is a witness that the God of Abraham, Isaac, and Jacob has remembered His covenant and that we are invited again to show that we remember what God has done for us.

Therefore, when ye shall receive this record [the Book of Ether and the Book of Mormon] ye may know that the work of the Father has commenced upon all the face of the land. Therefore, **repent** all ye ends of the earth, and **come unto me**, and **believe in my gospel**, and **be baptized in my name** [these are our tokens of covenantal loyalty to God]; for he that believeth and is baptized shall be saved; but he that believeth not shall be damned; and signs shall follow them that believe in my name [as evidence that they are part of the covenantal community]. And blessed is he that is found faithful [in the covenantal community] unto my name at the last day, for he shall be lifted up to dwell in the kingdom prepared for him from the foundation of the world [that is the promise of the Abrahamic covenant]. And behold it is I [the God of Abraham, Isaac, and Jacob] that hath spoken it. Amen. (Ether 4:17–19)

When the Jaredites landed in the promised land, their actions should be a model for all who want to live in covenantal community with God:

> And they did land upon the shore of the promised land. And when they had set their feet upon the shores of the promised land they bowed themselves down upon the face of the land, and did humble themselves before the Lord, and did shed tears of joy before the Lord, because of the multitude of his tender mercies over them. . . . And they were taught to walk humbly before the Lord [covenantal faithfulness on the covenant path]; and they were also taught from on high. (Ether 6:12, 17)

Notice that the Jaredite leaders inherently understood the significant threats that kingship posed to living faithfully and fruitfully in the promised land, so much so that like Nephi, everyone rejected kingship. Except for Orihah:

> And it came to pass that the people desired of them that they should anoint one of their sons to be a king over them. And now behold, this was grievous unto them. And the brother of Jared said unto them: Surely this thing leadeth into captivity. . . . And it came to pass that Orihah did walk humbly before the Lord, and did **remember how great things the Lord had done** for his father, and also taught his people how great things the Lord had done for their fathers. (Ether 6:22–23, 30; emphasis added)

Like Benjamin and Mosiah, Orihah was faithful to God and taught his people to be faithful. He walked the covenant path and taught his people to also walk the covenant path. He taught the people to remember God's great deeds (as a witness of God's loyalty to His covenant) and encouraged his people to likewise be loyal to God.

But the remainder of the Book of Ether is a sad tale of ongoing covenantal unfaithfulness often led by kings and false kings. We also see the rise of counterfeit covenants of power and mastery seeking to have a human provide peace and prosperity as a replacement to the humble covenant of choosing to have God be the provider of all good things.

Ether 7 reviews generations of warfare over who is to be the king of the land. With so much wickedness and destruction, with so many people forgetting that the true king of the land is God unto whom all loyalty is owed, prophets came to the land preaching faithfulness:

> And also in the reign of Shule there came prophets among the people, who were sent from the Lord, prophesying that the wickedness and idolatry of the people was bringing a curse upon the land, and **they should be destroyed if they did not repent** [that is the promise of the promised land]. And it came to pass that the people did revile against the prophets, and did mock them. And it came to pass that king Shule did execute judgment against all those who did revile against the prophets. And he did execute a law throughout all the land, which gave power unto the prophets that they should go whithersoever they would; and by this cause the people were brought unto repentance. . . . And there were no more wars in the days of Shule; and **he remembered the great things that the Lord had done for his fathers in bringing them across the great deep into the promised land** [covenantal devotion and fidelity]; wherefore he did execute judgment in righteousness all his days. (Ether 7:23–25, 27; emphasis added)

Regretfully, the peace did not last long. We all know where this sad tale led. Just when the people had turned to the Lord in covenantal fidelity, living true to true covenants, a false leader making false promises of prosperity and power offered false covenants (secret combinations) to the people. Murder and mayhem were the source these perverse covenants leading to a limited few who gained and controlled all, disrupting the covenantal peace of those who would seek to be on the covenant path. One wickedly ambitious prince named Jared battled his father for the kingdom. He won half, but later his brothers beat him in battle and restored the kingdom to their father. "And now Jared became exceedingly sorrowful because of the loss of the kingdom, for **he had set his heart upon the kingdom and upon the glory of the world**"

(Ether 8:7; emphasis added). Seeing his sorrow, Jared's daughter helped him resurrect corrupt and counterfeit covenants to obtain material resources and power by lying, deceit, and murder. She queried him, "is there not an account concerning them of old, that they by **their secret plans did obtain kingdoms and great glory**?" (Ether 8:9; emphasis added). Jared revived these corrupt plans and created a secret combination.

> And it came to pass that they all sware [pledged covenantal loyalty] unto him, by the God of heaven, and also by the heavens, and also by the earth, and by their heads, that whoso should vary from the assistance which Akish desired should lose his head; and whoso should divulge whatsoever thing Akish made known unto them, the same should lose his life.... **And [these perverse and damning covenants] were kept up by the power of the devil to administer these oaths unto the people, to keep them in darkness, to help such as sought power to gain power, and to murder, and to plunder, and to lie, and to commit all manner of wickedness and whoredoms**.... And it came to pass that they formed a secret combination, even as they of old; which combination is most abominable and wicked above all, in the sight of God; For **the Lord worketh not in secret combinations**, neither doth he will that man should shed blood, but in all things hath forbidden it, from the beginning of man. (Ether 8:14, 16, 18–19; emphasis added)

The rise of secret oaths of loyalty by those who would seek their own gain, rather than the gain of God and His people, led to the final demise and destruction of the Jaredites, as well as of the Nephites. And this story will be repeated again for any nation living in the promised land that glories in and supports corrupt leaders who demand loyalty to themselves instead of unswerving loyalty to the God of this land, even Jesus Christ.

What happens when a society has given itself over to corruption and to breaking the covenants of God? Do we not see this happening today in American society? If the American continents are the promised land, can we long stand living in such corruption and not suffer the consequences of a broken covenant?

> For so great had been the spreading of this wicked and secret society that it had **corrupted the hearts of all the people**; therefore Jared was murdered upon his throne, and Akish reigned in his stead. . . . And it came to pass that Akish begat other sons, and they won the hearts of the people, notwithstanding they had sworn unto him to do all manner of iniquity according to that which he desired. Now **the people of Akish were desirous for gain, even as Akish was desirous for power.** [Only true covenant keepers know that real gain and power is in the hands of God.] (Ether 9:6, 10–11)

This mutuality of corruption between people and leaders meant the abandonment of living the morals and values God has revealed through prophets. This corruption led to the destruction of the nation:

> The sons of Akish did offer [the people] money, by which means they drew away the more part of the people after them. And there began to be a war between the sons of Akish and Akish, which lasted for the space of many years, yea, unto the destruction of nearly all the people of the kingdom, yea, even all, save it were thirty souls, and they who fled with the house of Omer. (Ether 9:11–12)

As the house of righteous King Omer recovered, righteousness temporarily returned to the land:

> And thus the Lord did pour out his blessings upon this land, which was choice above all other lands; and **he commanded that whoso should possess the land should possess it unto the Lord** [the conditions of the covenant of faithfulness we make to God], or they should be destroyed when they were ripened in iniquity; for upon such, saith the Lord: I will pour out the fulness of my wrath. (Ether 9:20)

The Book of Ether continues to document the seesawing back and forth from faithful kings to faithless kings, from prosperity to destruction (see Ether 9–11). I can only imagine the heartache that filled Moroni's soul to document the ongoing generations of infidelity among the Jaredites that were just as awful as his own generation.

Moroni then paused the narrative of the Jaredites in Ether 12 to deliver to us readers a beautiful sermon on the power of faith. Remember that faith is a covenantal term signaling devotion and loyalty to God. As you read throughout this chapter, look for each mention of the word faith and replace it with any of these phrases: "covenantal love," "covenantal devotion," "covenantal fidelity," or "covenantal loyalty." As you re-read Ether 12 from this covenantal perspective, I hope you can see with fresh eyes the covenantal significance of faith within the gospel plan and how the Book of Ether and the Book of Mormon preserve and teach us the covenant path. This verse in particular makes the connection between faith and covenants:

> And it is by **faith** [covenantal love or covenantal loyalty] that my fathers have obtained the promise that these things [the covenantal instructions in the Book of Mormon] should come unto their brethren [their posterity] through the Gentiles; therefore the Lord hath commanded me, yea, even Jesus Christ [the giver of the covenant]. (Ether 12:22; emphasis added)

In Ether 13, Moroni shares Ether's prophecies of the coming New Jerusalem. This is the city where all who have been faithful to God will reside. Those who have not learned to live faithfully to God are not allowed citizenship in the city of New Jerusalem.

The closing chapters of Ether (chapters 13–15) read like the fall of the Nephites. Prophets warned the people to return to God. If they would return to Him, they would find peace and prosperity. Reject God and reject the land and be destroyed. Ether became a mute witness of this final destruction where the Jaredites in a futile attempt to on their own terms make real God's live promises destroyed everything they could ever desire:

> And so great and lasting had been the war, and so long had been the scene of bloodshed and carnage, that the whole face of the land was covered with the bodies of the dead. And so swift and speedy was the war that there was none left to bury the dead, but they did march forth from the shedding of blood to the shedding of blood, leaving the bodies of both men, women, and children strewed upon the face of the land, to become a prey to the worms of the flesh. . . . **And thus we see that the Lord did visit them in the fulness of his wrath, and their wickedness and abominations had prepared a way for their everlasting destruction** [the covenant of the land of promise is fulfilled]. (Ether 14:21–22, 25)

And the final conclusion that is the same story every time the people of God reject Him and His covenants is this:

> But behold, the Spirit of the Lord had ceased striving with them [no Spirit of the Lord means no prosperity], and Satan had full power over the hearts of the people; for they were given up unto the hardness of their hearts, and the blindness of their minds that they might be destroyed. . . . And the Lord spake unto Ether, and said unto him: Go forth. And he went forth, and beheld that the words of the Lord had all been fulfilled [to the complete destruction of the Jaredite people]. (Ether 15:19, 33)

The Book of Ether and the Book of Mormon were written, preserved, translated, and delivered to each us, for our day and time, that we might know of the covenants of the Lord, remember His all-encompassing goodness and covenantal faithfulness, and respond in kind with loving faithfulness and trust. The Book of Mormon invites us to know, enter, and endure on the covenant path.

# CHAPTER 25
## MORONI: EXHORTATION TO EXPERIENCE THE PRESERVED COVENANT PATH

The Book of Moroni is dedicated to preserving the covenantal ordinances and calling us to join the covenant path by gaining a witness of the truthfulness of the covenantal instructions preserved in the Book of Mormon.

Moroni did not think that his life would last longer than completing the Book of Ether. To our everlasting benefit, his life was preserved and he preserved some of the most precious elements of the covenant path in all of recorded scripture.

Moroni preserved the fundamental ordinances of the covenant path in Moroni 2–5. We remember that Jesus told His disciples that there should be no disputation about the basic order of the Church. That order is established by ordinances, and those ordinances are stepping stones on the covenant path. (The word "ordinances" comes from the word "order.") Moroni fulfilled Jesus's command to His disciples to avoid disputation about and create order surrounding the ordinances by recording how to conduct those ordinances. Now in the latter days we can move forward on the covenant path with confidence and without disputation, having surety about how to enact these ordinances.

Moroni 2 shared instructions for how to grant the gift of the Holy Ghost to disciples of Jesus Christ. In Moroni 3, Moroni explained how to ordain priesthood-bearing teachers of the covenant path. Moroni 4 and 5 review the most significant way we regularly demonstrate our covenantal loyalty to God—the ordinance of the sacrament. Moroni 6 instructs on the proper process for repentance and baptism. This same chapter also provides instructions for how and when the covenantal community should gather and what their activities should be: prayer and fasting, speaking to each other about the welfare of their souls and partaking of the sacrament. Moroni also provided instructions in this chapter for how the covenantal community (Church members and leaders) should handle the repentance process as well as how church meetings should be conducted.

God is not trying to confuse us. He has simple, easy-to-understand guidance for how to enter into and stay on the covenant path. Moroni 2–6 represent some of the shortest and easiest-to-understand chapters in all of scripture. They also represent foundational actions we can all adhere to as signs of our covenantal loyalty to God. We do not need to encumber the covenant path with more or less than these things. Live and love God and you will find life flowing back unto you again from God.

Before Moroni closed his writings, he included a sermon and several letters from his beloved father, Mormon. Moroni 7 focuses on the theme of love or charity. Fittingly, Mormon's name likely means "[God's] love endures forever" and the greatest speech anywhere in scripture is that of Mormon's in Moroni 7. Mormon may have simply been preaching the meaning of his own name to the people. What is significant from this chapter learning about covenants is that *love* is at the foundation of the covenant path. God loves us and He made covenants to share that love freely with us. He invites us to covenant to share our love with Him. As we do, we experience His love without end. When we walk away from His love, His love does not disappear, but we may not experience it as fully and as warmly. Mormon in Moroni 7 provided beautiful instruction for how we can love more fully and deeply.

In Moroni 8, Mormon expressed truths about foundational ordinances necessary for our salvation. He reviewed the what, how, and why of the covenant path: faith, repentance, baptism, reception of the presence of God (i.e., the Holy Ghost), and enduring to the end. Like we saw with Moroni 2–6, the path is so clear and simple. God is doing everything He can to tell us that all we have to do is choose Him and then be enduringly faithful and we receive all that we desire—eternal life in His presence.

I love Moroni 9. Moroni was all alone, having lost all who loved him: father, mother, possibly brothers and sisters, quite likely a wife and children. He wandered alone as a hunted fugitive, not knowing how long the Lord would preserve his life. I can just see/sense/feel Moroni treasuring the words of his father found in this letter that conclude with this soul-stirring exhortation from father to son:

> My son, be faithful in Christ; and may not the things which I have written grieve thee, to weigh thee down unto death; but may Christ lift thee up, and may his sufferings and death, and the showing his body unto our fathers, and his mercy and long-suffering, and the hope of his glory and of eternal life, rest in your mind forever. And may the grace of God the Father, whose throne is high in the heavens, and our Lord Jesus Christ, who sitteth on the right hand of his power, until all things shall become subject unto him, be, and abide with you forever. Amen. (Moroni 9:25–26)

The covenantal instruction manual known as the Book of Mormon concludes with a reverberating call to covenantal faithfulness. The most memorable and oft-quoted passage from Moroni 10 is this:

> Behold, I would exhort you that when ye shall read these things, if it be wisdom in God that ye should read them, that ye would **remember how merciful the Lord hath been**

**unto the children of men** [remember how God has fulfilled His covenantal obligations and be humble enough to be covenantally loyal!], from the creation of Adam even down until the time that ye shall receive these things, and ponder it in your hearts. And when ye shall receive these things, I would exhort you that ye would **ask God** [show covenantal loyalty by talking to God in faith], the Eternal Father, in the name of Christ, if these things are not true; and if ye shall ask with a sincere heart, with real intent, having faith in Christ, he will manifest the truth of it unto you, by the power of the Holy Ghost. And **by the power of the Holy Ghost ye may know the truth of all things**. (Moroni 10:3–5; emphasis added)

So stirring and powerful is this invitation from Moroni that most missionaries throughout the world today echo Moroni's exhortation to countless children of God seeking the truth.

We might pause a moment and wonder at the beautiful audacity of the Book of Mormon. What other book across all of human history so boldly declares its own authenticity and truthfulness? What other book ever to pass through the hands of human readers has challenged its readers to learn for themselves if the covenant path recorded, preserved, and revealed in its pages leads them to greater truth?

So stirring and bold is this invitation that many of us miss the significant covenantal assignment Moroni challenges us to take on. Look again. And consider what it truly would cost to fully fulfill this invitation from Moroni.

Remember how merciful the Lord hath been unto the children of men, from the creation of Adam even down until the time that ye shall receive these things, and ponder it in your hearts. (Mormon 10:3)

If we had enough years in our life that we could truly remember every last act of covenantal love & mercy God has ever dispersed across the generations amongst all His children, we would be so overwhelmed with the enormity of lovingkindness that we could do nothing else but fall to the earth and proclaim, "Great are the works of the Lord God!" Indeed His works are mighty and great! With all God's mercies in mind, can we doubt His covenant with us, His love for us, and the covenantal instructions He has provided in pages of the Book of Mormon?

When you remember what great things the Lord has done to be faithful and true to His covenantal commitment to Abraham, we are invited to be like God, to likewise be faithful and true to our covenantal obligations to learn and live the commandments. When we remember what great things the Lord has done, we are able to more firmly stay on the covenant path. The scriptures are powerful memory tools to help us remember what great things the Lord has done for His people across the ages. That is why we are commanded to read the scriptures on a regular basis so that we can remember God's covenantal faithfulness and thereby be humbly encouraged to likewise be covenantally faithful.

Moroni's concluding thoughts include reminding us of the nature of God:

> And I would exhort you, my beloved brethren, that ye **remember** that he is the same yesterday, today, and forever, and that all these gifts of which I have spoken, which are spiritual, never will be done away, even as long as the world shall stand, only according to the unbelief of the children of men. . . . And God shall show unto you, that that which I have written is true. (Moroni 10:19, 29; emphasis added)

Let us finish this book about the covenant path with Moroni's powerful final exhortation, replete with the doctrines and ideas of that path:

> And awake, and arise from the dust, O Jerusalem; yea, and put on thy beautiful garments, O daughter of Zion; and strengthen thy stakes and enlarge thy borders forever, that thou mayest no more be confounded, that **the covenants of the Eternal Father which he hath made unto thee**, O house of Israel, **may be fulfilled** [the Abrahamic promises]. Yea, **come unto Christ** [our covenantal obligation, this is how we receive the Abrahamic promises], and be perfected in him [be

covenantally loyal], and deny yourselves of all ungodliness; and if ye shall deny yourselves of all ungodliness, and love God with all your might, mind and strength [our covenantal obligations], then is his grace sufficient for you, that by his grace ye may be perfect in Christ; and if by the grace of God ye are perfect in Christ, ye can in nowise deny the power of God. And again, if ye by the grace of God are perfect in Christ, and deny not his power, then are ye sanctified in Christ by the grace of God, through **the shedding of the blood of Christ, which is in the covenant of the Father unto the remission of your sins** [for God to fulfill His promises to Abraham, God had to die that we might live], that ye become holy, without spot. And now I bid unto all, farewell. I soon go to rest in the paradise of God [the eternal promised land available to all the covenantally faithful], until my spirit and body shall again reunite, and I am brought forth triumphant through the air, to meet you before the pleasing bar of the great Jehovah, the Eternal Judge of both quick and dead. Amen. (Moroni 10:31–34; emphasis added)

The covenant path is as available to us today as it was to the Nephites, Lamanites, and other children of Abraham, including other members of the House of Israel. When we accept Jesus and pledge our lives to Him, we are on the covenant path. When we regularly renew our pledge of allegiance to God, we are holding to the rod. When we follow the living prophets, we are in the covenant path. When we seek the word of God in scripture and through personal revelation, we are prospering as God's Spirit is with us. The covenant path is alive and well. Are we?

## Conclusion to Part 4: The Covenant Path in the Book of Mormon

What is God's role in the covenant path? He has promised to provide a land so that posterity and prosperity can thrive. He did so for the Nephites, leading them to a new promised land. He sent prophets to teach them and he continued to protect them from their enemies, as they were faithful. He blessed them in all ways. Most important, God sent His son Jesus Christ to be the covenant path, to provide the way that all of us may return to God.

If we carefully read the Book of Mormon and tallied all the references to God's unconditional Abrahamic covenant and compared that against the number of references to the Mosaic covenant and the instructions related to the conditions of that covenant, we'd see that the Mosaic covenant is far more represented and discussed in the Book of Mormon.

This raises an important question. Why do we see so much of the Mosaic covenant (and related instructions) throughout the Book of Mormon? Because the Book of Mormon focuses deeply on what *we* must do to keep the door open to receive God's blessings. Those blessings are always available, always there. But if we turn away from God, we lose access until we return to Him again. God has sent prophets and revelation to explain our covenantal obligations. As we learned with the Abraham story, God expects our perfection, but not in the modern sense of never making a mistake. He wants our devoted love and loyalty. He wants us to demonstrate to Him how we love Him just as He has demonstrated His love to us. The stipulations of the covenant, or the instructions of the Mosaic covenant, provide guidance and guardrails for how we can stay on the covenant path, demonstrating our faith in God. Because we need instruction and reminders, God delivers multiple stories, ongoing revelation, updated instruction, and explanatory expansions on the covenantal instruction, all with the intent to help us to hold to the rod of iron. All of these words He has provided give us greater access for holding to the rod of iron. So as we reflect on the two covenant mountains from the Bible and where those symbolic mountains appear in the Book of Mormon, we shouldn't be surprised that the majority of the Book of Mormon is focused on revealing and clarifying how we, as God's people, can show trust in and love of Him as the covenant-making God who has promised to provide a way—the covenant path.

# CONCLUDING THOUGHTS AND RESOURCES FOR THE COVENANT PATH IN THE BIBLE AND THE BOOK OF MORMON

## Do These Covenants and Covenantal Instructions Still Matter Today?

If there is one theme stretching across the pages of the Book of Mormon (and throughout scripture) that I hope to echo here it is that the God of Abraham, the God of Isaac, the God of Jacob, and the God of Moses at Sinai is the same, yesterday, today, and forever. He is a God who we can trust. He is devoted and loyal to His covenantal obligations to offer us prosperity in our lands of promise *if* we demonstrate our devotedness to Him in return. His covenants are still in force; they are still available to us. We only need to show our commitment to God and the promises of the eternities are ours, if we endure to the end.

One of the simplest ways to describe the covenantal relationship God desires with us is to use the analogy of a marriage. When two people are married, what do they hope to experience from their marriage? Loyalty and devotion. Neither spouse expects the other to be perfect in the modern sense of how we define that term (where someone has no faults and no blemishes and never makes any mistakes). A mature spouse does not expect a perfect dinner, perfectly made beds, perfectly washed and dressed children, a perfect smile at all moments, a perfect hairdo. Well, some people do expect such perfection of their spouse in their marriage and it's a disaster. No one can achieve such a perfection in this life. And even if they could, perfect hair or perfect children are hardly qualifying requirements for getting on and staying on the covenant path.

What do the spouses really want? They want a devoted spouse who loves them no matter what. They want a spouse who keeps trying, despite their weaknesses. They want a spouse who is loyal, even if they happen to be late from time to time or perhaps forget a birthday or an anniversary. They want a spouse that is fully committed to the marriage, not someone who is committed for a few hours a week but then is off to other loves or other marriages. This is what God wants with us. He knows we aren't perfect (in the modern sense of the word). He knows that we cannot be perfect. He desires that we are devoted to Him, loyal to Him, committed to the relationship. That is perfection. That is the primary invitation of the covenant path.

### Where Is Jesus on the Covenant Path?

Jesus Christ is the Jehovah of the Old Testament. Jesus as Jehovah is the God of Abraham, Isaac, and Jacob. He it was who had Abraham ponder the stars and count the grains of sand on the seashore. Jehovah marked the covenant path when He passed through the sacrificial animals of Genesis 15, forever obligating Himself to Abraham and his descendants to make property, posterity, and prosperity available *if* they demonstrated their loyalty in return. Jesus as Jehovah appeared again in flaming tongues of fire at the burning of bush on Mount Sinai. As Jehovah, Jesus revealed the conditions by which His people demonstrate their loving commitment to Him. Jesus is in the Passover lambs who each year were sacrificed by Israelites as a grateful reminder that

Jehovah had saved them from enduring bondage. Jesus is in all the sacrifices offered over the ages at the tabernacle, the temple, and other sacred locations and altars, representing the great and last sacrifice He would give of Himself at the meridian of time. Before Jesus endured His sacrificial offering for all humankind, He instituted the ritual of sacrament. Each week we meet Jesus at His table of plenty. There under the blessing of appointed priests, we receive the symbols of Jesus's body and blood, broken that the covenant might be whole. When we partake, we signal that we are committed to Jesus. At the sacrament, we are com-mitting ourselves to the covenant relationship He revealed to Abraham, renewed with Moses, and rekindled at His death and Resurrection. The weekly Holy Supper reanimates the covenant relationship Jesus has always desired of us.

As we read about these covenants as expressed throughout scripture, we must not lose sight that Jesus is at the center. Jesus marks the covenant path. The presence of Jesus guides us on the path. Jesus is the mountain boundaries of Moriah and Sinai and He disciplines us within the covenantal boundaries.

Just as Jesus is advocate, judge, and law, He is the path, the guide, and the life of the covenant. Where there is no death, there can be no life. Something has to die for the covenant to live. Our old selves must be shed as we walk the path. For the gaping chasms we cannot cross on our own, Jesus lay down His own life to bridge us from here to eternity.

## Follow the Prophet! Modern-day Prophets Mark the Covenant Path. Don't Go Astray

Make no mistake. We should all recognize that God still speaks today through His covenant servants, the prophets. As crucial as revealed scripture is for us, far more important is the living word of God, showing us the way. What good is following an old path if God has shown an updated way to return to Him? I don't want to push the analogy too far. I hope no reader will now think that he or she shouldn't take scripture seriously. But we have an amazing advantage in these latter days. God has restored His Church, His priesthood, and His processes for delivering official good news. "Follow the prophet" literally means to stay on the covenant path. He knows and shows the way. We have no need to get ahead of the prophet in trying to reveal the path to others. We have no need to stray off into other paths. God has sent modern-day servants to mark the path for us.

I sometimes hear people wishing we would spend more time in church talking about the mysteries. I wonder if those same individuals have fully mastered faith, repentance, baptism, Holy Ghost, and enduring to the end. Aren't those the real mysteries? Aren't those the real matters? And isn't that the covenant path?

I show my covenantal loyalty by trusting that the God of Abraham, Isaac, and Jacob can save me. I show that trust and faith by repenting and getting back on His covenant path. My repentance demonstrates devoted commitment to God by the act of baptism and receiving the Holy Ghost. Or, if I've already been baptized, I show ongoing fidelity to my covenant relationship with God by regularly renewing my covenant through the sacrament. In the sacrament prayer, I promise to remember Jesus Christ in all things and in all places, thereby granting me access to the constant presence of the Holy Ghost. When I have the Holy Ghost—a member of the Godhead—with me, I am experiencing the prosperity God promised in the Abrahamic covenant. The Holy Ghost prospers me, or empowers me, to endure to the end. *That is the covenant path.* Yes, there are other important elements to the path such as receiving and participating in priesthood ordinances, receiving a temple endowment, and eternal marriage. We could list other aspects, but I want us to focus on the simple beauty of the gospel. God has not revealed a complex gospel or a complex covenant path. Sure, life is difficult. Holding on to the rod can be challenging when the storms of life buffet us and feel to drag us away. But God is not trying to weed people out of His kingdom. He invites all unto Him. The path is plain.

Jesus is the gate. Jesus is the way. Jesus is the life. Because of the life, death, and life of Jesus Christ, the path has been marked bright and clear. We should follow in His footsteps. The testimonies of prophets ancient and modern instruct us on the covenants (and our covenantal duties) and model for us what walking in the path of Jesus looks like.

> *"I, the Lord, am bound [Abrahamic covenant] when ye do what I say [Mosaic covenant]; but when ye do not what I say [Mosaic covenant], ye have no promise [Abrahamic covenant]"* (D&C 82:10).

As we come to the close of this book. I hope you feel the deep joy of knowing that God loves you wherever you are on the covenant path, or off. As the God of Abraham, Isaac, and Jacob, He is eternally obligated to make the incredible promises of eternal progress yours, if we simply look to Him, as He had requested the Israelites to do. God cannot withhold those promises from you. If He did, He would cease to be God. And God will never cease to be God. You can eternally trust that He is the same yesterday, today, and forever. The promises are yours if you simply show your covenantal loyalty. Reach out and hold on to the covenant instructions found in the word of God and represented in the rod of iron that marks the path to God's beckoning presence.

# APPENDIX 1
## SOME THOUGHTS ON THE RESTORATION OF THE COVENANT PATH

I hope that a convincing case has been made that the covenant path (beginning with Abraham and Moses) shines bright and clear throughout scripture, especially the Book of Mormon. But what about within other Restoration scripture like the Doctrine & Covenants? Or where is the covenant path in the Restoration?

**Doctrine and Covenants 1: The Covenant Path Marked for the Restoration**

Section 1 of the Doctrine and Covenants is also called the preface to the Doctrine and Covenants. Similar to the Book of Mormon Title Page that lays out the key themes of the Book of Mormon, section 1 orients our minds to some of the most important principles and ideas God wants us to pay attention to as we read these modern-day revelations. At this point in the book, you won't be surprised to see that D&C 1 interweaves the Abrahamic and Mosaic covenants into a cohesive and unified whole, as they should be as standards for the covenant path.

The first word of D&C 1 is "hearken"! This echoes the Mosaic covenant where God calls to the people from Sinai the covenantal mountain: "Hear, O Israel" (Deuteronomy 6:4). The underlying Hebrew word for "hear" suggests "listen with the intent to obey and follow"! After God had captured His people's attention in Deuteronomy, He reminded that the very first act of covenantal loyalty is to love Him and no other God.

Though some people feel that D&C 1 sounds like a fire and brimstone sermon, God is trying to wake up His people everywhere to their need to be covenantally faithful. The Book of Mormon was revealed for these latter days to provide evidence, like the Bible does, of the consequences of what happens to individuals, families, and nations who consistently and purposefully fail to show loving loyalty to God. Listen to how the two major covenants of the Bible are tied together in this opening act of revelation in the Doctrine & Covenants.

I've laid out key verses in D&C 1 above my covenantal commentary with the hope that this visual organization will help us to better see the covenant path.

**D&C 1:14.** *And the arm of the Lord shall be revealed; and the day cometh that they who will not hear the voice of the Lord, neither the voice of his servants, neither give heed to the words of the prophets and apostles, shall be cut off from among the people;*

The scriptures consistently use the symbol of "the arm of the Lord" to convey His awesome power to bless us and save us. This relates to the Abrahamic covenant, or God's covenantal duty to offer salvation to us. We see Lehi sharing this in his farewell address, "the Lord hath redeemed my soul from hell; I have beheld his glory, and I am encircled about eternally in the arms of his love" (2 Nephi 1:15).

But in the next breath where God offers His salvation (as promised under the Abrahamic covenant), He turns to highlight the stipulations and expectations of an updated Mosaic covenant—God's people must hearken to the voice of His servants the prophets, or they will be cut off from God's gathered people. Even the language of "cut off" has its origin in covenantal terminology.

**D&C 1:15.** *For they have strayed from mine ordinances, and have broken mine everlasting covenant;*

In this verse, God explains what the unfaithful have done to set themselves up for exclusion from God's covenant. They have consistently and purposely walked away from the covenant path—committing the act of breaking His everlasting covenant. What is the everlasting covenant? The Abrahamic covenant God offers to all people who have Abraham as their father of faith, plus the Mosaic covenant where we demonstrate loving loyalty to God. These two covenants are tied together by Jesus. In every sense of the word, He lived the Mosaic covenant perfectly and therefore received *all that the Father has, as promised in the Abrahamic covenant* (see D&C 84:38). Jesus then updated the Mosaic covenant, showing us a better way to show love and loyalty. And Jesus promised to share *everything* with us that He had received from the Father! What is expected? Devotion to God. When we stray from the order that He has created (the word "ordinances" comes from the word "order") we have broken the bands that bind us to God. These bands can be healed through repentance and faithfulness. But for those who never seek to heal the breach, they are everlastingly cut off from the everlasting covenant.

**D&C 1:16.** *They seek not the Lord to establish his righteousness, but every man walketh in his own way, and after the image of his own god, whose image is in the likeness of the world, and whose substance is that of an idol, which waxeth old and shall perish in Babylon, even Babylon the great, which shall fall.*

We saw with the ancient Israelites that they pursued their own paths and their own gods. God has consistently taught the covenant path and has asked in simplicity for us to follow. His first command, which was to love Him first above all others. When we invent our own paths, when we create our own gods and follow their supposed commandments, we are on the path that leads to the kingdom of Babylon and not the kingdom of God.

**D&C 1:17-19.** *Wherefore, I the Lord, knowing the calamity which should come upon the inhabitants of the earth, called upon my servant Joseph Smith, Jun., and spake unto him from heaven, and gave him commandments; And also gave commandments to others, that they should proclaim these things unto the world; and all this that it might be fulfilled, which was written by the prophets—The weak things of the world shall come forth and break down the mighty and strong ones, that man should not counsel his fellow man, neither trust in the arm of flesh—*

What does God do to help us stay on the covenant path? He brings forth prophets and gives them stipulations of faithfulness (i.e., commandments) to share with the world. Joseph Smith is the first prophet of the Restoration. God calls whomever He will. We should not expect God's servants to meet the world's expectations for success, though many prophets have. God ultimately looks on the heart. He seeks servants who *only* trust God, as Abraham did. In seeing their own fallen nature, they cast everything upon the Lord and therefore become strong because He is *the Mighty God!*

**D&C 1:20.** *But that every man might speak in the name of God the Lord, even the Savior of the world;*

Why does God reveal His covenant path? That we might all confess Jesus as the Christ, the pathway to God.

**D&C 1:21.** *That faith also might increase in the earth;*

Because of the Restoration of the covenant path and the restored knowledge of ancient covenant people like the Nephites, our faith can increase as we read and ponder the wondrous deeds of salvation God offered the faithful.

**D&C 1:22.** *That mine everlasting covenant might be established;*

Revelation and restoration have brought forth and re-established God's everlasting covenant, made sure through the sacrifice of Jesus Christ.

**D&C 1:23.** *That the fulness of my gospel might be proclaimed by the weak and the simple unto the ends of the world, and before kings and rulers.*

The fullness of the gospel includes the covenant path. From high to low, God will reveal His covenant path to all people.

**D&C 1:24.** *Behold, I am God and have spoken it; these commandments are of me, and were given unto my servants in their weakness, after the manner of their language, that they might come to understanding.*

God wants us to recognize the covenant path. He does not seek to hide it or obscure it. We cannot be saved in ignorance. God therefore reveals and communicates through means that reach to our understanding so that our agency is alive for showing faithfulness to Him.

My purpose in reviewing this small selection from the first section of the Doctrine and Covenants is to encourage readers to dive back in to search for and follow the covenant path throughout this Restoration scripture. I won't explore further sections of the Doctrine and Covenants beyond what I've shared with the hope that the taste of the covenant path we just experienced will be enticing enough to search further.

Before we close, we should remember that originally the Doctrine and Covenants was called *The Book of Commandments* (see D&C 1:6). Given what we've learned in our discussion in this book, we know that *The Book of Commandments* is modern-day instructions for how to live covenantally faithful to God. I love the fact that the covenantal purposefulness of the Doctrine and Covenants is written into the very title of the book. It turns out that both the Old Testament and the New Testament literally mean "Old Covenant" and "New Covenant" but Jerome, an ancient translator, thought that the best Latin word for the Hebrew word for "oath and covenant" was "testament," as in one's last will and testament, or the instructions that a beloved person leaves behind for those they love before they die. Because the word "testament" appears in the title of the two major sections of the Bible, many of us miss that these two sections of the Bible are focused on revealing God's covenants to His people and instructing His people to dutifully live the covenants.

# APPENDIX 2

## WHY DOES MY BOOK NOT INCLUDE MORE REFERENCES TO THE BOOK OF ABRAHAM AND THE PEARL OF GREAT PRICE?

One of my most treasured books in all of scripture is the Book of Abraham. Given the pervasive nature of talking about the Abrahamic covenant throughout the Bible, the New Testament, and the Book of Mormon, a reader might rightly ask, "Why isn't the Book of Abraham more often referenced in this book?" The answer is simple. Though the evidence for the historical authenticity of the Book of Abraham is overwhelming, there is little evidence that its form was available to ancient Biblical writers or that they structured their stories on the basis of the Book of Abraham as we have it today. Though the Book of Abraham provides revealing pearls of great price about Abraham, God's covenant with him, the gospel, the plan of salvation, and the covenant path, the books of the Bible appear to be following the story and structure of the Abraham saga as expressed in Genesis 12–25. So for simplicity, I've followed the covenant path as expressed in the Bible starting in Genesis 12–25 and sought to trace that covenant throughout the Old Testament and the Book of Mormon. As for the Book of Mormon, our best evidence is that Nephi had access to some version of Genesis that would have been similar to our version, including Genesis 12–25. We have little evidence that Nephi had access to or was influenced specifically by the Book of Abraham. Because we have strong evidence that Nephi was influenced by the writings we have from the Bible compiled before he left Jerusalem, which are full of the Abrahamic (and Mosaic) covenant, I continued tracing the Abrahamic covenant thread into the Book of Mormon as it is expressed in the Bible (and not as expressed in the Book of Abraham).

I love the Book of Abraham and urge anyone taking seriously the covenants of God to read that book. In order to see the "flavor" of expression of the Abrahamic covenant throughout the Old and New Testament and the Book of Mormon, I believe we should start with Genesis 12–25 and supplement all those discoveries with the unmatched beauties flowing from the Book of Abraham.

# APPENDIX 3
## GLOSSARY OF COVENANTAL TERMS IN SCRIPTURE

In the ancient Biblical world, covenants were paramount for defining and binding together relationships among people and of people to God. This book discusses the two most significant covenants that emerged in the Old Testament and then permeated the New Testament and the Book of Mormon. The first covenant is the one God vowed to Abraham at Mount Moriah. The other covenant is the one the people of Israel vowed to God at Mount Sinai. Anyone wanting to understand God's message to humanity in scripture must begin with understanding the two major covenants of the Bible. In order to understand God's covenants, we need to recognize and understand covenantal language.

Let's use a modern example of why understanding covenantal language is so important. Imagine that you are buying a house. There are all sorts of agreements expressed via legal documents that you and the bank sign. These agreements may use words that are unfamiliar to you and which have specific legal and promissory meanings. Furthermore, there may be other words used in these agreements that *are* familiar to you, but you can see that these words are used in unfamiliar, technical, and legal ways. Of course, you'd want to familiarize yourself with the meaning of these terms before you signed any obligating documents.

Similarly, the scriptures are full of covenantal terminology describing, explaining, and elucidating the agreements between God and His people. We would be wise to familiarize ourselves with what these words mean in their covenantal context. Words serve as templates or frames, helping to make sense of what we are seeing.

**When you see in scripture these English words I've listed below, remember that these words typically have covenantal meaning and *not* the familiar meaning we may use in our everyday speech.**

I hope that this verbal clarity will make the scriptures more accessible, understanding, engaging, and meaningful. I hope that this list helps you to see the beautiful covenantal themes that saturate and bring meaning to the Bible and the Book of Mormon.

**Affection**: A focus on covenants made with God.

> *Example:* "Yea, and cry unto God for all thy support; yea, let all thy doings be unto the Lord, and whithersoever thou goest let it be in the Lord; yea, let all thy thoughts be directed unto the Lord; yea, let the **affections** of thy heart be placed upon the Lord forever" (Alma 37:36; emphasis added).

**Belief / Believe** (Hebrew = amen): Trusting the God of Abraham, Isaac, and Jacob.

> *Example:* "And [Abraham] **believed** in the LORD; and [the Lord] counted it to him for righteousness" (Genesis 15:6; emphasis added).

**Do not add or take away**: The covenantal agreement from God should *not* be modified by humans. However, God can, through revelation and prophets, make amendments to the covenantal expectations.

> *Example:* "You shall **not add** to the word which I am commanding you, **nor take away** from it, that you may keep the commandments

of the LORD your God which I command you" (Deuteronomy 4:2, NIV; emphasis added).

*Example:* "I testify to everyone who hears the words of the prophecy of this book: if anyone **adds** to them, God will add to him the plagues which are written in this book" (Revelation 22:18, NASB; emphasis added).

**Faith / Faithful**: Covenantal fidelity.

*Example:* "Know therefore that the LORD thy God, he is God, the **faithful** God, which keepeth covenant and mercy with them that love him and keep his commandments to a thousand generations" (Deuteronomy 7:9; emphasis added).

**Forget**: Not keeping covenantal promises, covenantally disloyal.

*Example:* "Then beware lest thou **forget** the LORD, which brought thee forth out of the land of Egypt, from the house of bondage" (Deuteronomy 6:12; emphasis added).

**Friend / Friendship**: One within the covenant relationship (i.e., Abraham was the "Friend of God"; therefore, he was in a covenant relationship with God).

*Example:* "And the LORD spake unto Moses face to face, as a man speaketh unto his **friend**" (Exodus 33:11; emphasis added).

**Good**: Keeping God's commandments as an expression of covenantal loyalty to God.

*Example:* "Behold, my sons, I desire that ye should remember to keep the commandments of God . . . and when ye remember their works [of the ancestors you are named after] ye may know how that it is said, and also written, that they were **good**. Therefore, my sons, **I would that ye should do that which is good**, that it may be said of you, and also written, even as it has been said and written of them" (Helaman 5:6–7; emphasis added).

(Author's note: Nephi's name in Egyptian means "good" because he was covenantally loyal to God! In contrast, Laman's name may mean La (not) aman (faithful)—*not believing, not faithful, or not in the covenant.* For more on the meanings of Book of Mormon names, look for the writings of Dr. Matt Bowen, professor of religion at BYU–Hawaii.)

**Grace**: Granting or fulfilling the blessings promised in the covenant.

*Example:* "But Noah found **grace** in the eyes of the LORD" (Genesis 6:8; emphasis added).

**Hate**: No covenantal devotion, *not* in a covenant relationship with God (compare to "love" below).

*Example:* "And I [the Lord] **hated** Esau[/Edom]" (Malachi 1:3; emphasis added).

**If ye keep my commandments, ye shall prosper in the land**: Summary statement of the conditional covenant God made with Israelites at Sinai. This statement has several variants in scripture.

*Example:* Inasmuch as ye shall keep my commandments ye shall prosper in the land; but inasmuch as ye will not keep my commandments ye shall be cut off from my presence (see 2 Nephi 2:1).

**Just / Justice / Judgment**: Living the expectations of the covenant.

*Example:* "Noah was a **just** man and perfect [covenantally loyal] in his generations, and Noah walked with God" (Genesis 6:9; emphasis added).

*Example:* "[God said] For I know [Abraham], that he will command his children and his household after him, and they shall keep the way of the LORD, to do **justice** and **judgment**; that the LORD may bring upon Abraham that which he hath spoken of him" (Genesis 18:19; emphasis added).

**Keep**: Covenantal loyalty to God (i.e., keep the commandments).

*Example:* "Now therefore, if ye will obey my voice indeed, and **keep** my covenant, then ye shall be a peculiar treasure unto me above all people: for all the earth is mine" (Exodus 19:5; emphasis added).

**Kindness / Loving-kindness (Hebrew = hesed)**: Covenantal faithfulness.

*Example:* "I will betroth thee unto me for ever . . . in **lovingkindness**" (Hosea 2:19; emphasis added).

*Example:* "How excellent is thy **lovingkindness**, O God! therefore the children of men put their trust under the shadow of thy wings" (Psalm 36:7; emphasis added).

**Love**: Covenantal devotion, in a covenant relationship with God (compare to "hate" above).

*Example:* "I [the Lord] **loved** Jacob[/Israel]" (Malachi 1:2; emphasis added).

**Mercy**: Granting or fulfilling the blessings promised in the covenant.

*Example:* "But the LORD was with Joseph, and shewed him **mercy**, and gave him favour in the sight of the keeper of the prison" (Genesis 39:21; emphasis added).

**Observe**: Keep the commandments of the covenant.

*Example:* "Wherefore the children of Israel shall keep the sabbath, to **observe** the sabbath throughout their generations, for a perpetual covenant" (Exodus 31:16; emphasis added).

**Perfect**: Covenantal loyalty.

*Example:* "Be ye therefore **perfect [being loyal to God's covenants]**, even as your Father which is in heaven is **perfect**" (Matthew 5:48; emphasis added).

**Prosper**: To have God's covenantal presence with them.

*Example:* "The Lord, before whom I walk, will send his angel with thee, and **prosper** thy way" (Genesis 24:40; emphasis added).

*Example:* "Inasmuch as ye shall keep my commandments ye shall **prosper** in the land" (2 Nephi 4:4; emphasis added).

**Not Prosper**: Be outside God's covenantal protection and presence.

*Example:* "Inasmuch as ye will not keep my commandments ye shall **not prosper** in the land" (Omni 1:6; emphasis added).

**Remember**: Bring back to memory covenantal promises.

*Example:* "And I will **remember** my covenant, which is between me and you and every living creature of all flesh; and the waters shall no more become a flood to destroy all flesh" (Genesis 9:15; emphasis added).

**Righteous / Righteousness**: Committed to a covenant with God.

*Example:* "And [Abraham] believed in the LORD; and [the Lord] counted it to him for **righteousness**" (Genesis 15:6; emphasis added).

*Example:* "For I say unto you that unless your **righteousness** shall exceed the **righteousness** of the scribes and Pharisees, ye shall in no case enter into the kingdom of heaven" (Matthew 5:20; emphasis added).

**The God of Abraham, Isaac, and Jacob**: The God who is trustworthy, the God who makes and keeps covenants, the covenant-making God who vowed to fulfill certain promises to the patriarchs and their descendants.

*Example:* "And God said moreover unto Moses, Thus shalt thou say unto the children of Israel, The LORD God of your fathers, **the God of Abraham, the God of Isaac, and the God of Jacob**, hath sent me unto you" (Exodus 3:15; emphasis added).

**Walk / Walk with or before God**: Being on the covenant path, showing devoted loyalty to God and His covenants.

*Example:* "Noah was a just man and perfect [covenantally loyal] in his generations, and **Noah walked with God**" (Genesis 6:9; emphasis added).

*Example:* "And I will **walk** among you, and will be your God, and ye shall be my people. . . . [But] if ye **walk** contrary unto me, and will not hearken unto me; I will bring seven times more plagues upon you according to your sins" (Leviticus 26:12, 21; emphasis added).

Other words or terms that may have covenantal significance: bond, bondage, captivity, afflictions, trust, power, deliverance, oath, brotherhood, peace, truth, establishing a covenant, instituting a covenant.

# APPENDIX 4

## FOUNDATIONAL READINGS ON COVENANTS IN SCRIPTURE

The insights that I have discovered and shared in this book are based on the inspiration and influence I have experienced reading a variety of Biblical scholarly writings on covenants in the Ancient Near East. These works have had lasting and transformative influence on my thinking about and reading of scripture. I cannot read the scriptures now except to see God's covenants *everywhere* and His call to all of us to be covenantally loyal and devoted to Him.

Baltzer, Klaus. *The Covenant Formulary: In Old Testament, Jewish, and Early Christian Writings*, translated by David E. Green (Philadelphia: Fortress Press, 1971).

Benson, RoseAnn and Stephen D. Ricks. "Treaties and Covenants: Ancient Near Eastern Legal Terminology in the Book of Mormon," *Journal of Book of Mormon Studies*, 14.1 (2005), pp. 48–61, 128–129.

Levenson, Jon. *Sinai and Zion: An entry into the Jewish Bible*, (San Francisco: HarperSanFrancisco, 1987).

McCarthy, Dennis (D. J.) .*Treaty and Covenant, Second Edition*, (Rome: Pontifical Biblical Institute, 1978).

Mendenhall, George. "Covenant Forms in Israelite Tradition," *The Biblical Archaeologist*, 17.3 (September 1954), pp. 49–76.

*Monumental Inscriptions from the Biblical World, Volume 2 of The Context of Scripture*, edited by William W. Hallo and K. Lawson Younger Jr. (Leiden: Brill, 2000).

Ricks, Stephen D. "King, Coronation, and Covenant in Mosiah 1–6," *Rediscovering the Book of Mormon*, edited by John L. Sorenson and Melvin J. Thorne (Salt Lake City: Deseret Book and FARMS, 1991), pp. 209–219.

———."The Treaty/Covenant Pattern in King Benjamin's Address (Mosiah 1–6)." *BYU Studies*, 25.2 (Spring 1984), pp. 151–162.

Weinfeld, Moshe. "Covenant Terminology in the Ancient Near East and Its Influence on the West," *Journal of the American Oriental Society*, 93.2 (April–June 1973), pp. 190–199.

———. "Covenant-making in Anatolia and Mesopotamia," *Journal of Ancient Near Eastern Society*, 22.1 (1993), pp. 135–139.

———. *Deuteronomy and the Deuteronomic School*, (Winona Lake, Indiana: Eisenbrauns, 2014, reprint of 1972 edition).

———. "The Covenant of Grant in the Old Testament and in the Ancient Near East," *Journal of the American Oriental Society*, 90.2 (April–June, 1970), pp. 184–203.

———. "The Loyalty Oath in the ancient Near East." *Ugarit-Forschungen*, 8 (1976), pp. 379–414.

# APPENDIX 5
## LIST OF REFERENCES TO THE NAME ABRAHAM IN THE BOOK OF MORMON

| | |
|---|---|
| 1 Nephi 6:4 | Alma 29:11 |
| 1 Nephi 15:18 | Alma 36:2 |
| 1 Nephi 17:40 | Helaman 8:16 |
| 1 Nephi 19:10 | Helaman 8:17 |
| 1 Nephi 22:9 | Helaman 8:18 (two times) |
| 2 Nephi 8:2 | Helaman 8:19 |
| 2 Nephi 27:33 | 3 Nephi 4:30 |
| 2 Nephi 29:14 | 3 Nephi 20:25 |
| Jacob 4:5 | 3 Nephi 20:27 |
| Mosiah 7:19 | Mormon 5:20 |
| Alma 5:24 | Mormon 9:11 |
| Alma 7:25 | Ether 13:11 |
| Alma 13:15 (two times) | |

# APPENDIX 6

## LIST OF REFERENCES TO THE NAME MOSES IN THE BOOK OF MORMON

| | | |
|---|---|---|
| 1 Nephi 4:2 | Jacob 1:5 | Alma 31:9 |
| 1 Nephi 4:15 | Jacob 7:7 (two times) | Alma 33:19 |
| 1 Nephi 5:11 | Jarom 1:5 | Alma 34:7 |
| 1 Nephi 17:22 | Jarom 1:11 | Alma 34:13 |
| 1 Nephi 17:24 | Mosiah 2:3 | Alma 45:19 (two times) |
| 1 Nephi 17:26 | Mosiah 3:14 | Helaman 8:11 |
| 1 Nephi 17:29 | Mosiah 3:15 | Helaman 8:13 |
| 1 Nephi 17:30 | Mosiah 12:28 | Helaman 8:16 |
| 1 Nephi 17:42 | Mosiah 12:29 | Helaman 13:1 |
| 1 Nephi 19:23 | Mosiah 12:31 (three times) | Helaman 15:5 |
| 1 Nephi 22:20 | Mosiah 12:32 | 3 Nephi 1:24 |
| 1 Nephi 22:21 | Mosiah 12:33 | 3 Nephi 9:17 |
| 2 Nephi 3:9 | Mosiah 13:5 | 3 Nephi 15:2 |
| 2 Nephi 3:10 | Mosiah 13:27 | 3 Nephi 15:4 |
| 2 Nephi 3:16 | Mosiah 13:28 | 3 Nephi 15:8 |
| 2 Nephi 3:17 | Mosiah 13:33 | 3 Nephi 20:23 |
| 2 Nephi 5:10 | Mosiah 16:14 | 3 Nephi 21:11 |

| 2 Nephi 11:4  | Mosiah 24:5            | 3 Nephi 25:4           |
| 2 Nephi 25:20 | Alma 25:15 (four times) | 3 Nephi 27:8 (two times) |
| 2 Nephi 25:24 | Alma 25:16 (two times) | 4 Nephi 1:12           |
| 2 Nephi 25:30 | Alma 30:3 (two times)  | Ether 12:11            |

# APPENDIX 7

## LIST OF REFERENCES TO THE WORD COVENANT IN THE BOOK OF MORMON

| Title Page | Mosiah 9:6 | 3 Nephi 6:3 |
|---|---|---|
| 1 Nephi 13:23 (two times) | Mosiah 18:10 | 3 Nephi 6:28 (three times) |
| 1 Nephi 13:26 | Mosiah 18:13 | 3 Nephi 6:29 |
| 1 Nephi 13:30 | Mosiah 21:31 | 3 Nephi 6:30 |
| 1 Nephi 14:5 | Mosiah 21:32 | 3 Nephi 7:11 |
| 1 Nephi 14:8 | Mosiah 24:13 (two times) | 3 Nephi 10:7 |
| 1 Nephi 14:14 | Mosiah 26:20 | 3 Nephi 15:5 |
| 1 Nephi 14:17 | Alma 7:15 | 3 Nephi 15:8 |
| 1 Nephi 15:14 | Alma 24:18 | 3 Nephi 16:5 |
| 1 Nephi 15:18 (two times) | Alma 37:27 | 3 Nephi 16:11 |
| 1 Nephi 17:40 (two times) | Alma 37:29 | 3 Nephi 16:12 |
| 1 Nephi 19:15 | Alma 43:11 | 3 Nephi 20:12 |
| 1 Nephi 21:8 | Alma 44:14 | 3 Nephi 20:19 |

## Appendix 7

| | | |
|---|---|---|
| 1 Nephi 22:6 | Alma 44:15 (two times) | 3 Nephi 20:22 |
| 1 Nephi 22:9 | Alma 44:19 | 3 Nephi 20:25 |
| 1 Nephi 22:11 | Alma 44:20 | 3 Nephi 20:26 |
| 2 Nephi 1:5 (two times) | Alma 46:20 | 3 Nephi 20:27 |
| 2 Nephi 3:4 | Alma 46:21 | 3 Nephi 20:29 (two times) |
| 2 Nephi 3:5 | Alma 46:22 (two times) | 3 Nephi 20:46 (two times) |
| 2 Nephi 3:7 | Alma 46:31 | 3 Nephi 21:4 (two times) |
| 2 Nephi 3:12 | Alma 46:35 (two times) | 3 Nephi 21:7 |
| 2 Nephi 3:21 | Alma 50:36 | 3 Nephi 21:11 |
| 2 Nephi 3:23 | Alma 51:6 | 3 Nephi 21:22 |
| 2 Nephi 6:12 | Alma 53:15 | 3 Nephi 22:10 |
| 2 Nephi 6:13 | Alma 53:16 | 3 Nephi 24:1 |
| 2 Nephi 6:17 | Alma 53:17 (two times) | 3 Nephi 29:1 |
| 2 Nephi 9:1 (two times) | Alma 53:18 | 3 Nephi 29:3 |
| 2 Nephi 9:53 | Alma 56:6 | 3 Nephi 29:8 |
| 2 Nephi 10:7 | Alma 56:7 | 3 Nephi 29:9 |
| 2 Nephi 10:15 | Alma 56:8 | Mormon 3:21 |
| 2 Nephi 11:5 | Alma 60:34 | Mormon 5:14 |
| 2 Nephi 29:1 | Alma 62:16 | Mormon 5:20 |
| 2 Nephi 29:4 | Alma 62:17 | Mormon 7:10 |
| 2 Nephi 29:5 | Helaman 1:11 | Mormon 8:15 |
| 2 Nephi 29:14 | Helaman 1:12 | Mormon 8:21 (two times) |
| 2 Nephi 30:2 (two times) | Helaman 2:3 | Mormon 8:23 |
| Enos 1:16 | Helaman 6:21 | Mormon 9 |

| Enos 1:17 | Helaman 6:22 (two times) | Ether 4:15 |
| Mosiah 5:5 | Helaman 6:25 | Ether 13:11 |
| Mosiah 5:6 (two times) | Helaman 6:26 | Moroni 7:31 |
| Mosiah 5:7 | Helaman 6:30 | Moroni 7:32 |
| Mosiah 5:8 | 3 Nephi 5:4 | Moroni 10:31 |
| Mosiah 6:1 | 3 Nephi 5:5 | Moroni 10:33 |
| Mosiah 6:2 | 3 Nephi 5:25 (five times) | |

# ABOUT THE AUTHOR

Taylor Halverson is an aspiring master learner and an Entrepreneurship Professor in the BYU Marriott School of Business. He has discovered his life purpose to help people find and act on the best ideas and tools in order to experience enduring joy.

As an executive coach and entrepreneur, Taylor builds leaders and businesses while creating transformative professional and personal development experiences.

Taylor leads acclaimed travel tours to incredible locations throughout the world (Israel, China, India, Europe, Central America, and America's National Parks). Tour members have loved his irresistible enthusiasm, encyclopedic knowledge, spirit of adventure, and sense of fun.

Taylor is a prolific author and editor of twenty books and more than three hundred articles and a developer of breakthrough scripture study resources with Book of Mormon Central (ScripturePlus app & Come, Follow Me Insights videos with Tyler Griffin) and BYU's Virtual Scripture Group (3D Ancient Jerusalem project).

# About the Author

Taylor lives in Springville, Utah, with his wife Lisa and their two kids. He loves to spend time with his family on all sorts of adventures including exploring the nooks and crannies of the American West and Southwest, participating with geology and archaeology teams on location, creating and mixing electronic music, watching and discussing edifying shows, reading good books, playing games, learning, and laughing.

Taylor's academic training includes:

>BA, Ancient Near Eastern Studies, Brigham Young University
>MA, Biblical Studies, Yale University
>MS, Instructional Systems Technology, Indiana University
>PhD, Instructional Systems Technology, Indiana University
>PhD, Judaism & Christianity in Antiquity, Indiana University

Would you like a free humorous ebook from Taylor? Go here to request *Memoirs of The Ward Rumor Control Coordinator*: shorturl.at/koqO5.

Learn more at taylorhalverson.com.

www.ingramcontent.com/pod-product-compliance
Lightning Source LLC
Chambersburg PA
CBHW021848230426
43671CB00006B/304